TREASURE CHEST
OF GROUP ACTIVITIES

Susanna Palomares   **Dianne Schilling**   **Cathy Winch**

Innerchoice Publishing

© 2018 by Innerchoice Publishing.
15079 Oak Chase Court
Wellington, Florida, 33414
561-790-0132
www.InnerchoicePublishing.com

All rights reserved.

ISBN-13: 978-1-56499-098-3

ISBN-10: 1-56499-098-2

NOTICE: Innerchoice Publishing grants permission to the purchaser of this material to make unlimited copies of the reproducible student pages for teaching or counseling purposes.

Duplication of this material for commercial use is prohibited

Printed in the United States of America

INNERCHOICE Publishing

15079 Oak Chase Court
Wellington, FL 33414

www.InnerchoicePublishing.com

Contents

Introduction 1

Life-Skills 9

Learning Strategies 67

Health and Wellness 93

Emotional Intelligence 151

Diversity 179

Conflict Management 207

Character Education 265

Careers 293

Introduction

Introduction

A book filled with instructional activities cannot rightfully be called a treasure chest unless it holds something of considerable value. When *Treasure Chest* was compiled, the objective was to create an expansive resource of activities that foster development of the whole child – not only the parts of the child that read and solve mathematical equations, but the parts that feel, create, relate, communicate, cooperate, solve problems, and make moral decisions. We consider these facets of the whole child to be extremely valuable.

By choosing this collection of activities, in many ways you have become a steward of education's lost treasure. The physical, emotional, and social development of children were once considered essential components of a comprehensive approach to teaching and learning. Unfortunately, in recent years they have been partially buried under the weight of standardized performance expectations in reading and mathematics.

Today's narrow, somewhat impoverished approach to education keeps teachers so busy preparing students for frequent make-or-break testing that most have little time to address the needs of the whole child. We are grateful to the counselors and teachers who are doing their best to fill this gap.

Students respond to educational experiences not just cognitively, but emotionally and socially as well. While not the same as numerical scores compared with the scores of thousands of other students, we can teach and measure the achievement of emotional and social skills. We can measure students' self-awareness or emotional intelligence, social competence, creativity, and readiness for democratic participation through deliberate lessons with well-formed objectives. *Treasure Chest* activities identify objectives aligned with the ASCA National Standards for School Counseling Programs (Campbell & Dahir, 1997).

Historically, public schools in the U.S. were established as much for social and moral as for academic instruction. The recent laser-like focus on academic achievement to the exclusion of other developmental concerns is not in the best interests of children, families, democratic institutions, or the emerging global marketplace. We need to develop young people who understand themselves, have empathy and compassion for others, can think on their feet, and are ready to participate in innovative ways to solve the nation's and the planet's many grave problems.

The Association for Supervision and Curriculum Development (ASCD) has powerfully and eloquently urged a return to educating the whole child. The September, 2005 issue of the organization's publication, *Educational Leadership*, states:

The ASCD Position Statement on the Whole Child, derived from positions adopted by ASCD's Leadership Council in 2004, calls for schools and communities to pay attention to each student's academic, physical, emotional, social, and ethical well-being. The statement reaffirms what ASCD educators value: a challenging and engaging curriculum, evidence-based instruction and assessment, safe and trusting classrooms and schools, and a climate that supports students and their families (Scherer, 2005, p. 7).

A feature article in the same issue observes that "students can develop reading, writing, speaking, and mathematical skills as they plan and stage dramatic performances, design classroom murals, compose a school paper, and participate in establishing classroom rules" (Noddings, 2005, pp. 8-13). It is unfortunate that in today's educational climate such an obvious notion needs to be vigorously promoted.

Activities for the Whole Child

Treasure Chest is made up of predominantly group activities in several vital areas that promote the development of the whole child.

Life Skills

As the name implies, life skills serve as passports to effective day-to-day living. They build independence, social competence, and interpersonal versatility, enabling students to handle themselves well in whatever circumstances life presents. These activities teach students to communicate effectively, respond assertively, nurture friendships, manage their time, solve problems, and work productively in teams.

Learning Strategies

Teachers and counselors have always played an important role in helping students to acquire personal habits that enhance school performance. These activities focus on the development of effective study skills, self-management techniques, and preferred learning styles. They also address factors that greatly influence academic performance, including brain functioning, nutrition, and stress management.

Health and Wellness

This group of activities deals with some of the most important issues facing schools today, such as how to create a safe environment, how to respond to crises, and instructional approaches to combating childhood obesity. Activities address emotional balance, nutrition, exercise and stress management, as well as potentially difficult topics such as fear, grief, unwelcome touching, safety, the effects of TV viewing, refusal skills, and smoking.

Emotional Intelligence

Counselors recognize that emotional intelligence is the silent partner of rational intelligence—equal in importance, yet frequently overlooked and rarely schooled. Curiosity, interest, determination, and satisfaction are as much feelings as they are cognitive states, and profoundly impact performance. This group of activities builds self-awareness, self-esteem, recognition and acceptance of feelings, healthy self-talk, and peer inclusion and cooperation.

Diversity

Cultural clashes occur countless times each day in schools throughout the U.S. Sometimes they are satisfactorily resolved, but many times they go completely unnoticed. Every time this happens an opportunity to improve the educational experience of a student is lost. These activities directly examine cultural heritage, discrimination, disabilities, stereotypes, prejudice, and the attitudes and values needed to promote tolerance and the full appreciation of diversity.

Conflict Management

Conflict is not only a fact of school life, it reflects a powerful human predisposition. Administrators and teachers are charged with handling the disciplinary side of conflict, which gives counselors an opportunity to deal with prevention and management. This group of activities aids in that effort by addressing various causes of conflict, empathy development, anger management, self-control and bullying, and by providing proven conflict-management processes and strategies.

Character Education

The importance of moral education and recognized and promoted by such luminaries as Thomas Jefferson and Benjamin Franklin, and its place in public education has been more or less secure for centuries. Whether by design or default, schools teach ethics and values in the priorities they model and the behaviors they praise and punish. This group of activities deliberately instills such universal moral values as fairness, friendship, responsibility, truthfulness, promise-keeping, service, courage, environmentalism, respect, and citizenship through activities dealing with classroom rules, current events, cheating, lying, moral dilemmas, and more.

Careers

Counselors are traditionally expected to help students assess their aptitude for, and interest in, various careers. In addition, career activities can and should be integrated within existing academic subject areas. This group of activities asks students to investigate local businesses, survey occupations, practice job-search skills, test cooperative vs. competitive behaviors, practice teamwork, and trace the career paths of people in the community.

Benefits of Group Work

There are many advantages to working with students in groups. Aside from the obvious fact that groups allow more students to benefit during a given period of time, several other points are worth mentioning.

Groups are usually preferable if your intent is to instruct, as it is with these activities. In the process of completing an activity, students often learn as much from one another as they do from the lesson itself. They share experiences, reactions, and ideas. Increased brainpower produces greater creativity and, often, better results.

Students experience safety in numbers. No one student feels singled out or "on the spot" when several students are presented with the same information, problems and questions. In *Learning Smarter: The New Science of Teaching*, authors Eric Jensen and Michael Dabney link group learning with an increased sense of safety:

Research has found that supportive, safe learning environments (including those involving peer collaboration) engage the emotions in a positive way and stimulate attention, meaning, and memory in the brain. Researchers believe this enhanced learning results from both psychological and physiological components found in safe environments. Most of us experience security in numbers since the chance of being singled out is reduced. With others around us to provide a sense of social safety, the brain's fear response is less likely to be triggered (Jensen & Dabney, 2000, p. 15).

Greater safety allows reticent students to assert themselves more easily, so groups eventually benefit from the views and opinions of all members.

Groups are laboratories for the advancement of communication skills—more constraining than classrooms, but less intimidating than one-to-one sessions. When students talk to one another in groups, your role becomes that of coach, encouraging clear statements, good listening, and congruent body language. Good communication is likely to be a secondary objective of every group, regardless of the main topic of inquiry.

Cooperation and collaboration are encouraged in groups, particularly when instructional activities call for decision making or problem solving of some sort. It's hard to imagine a better venue for practicing aspects of the democratic process. Your ability to facilitate and take advantage of teachable moments will make the most of these opportunities.

Finally, groups build a sense of connection and community. Because of their association in the group, students who otherwise might not get to know one another often develop friendships outside the group. These connections in turn promote cross-connections between grade-level, interest-based and ethnic groups on the campus, which strengthens the entire school.

Awareness, Social Competency, and Mastery

The activities in *Treasure Chest* are designed to develop in students three critical areas of human functioning: awareness, social competency, and mastery. These areas comprise the underlying theoretical components of the entire collection.

Awareness

Awareness is a critical element of self-esteem. Aware students do not hide things from themselves. They are in touch with the inner world of feelings and thoughts, and they are in control of their actions. They understand that other people feel, think, and behave, too. They are also in touch with the reality of the past, the possibilities of the future, and the certainty of the present. Awareness allows students to order their lives flexibly and effectively on a moment-to-moment basis.

By contrast, relative unawareness sets the stage for lack of congruence between what a student believes or feels and how the student behaves. Feelings of isolation ("I'm the only one who has ever felt like this") occur when students are unaware that everyone experiences similar feelings, thoughts, and behaviors. Without awareness, students cannot effectively direct the course of their school experience, or their lives.

Social Competency

Students who are effective in their social interactions are capable of understanding other people. They know how to interact with others flexibly, skillfully, and responsibly, without sacrificing their own needs and integrity. They have a good sense of timing and are effective at being heard and making needed changes to their environment.

Socially competent students realize that people have the power to affect one another. They are aware, not only of how others affect them, but of the effects of their behavior on others, and they take accompanying responsibility for their actions.

Without social skills, individuals confuse situations and give inappropriate responses. They lack positive communication skills, fail to develop lasting friendships, have difficulty resolving conflicts, and do not work effectively in teams.

Mastery

Masterful students believe in themselves. They perceive themselves as being capable. They are not debilitated by knowledge of their weaknesses, and have a healthy degree of self-esteem and a feeling of mastery or self-confidence. They try new challenges and do not strongly fear failure.

Students are more likely to achieve mastery in their endeavors when they have a feeling of mastery about themselves. Generally, those who believe in themselves are the ones who continue to succeed, and the more they succeed, the more they believe in themselves. Thus a beneficial cycle is created.

The ways in which significant others respond to what students do plays a critical role in whether or not they see themselves as masterful. If others recognize their efforts and comment positively when they try or succeed, their awareness that they have capabilities increases. Conversely, without favorable comment, they are less aware of their capabilities, even if they experience success. This explains why so many brilliant students do not regard themselves as such. Rather, they are painfully aware of their limitations and shortcomings and miss many opportunities to actualize their potential.

Guidelines for Implementation

Whether you use these activities as a classroom teacher, a guest facilitator in the classroom, or conduct group counseling sessions in a separate venue, the following suggestions are intended to maximize both your success and the benefits to students.

Begin by developing a safe and trusting atmosphere. As a teacher or counselor, you understand that groups develop in a fairly predictable way, maturing and becoming more effective as members spend increasing time together. To facilitate this process, start with activities that promote communication and trust-building and save the more challenging activities for later. Establish ground rules that safeguard confidentiality, promote respect and good listening, and encourage everyone to participate.

Assess the needs of the group before proceeding. Each group is different, with a unique amalgam of interests, talents, and concerns. Depending on your purpose in forming a particular group, consult with referring adults (teachers, administrators, parents) regarding individual members.

Choose activities that deal with the values and interests you wish to promote. For example, if your aim is to encourage personal accountability, you will find appropriate activities in several of the theme areas. If you are working with an anger-management group, Emotional Intelligence and Conflict Management will offer many directly relevant activities. An alternative approach is to announce the formation of a group devoted to a particular theme area and then recruit students who already have an interest in exploring that area.

Modify activities to suit the ages, ability levels, cultural/ethnic backgrounds, and interests of your students. You will know best how to maximize the appropriateness and impact of each activity, so please take those liberties. For example, if the instructions call for the students to write a story and you are working with pre-writing students, you might choose to have them draw pictures instead.

Conclude activities with a summary discussion. Discussion questions are listed at the end of each activity. They are designed to help the students think about and articulate what they have learned from the activity, to apply concepts in different ways, and to contrast and compare ideas. All of this helps the students internalize the main points of the lesson, committing them to long-term memory.

When asking questions, maximize participation by allowing sufficient time for the students to answer. Typically, discussion leaders allow one to three seconds before calling on someone or supplying an answer themselves. This is not enough time for most students to transfer information from long-term memory. Though it may seem awkward at first, discipline yourself to wait longer. After a period of silence, if no one has volunteered, offer a few key words to spark ideas.

Create your own discussion questions based on what has transpired in the group. This is an effective way to lend immediacy to the session. Watch and listen for relevant side issues and personal examples that can be expanded to have universal application. For example, in a conflict management session, if a student touches on the issue of inner (intrapersonal) conflict, you might want to formulate a discussion question that asks the students how they would apply conflict management strategies to conflicting values, opinions, or desires within themselves.

Finally, take full advantage of your knowledge and skills as a counselor. While these are instructional activities, your training has prepared you to give each one a humanistic overlay that can't be conveyed by the printed word. Trust your instincts in this regard. Make the activities work for you.

References

Brokenshire, D. (2001). *The tough stuff elementary series*. Austin, TX: PRO-ED, Inc.

Campbell, C.A. & Dahir, C.A. (1997). *Sharing the vision: National standards for school counseling programs*. Alexandria, VA: American School Counselor Association.

Jensen, E. & Dabney, M. (2000). *Learning smarter*. San Diego, CA: The Brain Store, Inc.

Kübler-Ross, E. (1997). *On death and dying*. New York, NY: Macmillan Publishing Co., Inc. (see www.elisabethkublerross.com and www.ekrfoundation.org).

Noddings, N. (2005). What does it mean to educate the whole child? *Educational Leadership*, September, 8-13.

Rokeach, M. (1960). *The open and closed mind*. New York, NY: Basic Books.

Scherer, M. (2005). Valuing children. *Educational Leadership*, September, 7.

Schilling, D. & Palomares, S. (1999). *50 activities for teaching emotional intelligence, level III*. Wellington, FL: Innerchoice Publishing.

Life-Skills

Life Skills

Getting to Know Someone New

Objectives

The students will:
- Practice communication skills by listening attentively and speaking in front of the group.
- Become aware of similarities and differences between themselves and others.
- Practice using questions to become acquainted with another person.

ASCA Standards

PS:A2.8   Learn how to make and keep friends
PS:A2.3   Recognize, accept, respect, and appreciate individual differences

Materials

One copy of the experience sheet, *Getting to Know You*, for each student

Procedure

Introduce the activity by saying, "Just about everyone thinks that having friends is important. We go places and do things with our friends. We talk to them about our experiences and problems. We grow up with our friends and sometimes remain friends forever. If you've ever felt left out of a group, or wished you had more friends, today's activity may help. Each of us is going to become acquainted with someone new, which is the first step to becoming friends."

Have each student choose a partner—someone they don't know very well. Tell them to decide which person is "A" and which is "B."

Give each person an experience sheet. Explain that person A is to interview person B, asking the questions on the sheet and writing their responses in the spaces provided. They will have 10 minutes to complete the interview. Then person B will interview person A using the same questions and recording the answers in the same manner.

Life Skills

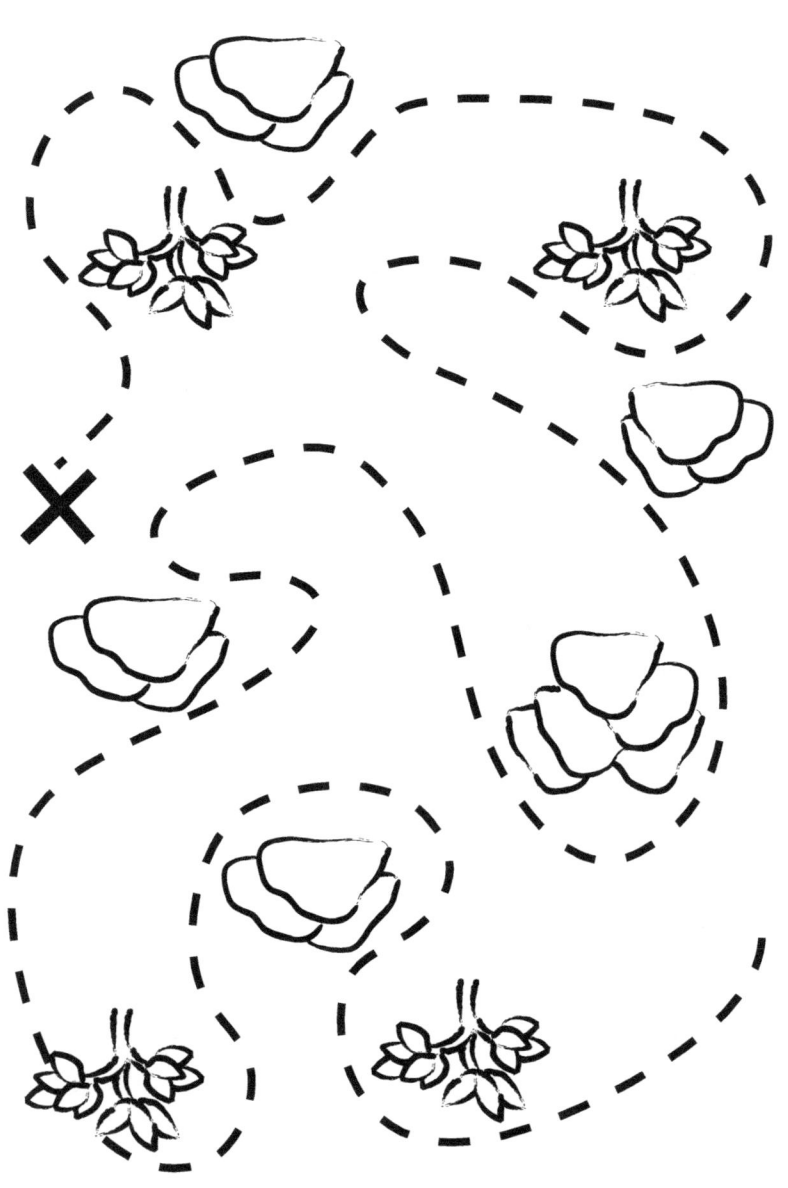

Following the interviews, reconvene the group. Instruct the students to take a couple of minutes to review their notes and think about the most interesting things they learned about their partner.

Go around the group and ask each student to introduce his/her partner, sharing interesting facts from the interview. Encourage the students to do their introductions from memory, not by reading their notes.

Discussion Questions

1. How was the person you interviewed different from you?
2. In what ways are you and your partner the same?
3. How do you benefit by having friends who are different from you?
4. How do you benefit when you and a friend are alike?
5. If you wanted to get to know someone, what kinds of questions would you ask?

Assessment

- Were students able to elicit appropriate responses from their partners?
- Were the students able to verbalize specific differences and similarities between themselves and their partners?
- Were students able to formulate questions they would ask someone they wanted to get to know?

Getting to Know You

1. Partner's full name: _____

2. Birthdate: _____

3. Where were you born? _____

4. How many brothers and sisters do you have? _____
   _____

5. Have you ever lived somewhere else? _____

   Where? _____

6. What do you like to do outside of school? _____
   _____

7. Do you have a pet? _____

8. What is it? _____

   What is its name? _____

   Where were you born? _____

9. What is your favorite food? _____

10. What is your favorite breakfast cereal? _____

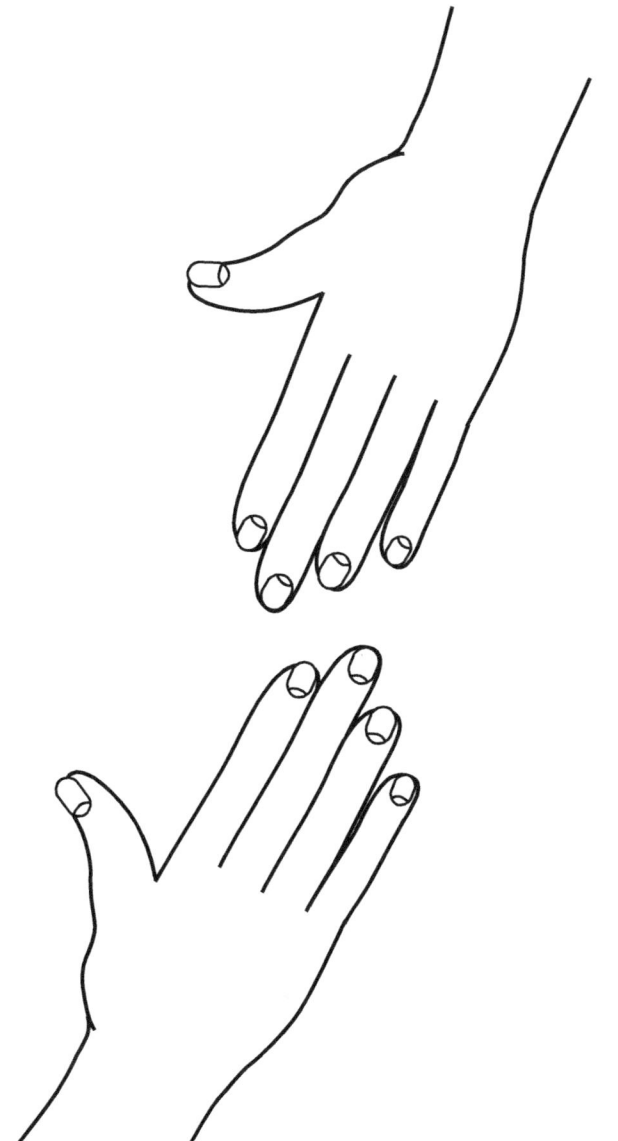

Life Skills

Life Skills

The Shape of Friendship

Objectives

The students will:
- Describe qualities and behaviors that they value in a friend.
- Describe qualities and behaviors that weaken friendships or prevent their development.

ASCA Standards

PS:A1.6   Distinguish between appropriate and inappropriate behavior

PS:A2.8   Learn how to make and keep friends

Materials

One copy of the experience sheet, *What Is a Friend?*, for each student; three or more large pieces of butcher paper; masking tape; marking pens in assorted colors

Procedure

This is the first of a two-part focus on friendship behaviors. It deals with generally helpful and damaging interpersonal behaviors. The next activity, *How to Be a Good Friend*, personalizes the analysis to the student's own behaviors.

Use the experience sheet as a prelude to this activity. Distribute the sheet and go over the directions. Give the students some examples of behaviors they might list on their sheets, then allow time for writing. When the students have finished, ask volunteers to share items from their lists.

Divide the students into small groups. Distribute a large piece of butcher paper and several markers to each group. Give these directions:

Choose one person from your group to lie down on the paper, assuming any position he or she wishes. Have a second person trace around the prone body with a marking pen to make a "person shape." When you have finished, turn the paper over and hand your markers to two other members of your group. The new pair will repeat the process using the reverse side of the paper.

Life Skills

Have the students label one side of the paper, "Things Good Friends Do," and the other side of the paper, "Things Friends Don't Do."

Direct the groups to brainstorm qualities or behaviors that they value in a friend. These might include honesty, loyalty, listening well, being friendly, showing affection, helpfulness, and so forth. When a student has an idea, he or she must pick up a marking pen, go up to the drawing and write the idea inside the person outline. At the same time, the student is to explain the idea to the rest of the group. Encourage all group members to get involved.

Circulate and stimulate discussion within each group. Get the students to focus on the values they are expressing. For example, say, "Cindy, you mentioned that you value being friendly. Would you please explain what that means to you?" or "Jack, you and Lu both said friends are always honest. How do you feel if a friend lies to you?"

When the groups have finished filling in their person shapes, have them turn the paper over and use the other side to record qualities or behaviors they *dislike* in a friend. These might include lying, tattling, backbiting, pressuring, name-calling, and putting others down. Encourage the students to think of their own experiences and fill up the drawing with ideas.

Have the groups tape their drawings to different walls around the room, with the "Things Good Friends Do" side up.

Have each group share its completed drawing (front and back) with the entire class. Facilitate discussion.

Discussion Questions

1. What ideas were recorded by all of the groups?
2. What ideas did you get from the drawings that you hadn't considered before? What are your thoughts about these ideas?
3. How will you use what you learned during this activity in your own friendships?

Extension

Challenge the students to use some of the ideas generated during this activity to make a new friend or strengthen an existing friendship. In two weeks, ask volunteers to share their experiences.

Assessment

- Were students able to verbalize several specific qualities and behaviors that strengthen and weaken friendships?
- Did students demonstrate an understanding of the cause-and-effect relationship between a person's behavior and his/her ability to make and keep friends?

What Is a Friend?

Put a checkmark beside the things you have done to make or keep a friend.
Put an X beside the things you have done that have hurt a friendship.

List things that help to make good friendships.

_____
_____
_____
_____
_____
_____
_____
_____
_____
_____

List things that can hurt a friendship.

_____
_____
_____
_____
_____
_____
_____
_____
_____
_____

How to Be a Good Friend

Objectives

The students will:
- Identify what they and others like about their friendship behaviors.
- Describe negative friendship behaviors.
- Develop a goal and plan for improving one friendship behavior.

ASCA Standards

PS:A1.6   Distinguish between appropriate and inappropriate behavior

PS:A2.8   Learn how to make and keep friends

Materials

One copy of the experience sheet, *My Friendship Goal*, for each student; whiteboard or chart paper

Procedure

This is the second of a two-part focus on friendship behaviors. It asks the students to assess their own behavior and develop a plan that will help them make and keep friends more easily.

Begin by reminding the students of the previous activity. Announce that, in this session, the students are going to concentrate on evaluating their own friendship behaviors.

Ask several volunteers to name things they could begin doing (or stop doing) that would make them a better friend. List ideas on the board, such as:

- Learn how to start a conversation with a new person.
- Volunteer to help someone study for a test.
- Reach out to someone of a different race or cultural background.
- Include someone with a disability in activities.
- Invite someone to eat lunch with me.
- Help a friend learn a new skill or game.
- Stick up for my friends (be loyal).
- Learn how to settle conflicts and negotiate differences.
- Practice giving compliments.
- Smile and use good eye contact when talking with others.
- Bring together friends from different groups in some common activity.

Life Skills

Ask the students to name behaviors that others respond to positively, as well as some that seem to turn others off. Offer three positive and one negative examples from your own experience. For example, say, "My positive friendship behaviors are that I always do what I say I'm going to do, so my friends can count on me. In addition, I have a generally positive attitude. I smile a lot, and I try to remember to tell people when I like their work, or behavior, or the way they look. A negative behavior I need to work on is letting my thoughts jump ahead during conversations, because when I jump ahead I tend to interrupt the person who is speaking."

Take additional examples from the group until you think the students have the idea. Then distribute the experience sheet, "*My Friendship Goal.*" Go over the directions, answering any questions. Allow the students time to complete the sheet.

Have the students pair up. Instruct the partners to take turns sharing three positive behaviors and one negative behavior, as you did in your earlier example. Suggest that they select from their experience sheet those behaviors they would most like to discuss. Allow about 5 minutes for sharing, signaling the partners at the halfway point.

Get the attention of the pairs and take a few moments to talk about the importance of goals in changing behavior. Point out that no one is born knowing how to make and keep friends; rather, these behaviors are learned. When behaviors are learned, they can also be changed. Change involves setting goals for new behaviors and implementing step-by-step plans for achieving those goals.

Give the partners an additional 5 to 20 minutes to share their goals and action plans. Suggest that they help each other formulate steps for achieving their goals. Urge them to make a mutual contract to support each other through continued informal sharing and discussion over the next few weeks. Lead a culminating class discussion.

Discussion Questions

1. How do you explain the fact that some people have so many friends and others have so few?
2. Why are friendships important? What do we gain from having friends?
3. What kinds of help and support do you need to achieve your friendship goal? How and from whom will you get that help and support?

Assessment

- Were most students able to recognize and describe at least one behavioral shortcoming that affects their ability to make and keep friends?
- Did the students set workable friendship goals?
- Did the students verbalize what they needed to do (action steps) to reach their goals?

My Friendship Goal

Friends are important! If you could take three people with you on a trip around the world, whom would you take? Why?

1. Name _____
   Reason _____
2. Name _____
   Reason _____
3. Name _____
   Reason _____

Do you have a friendship with someone that just keeps getting better? What have you done to keep it growing?
_____
_____

Have you ever had a friendship go bad? What was it about the friendship that didn't work out? _____
_____

Name five of your own friendship behaviors that others seem to like:
1. _____
2. _____
3. _____
4. _____
5. _____

Name two behaviors that seem to turn off others (your friends included).
1. _____
2. _____

Think of one way in which you would like to improve your friendship behaviors. Write your GOAL here: ____
_____

To achieve your goal, you need a PLAN—a systematic way of putting your goal into action. What are some of the first steps you will take?
Step 1. _____
Step 2. _____
Step 3. _____
Step 4. _____
Step 5. _____

Things to think about:
- How do you make friends with someone who speaks a different language?
- What should you do if a friend starts doing something that is wrong or dangerous?
- How could you make friends with someone who is blind? …someone who is deaf?

Life Skills

How to Reach a Goal

Objectives

The students will:
- Explain that having a goal is the first step to achieving what one wants.
- Identify specific steps for attaining goals.
- Develop skills in setting practical and achievable goals.
- Experience goal attainment.

ASCA Standards

PS:A1.6   Learn how to set goals
PS:A1.3   Learn the goal-setting process
PS:B1.9   Identify long- and short-term goals
PS:B1.10   Identify alternative ways of achieving goals
PS:B1.12   Develop an action plan to set and achieve goals

Materials

Pens or pencils; blank note paper; one copy of the experience sheet, *You Can Reach Your Goals!*, for each student

Procedure

Explain to the students that successful people have a habit of setting clear goals concerning things that they want to accomplish. Explain that in this activity the students will set a goal and experience the feeling of success that comes with attaining it.

Point out that when we think of goals, we usually picture big important things like cars, vacations, or what we want to be when we grow up. However, most people set dozens of smaller goals each day. Ask volunteers to share some of the things they want to accomplish today. Point out that stating these things is the simplest form of goal setting.

Distribute the experience sheets and spend a few minutes talking about each section. Make sure that the students understand the five "tips" for writing goals. Provide additional examples to clarify each tip.

Give the students a few minutes to write a goal statement. Circulate and assist any who have difficulty. Ask a few students to share their goal with the class.

Life Skills

Explain that goals are achieved in steps. Success is measured as each step is completed. State that the next part of the experience sheet helps the students break down their goals into easily managed steps.

Allow 10 to 15 minutes for the students to write down the steps for achieving their goal. Offer assistance while they are writing.

Direct the students to keep their experience sheets and refer to them daily as they work toward their goals. Review the progress of the students weekly or bi-weekly in class.

Discussion Questions

1. Why is having goals important?
2. Why is it important to have a plan for reaching each of your goals?
3. What would happen if you didn't have a plan?
4. How do you feel when you achieve a goal?
5. How do you feel when you set a goal and never reach it?
6. When you need the help of others to achieve a goal, how can you build in that requirement as part of your plan?

Assessment

- Were most students able to write a clear, specific, measurable goal?
- Did students verbalize an understanding of the importance of goals?
- Were students able to break down their goal into specific, doable steps?

You Can Reach Your Goals!

What Are Goals?

A goal is a target—something to aim for. Just like the goal line in soccer or football, it is something you try your best to reach. Goals can center on having something, like clothes or money, or on achieving something, like good grades.

Tips for Writing Goals

Short-term goals include things like making phone calls, finishing your homework, cleaning your room, doing your chores, or making plans for the weekend. Long-range goals might include planning a summer vacation with your family or saving money for college.

It's best to write goals so that they are:
1. *Clear.* Describe exactly what you want in simple words.
2. *Positive.* State your goal in positive, not negative terms. For example, write, "I will earn a B on Friday's quiz," not "I won't flunk Friday's quiz." See the difference?
3. *Personal.* Don't write goals about other people or things you can't control. Your goals should be about you. For example, write, "I will make two new friends this year," not "I'll get Sue to like me this year."
4. *Realistic.* Don't waste your time writing goals that are impossible to reach.
5. *Measurable.* How will you know that you have reached your goal? An "A" in math is measurable. "Good grades" in math is not as specific, so it's harder to measure.

Goal-Setting Practice

Take a few minutes to write down <u>one</u> of your goals. Check whether the goal is short-term or long-range, and write the date by which you plan to accomplish it.

Goal:

Short-term: _____   Long-range: _____

Target Date: _____

Come Up with a Plan

Think of a time when you wanted something very much. Right away, you probably started thinking of things you needed to do in order to get it. Maybe you even figured out the order in which those steps needed to be taken. That's planning. By developing a step-by-step plan to reach your goal, you increase your chances of achieving it.

Brainstorm all of the things you need to do to reach your goal. List them on the back of this paper. Be very specific. Don't worry about the order of the steps until after you have listed everything. Then go back and figure out which step to take first, second, third, and so on. Put a number beside each step in your plan.

Life Skills

These are the steps I need to take to reach my goal:

How I Spend My Time

Objectives

The students will:
- Evaluate their use of time.
- Identify time-wasters and ways to reduce or eliminate them.
- Explain the relationship between time management and goal attainment.

ASCA Standards

PS:A2.1 Apply time management and task management skills

PS:B2.1 Establish challenging academic goals in elementary school

PS:E1.1 Demonstrate the ability to balance school, students extracurricular activities, leisure time, and family life

Materials

One copy of the experience sheet, *Control Your Time*, for each student

Procedure

Begin by reminding the students of the importance of goals. Review the goal-setting process. Point out that one of the hardest things about attaining goals, particularly long-range goals, is making the time to do what's needed to reach them.

In your own words, explain:

Most of us are pretty good at reaching short-term goals. We do it everyday. One reason is that short-term goals usually have short-term deadlines. For example, if you don't stop at the library this afternoon, you won't have the book you need to finish your report by tomorrow's deadline. If you don't finish your homework early, you won't be able to watch TV. If you don't repair your skateboard before the weekend, you can forget about going to the skateboard park on Saturday.

Long-range goals often don't have deadlines at all. At least not at first. Instead, they require careful planning and the completion of lots of small tasks. Getting to the finals of the National Science Fair takes both planning and dedication. Between choosing a project and finally winning a top prize, there are many, many steps to take. A long-range goal without a plan is just a dream.

Life Skills

Try to get in the habit of writing down all the steps required to reach a goal. Then start taking those steps right away. Even if your goal is five years down the road, there are things that you can do about it now. Getting control of your time will allow you to take daily, weekly, or monthly steps toward your long-range goals.

Distribute the experience sheets. Go over the directions. Draw a "day pie" on the board and divide it up to show the major activities in your own day.

Give the students a few minutes to complete the sheet. Then have them form small groups and share their "day pies" and identified time-wasters. Suggest that the groups generate ideas for controlling and eliminating time-wasters.

Discussion Questions

1. What did your "day pie" tell you about the time you spend doing various things?
2. What changes would you like to make in your use of time?
3. What were the biggest time-wasters in your group?
4. What ideas did you come up with for reducing or eliminating time-wasters?
5. What have been the biggest time-wasters in organizations and groups to which you have belonged?
6. How does good time management help you achieve your goals?

Assessment

- Were students able to estimate the fraction of each day they spend in major categories of activity?
- Did students identify major time-wasters and ideas for controlling them?
- Were students able to verbalize the relationship between time management and goal attainment?

Control Your Time

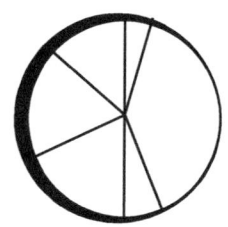

Are you satisfied with how you spend your time?

Where can you fit in the steps you must take to reach your goals?

Make a "Day Pie"

Estimate how many hours or parts of hours you spend in school, sleeping, doing homework, eating, watching TV, playing, reading, working, and other things. Label each piece of your "day pie" to show the major activity it represents. Once you've completed the pie, take a good look at it.

Control Time Wasters

We all waste time in different ways. What are your biggest time-wasters? Put a check mark beside activities that take too much of your time. Add other time-wasters that are not on the list.

Time-Wasters	Ideas for Reducing
__ Phone calls/texting	_____
__ TV/Video games	_____
__ Surfing the Internet	_____
__ Cluttered room or desk	_____
__ Socializing	_____
__ Poor communication	_____
__ Poor study habits	_____
__ Putting things off (procrastination)	_____
__ _____	_____
__ _____	_____
__ _____	_____

Group Think

Help your classmates come up with ideas for reducing or eliminating their worst time-wasters—and yours.

Life Skills

Solo Versus Team Efforts

Objectives

The students will:
- Demonstrate the power of team efforts.
- Describe advantages of working with a team and of working alone.
- Identify their preferred way of working: alone or with other students.

ASCA Standards

PS:A3.2   Demonstrate the ability to work independently, as well as the ability to work cooperatively with other students

PS:A2.1   Acquire employability skills such as working on a team, problem-solving and organizational skills

PS:C2.3   Learn to work cooperatively with others as team members

PS:A1.9   Demonstrate cooperative behavior in groups

PS:A1.4   Learn how to interact and work cooperatively with others

Materials

Stop watch or other time piece that displays seconds; whiteboard; writing materials for each student

Procedure

Have the students form teams of four or five. From the following list, select one word for each team. Write the assigned words on the board so all of the groups can see them.

> identification
> reverberation
> heterogeneous
> responsiveness
> haberdasher
> refrigeration
> significantly
> predetermination
> simultaneous

Explain to the students that, working individually, they are to write as many words as they can using the letters in the word that has been assigned to them. Go over these rules:

- No talking is permitted.
- Write real words of two or more letters.
- Use only the letters in the assigned word.
- Time limit is 5 minutes.

Life Skills

Call time at the end of 5 minutes. Explain to the students that in the second round of the activity, they are to follow the same rules, however, this time they will be working together as a team. Assign each team a new word from the list. Again, allow 5 minutes for brainstorming and then call time.

Poll the teams to find out how many words they came up with while working alone and how many they came up with while working as a team. (Chances are the team efforts produced more words.) Encourage the students to speculate as to why they obtained the results they reported.

Discussion Questions

1. How did you feel when you were working alone?
2. How did you feel when you were part of a team?
3. Under which circumstances, alone or with a team, did you produce more words? Under which circumstances did you enjoy yourself more?
4. Why do team efforts often produce better results than individual efforts?
5. If you prefer working with a team, what are some things you can do to be more successful in school?

Assessment

- Did the students work successfully alone?
- Did the students work successfully in teams?
- Did the students exhibit cooperative behaviors (taking turns, not interrupting, leading, following, encouraging each other) when working in teams?
- Did the students verbalize which way they preferred to work?
- How well did the students explain the results they achieved?

A Team Experiment

Objectives

The students will:
- Demonstrate cooperative and competitive behaviors while completing a task.
- Describe how one person's actions affect the actions of others.
- Explain how cooperative behaviors aid in goal attainment.

ASCA Standards

PS:A3.2   Demonstrate the ability to work independently, as well as the ability to work cooperatively with other students

PS:A2.1   Acquire employability skills such as working on a team, problem-solving and organizational skills

PS:C2.3   Learn to work cooperatively with others as team members

PS:A1.9   Demonstrate cooperative behavior in groups

PS:A1.4   Learn how to interact and work cooperatively with others

Materials

Sixteen (16) toothpicks and one small-necked bottle (eight-ounce plastic juice bottles are ideal) for each group of six to eight students

Procedure

Ask the students to form groups of six to eight and sit in a circle. Give each person two toothpicks. Hand a bottle to one person in each group. Direct that person to place one toothpick across the opening of the bottle and then pass the bottle to the next person. Have that person repeat the procedure using one toothpick. Continue passing the bottle around the circle, adding one toothpick at a time until all of the toothpicks have been successfully placed across the opening of the bottle. Tell the students that if even one toothpick drops, they must start over.

Note on the board how long it takes each group to successfully complete the task. (Use time-keeping to document performance, not to encourage competition between groups.)

When all of the groups have finished, lead a discussion. Focus on cooperative versus competitive behaviors. If groups have to start over due to competitive behaviors, focus on the resulting frustration and loss of time.

Life Skills

Life Skills

Discussion Questions

1. How did you feel when it was your turn to put a toothpick on the bottle?
2. What did you think about when you decided how to place your toothpick?
3. How did your behaviors affect the person who came after you?
4. How would you place your toothpick if you wanted the next person to succeed?
5. How would you place your toothpick if you wanted the next person to fail?
6. How would you pass the bottle if you wanted the next person to succeed?... to fail?
7. What cooperative behaviors did you see in this activity? What competitive behaviors did you see?
8. Which type of behavior—competitive or cooperative—helped your group to complete the task?
9. What did you learn from this activity about cooperating with others?

Variations

For older students, increase the number of toothpicks per student to three. Have the students place straws or pencils across an open box or basket. Very young students could use popsicle sticks.

Assessment

- Did the students recognize the need for cooperative behaviors without being told?
- Were the students able to articulate the cause-and-effect relationship of cooperative and competitive behaviors?
- Were the students able to explain why cooperative behavior is needed in team situations?

How to Be a Good Listener

Objectives

The students will:
- Demonstrate good listening skills.
- Relate good listening to incidents in their own lives.

ASCA Standards

PS:A2.6   Use effective communication skills
PS:A2.7   Know that communication involves speaking, listening, and nonverbal behavior

Materials

One copy of the experience sheet, *What Makes a Good Listener?*, for each student

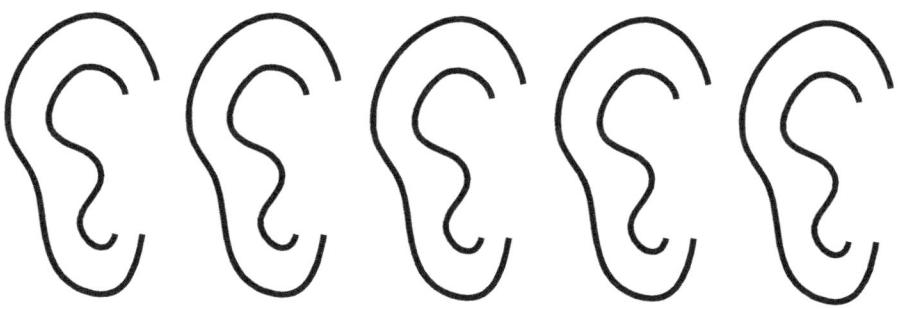

Procedure

Introduce the activity by saying:

Being a good listener means that you carefully listen and try to understand the point of view, and the feelings or ideas, of the person who is speaking. Good listening is not as easy as you might think. To be a really good listener takes focus and concentration.

Distribute the experience sheets. Go over the tips for good listening with the students. Use some examples to demonstrate the meaning and importance of each tip. Ask volunteers to share in their own words what various tips mean to them.

Give the students 10 to 20 minutes to complete the sheet. Circulate and assist. If students have trouble thinking of anyone to write about, ask them questions to help them recall specific incidents.

Reconvene the group and ask volunteers to share their stories. Intersperse discussion questions between stories. Point out and praise good listening throughout the sharing session.

Life Skills

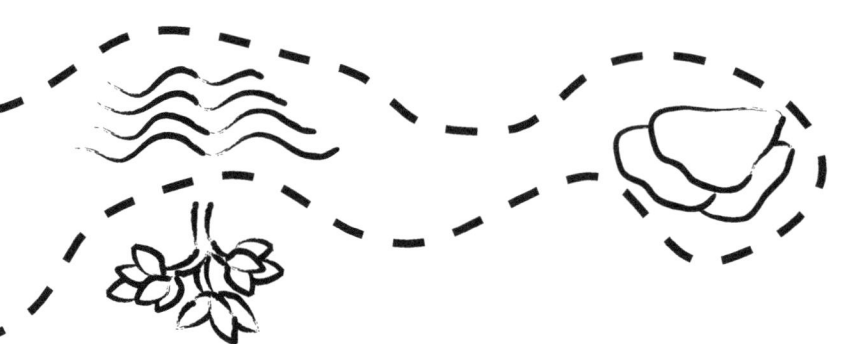

Discussion Questions

1. What made the person you wrote about a good listener?
2. How can you tell when the person you are speaking to is not really listening?
3. How do you feel when you talk with someone who is a poor listener?
4. What do you find hardest about being a good listener?
5. How do you let people know that you are listening to them?

Assessment

- Did the students demonstrate good listening skills during discussion?
- Did the students describe good listening skills in their writing assignments?

What Makes a Good Listener?

Tips for Good Listening

1. Instead of thinking about what you want to say next, think about what the speaker is saying.
2. Give the speaker your full attention. Look at the speaker when he or she is talking. Maintain eye contact.
3. Don't interrupt.
4. If you don't understand what the speaker is saying, ask for an explanation.
5. Try to understand how the speaker is feeling by asking yourself, "How would I feel if this happened to me?"

Some people are easy to talk with. They listen carefully to what you say and they seem to understand your feelings.

In the space to the right, write about a time when someone listened well to you—and it helped! Maybe you needed to talk over a problem. Maybe you wanted to tell someone about an exciting experience. Describe what happened and how you felt. Describe what the person did to show that he or she was listening.

Life Skills

One-Way Communication

Objectives

The students will:
- Practice giving clear instructions to each other.
- Listen to and follow directions accurately.
- Understand why good listening is vital in a variety of situations.

ASCA Standards

PS:A2.6   Use effective communication skills
PS:A2.7   Know that communication involves speaking, listening, and nonverbal behaviors

Materials

Drawing paper and pencils or markers

Procedure

Begin by asking the students: *How do you know when someone is listening to you?*

Accept all responses, jotting ideas on the board.

For example, the students might say that the listener usually…
…looks at me
…is quiet
…shows understanding
…asks questions that make sense
…doesn't interrupt

Point out that while conversations are an example of two-way communication, there are also many times when communication is mostly one-way. Some of them are very important. Ask the students to help you think of examples of one-way communication in which good listening is very important. Generate a list that includes:

- When you ask for directions to a place you've never been
- When your teacher gives an assignment
- When your parents tell you where and when to meet them
- When someone is teaching you a new skill
- When the principal is explaining a change in schedule over the intercom
- When the doctor is telling you how to care for an injury

Announce that the students are going to see how good they are at listening to one-way communication. Tell them to start right now by listening carefully to your instructions.

Tell the students that they have 1 minute to draw a simple design using a circle, a triangle, a rectangle, one curved line, and two straight lines. List the elements on the board. Tell the students to arrange the elements any way they wish in any size they wish.

When the students have finished, tell them to fold their drawings to hide them from view. Then have them form dyads by teaming up with one other person.

In your own words, explain:

First, decide who is A and who is B. Then, turn your desks or chairs and sit back to back. When it is your turn to be the speaker, open your drawing and slowly and clearly describe it to your partner. Your partner will attempt to duplicate the drawing on the back of his or her own sheet. When you are the listener, do not speak or turn around, just listen and draw. You will have 2 minutes to complete the drawing. When I call time, switch roles. Repeat the process for another 2 minutes. The A's will be the first speakers.

Clarify and answer questions. Then start the exercise, keeping time and signaling the students to switch roles after 2 minutes. When both rounds have been completed, tell the partners to turn around and compare their drawings. Urge them to comment on each other's effectiveness as a speaker and listener.

Discussion Questions

Lead a follow-up discussion.

Ask the students to pay attention to the words you use as you systematically and clearly describe your drawing.

Note: If you have time, demonstrate the process by sitting back-to-back with a student and describing a simple drawing that you have done using the assigned elements.

1. What was the hardest part about this exercise? What was the easiest part?
2. What was it like when you were the speaker?
3. What role does listening play in following directions?
4. What kinds of things can happen as a result of poor listening?
5. What kinds of things make it hard to understand directions and other kinds of one-way communication?
6. What should you do if you don't understand a direction?

Assessment

- Did most dyads succeed in duplicating each other's drawings with a fair degree of accuracy?
- Were the students able to articulate the importance of listening carefully to directions?

Communicating Effectively

Objectives

The students will:
- Demonstrate attentive listening with a series of partners.
- Explain how to show others that they are listening.

ASCA Standards

PS:A2.6 Use effective communication skills
PS:A2.7 Know that communication involves speaking, listening, and nonverbal behaviors

Materials

One copy of the experience sheet, *How to Recognize a Good Listener*, for each student

Procedure

Assign the students to groups of eight or ten. (An even number in each group is essential for this activity to work. If a group is one short, join that group during the activity.)

Ask the students to choose a partner. Explain that both people will take turns speaking to the same topic. As the first person (A) speaks for 1 minute, the second person (B) must listen very carefully, gathering information very much like a voice recorder. The listener should not interrupt or ask questions, except for clarification. When time is called, B will have 1 minute to "play back" to A as accurately as possible what he or she heard. Then A and B will switch roles. B will become the speaker and talk about the same topic for 1 minute while A listens. Then A will have 1 minute to "play back" what she or he heard. This will complete the first round, and the students will find new partners within their group.

Signal the end of each minute and give clear instructions. Conduct enough rounds so that every person is paired once with every other person in his or her group. (For example, if groups contain eight students, conduct seven rounds.)

Life Skills

Life Skills

Suggested Dyad Topics

My Favorite Hobby or Pastime
My Favorite Food
My Favorite TV Show or Movie
My Favorite Story, Poem, Book, or Magazine
My Favorite Animal
My Favorite Game or Sport
My Favorite Song or Musical Group
Something That Makes Me Happy
Something I Want to Do This Weekend
Something I'm Looking Forward To

Distribute the experience sheets. Read through the "Good Listening Checklist" together with the group. Discuss each behavior, giving examples where appropriate. Ask the students to check off behaviors that they demonstrated during the dyad activity. Point out that they were asked to listen like tape recorders, so they could not summarize or give feedback. However, these behaviors are also important in good listening. If possible, demonstrate how these behaviors look when done correctly.

Ask questions 6 - 8 to encourage discussion of how good listening applies to everyday interactions. Finally, give the students a few minutes to answer the questions on the experience sheet.

Lead a culminating discussion, using questions 1 - 5.

Discussion Questions

1. How did you feel as the speaker during this exercise? How did you feel as the listener?
2. What was hardest about listening like a tape recorder?
3. Did speaking and/or listening get harder or easier as you went from partner to partner?
4. How does silent, attentive listening lead to effective communication?
5. Why is it a good idea to "play back" what you hear?
6. How do you feel when the person you are talking to doesn't look at you or is busy doing something else?
7. What should you do if your teacher starts talking to you while you are busy on a project? What should you do if a friend tries to talk with you while you are listening to someone else?
8. What are some situations in which good listening is particularly important?

Assessment

- Did the students demonstrate good listening skills during the exercise?
- Did the students name multiple situations where good listening is important?

How to Recognize a Good Listener

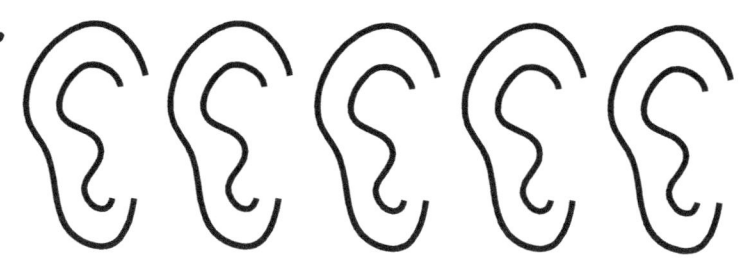

Listening is a very important part of good communication. Listed below are behaviors used by good listeners. Check the ones that describe how you behaved during the listening activity.

Good Listening Checklist

A good listener:

____ Faces the speaker.
____ Gives the speaker full attention.
____ Looks into the speaker's eyes.
____ Is relaxed but alert.
____ Keeps an open mind.
____ Listens to the words and tries to picture what the speaker is saying.
____ Doesn't interrupt or fidget.
____ Waits for the speaker to pause to ask clarifying questions.
____ Tries to feel what the speaker is feeling.
____ Nods and says, "uh huh," or summarizes to let the speaker know he or she is listening.

What is your strongest quality as a listener?

_____
_____
_____

What is your weakest quality as a listener?

_____
_____
_____

How can you become a better listener?

_____
_____
_____
_____

Life Skills

Life Skills

Conveying Feelings and Needs

Objectives

The students will:
- Learn the components of an assertive I-statement.
- Recognize the value of using I-statements over you-statements.
- Practice constructing I-statements.

ASCA Standards

PS:A1.5   Identify and express feelings.
PS:A2.6   Use effective communication skills
PS:B1.4   Develop effective coping skills for dealing with a problem
PS:B1.6   Know how to apply conflict resolution skills
PS:C1.10 Learn techniques for managing stress and conflict

Materials

One copy of the experience sheet, *I-Statements in Action*, for each student

Procedure

Introduce the topic to the class by explaining in your own words:

Sending a clear message is important if you want to be heard and understood. A good way to accomplish this is to use I-statements. I-statements get their name from the fact that they begin with the word, "I." With an I-statement you can express your own concerns, feelings, or needs in a way that doesn't upset listeners or make them defensive or resistant.

You-statements are the opposite of I-statements. You-statements are often blaming, judgmental, or hurtful. When you make an accusation using "you" (for example, "You took my book."), the listener may feel criticized, judged, and may think you are angry. The listener thinks about defending himself and can't hear the message or request you are trying to convey.

On the board, write the three components of an I-statement:
1. The problem
2. Your feelings
3. Your need

Life Skills

Provide several examples:

"When people cut into line (the problem), I feel angry because I've been waiting for my turn and shouldn't have to wait longer (your need)."

"When my ruler is missing (the problem), I get worried (your feeling) because I know I will need it for math class (your need)."

"When people call me names (the problem), I feel sad because I would like to be friends (your need)."

Distribute the experience sheets and go over the directions. Have the students complete the sheets. Then reconvene the group and ask volunteers to share what they have written. Encourage discussion by asking appropriate questions throughout the sharing.

Discussion Questions

1. Why are I-statements helpful in a conflict situation?
2. How do you feel when someone criticizes, blames, or accuses you?
3. What is the hardest thing about making I-statements?
4. Why is it easier to change your behavior when a person makes an I-statement than when he or she makes an accusation?
5. Why do you think using an I-statement is more effective than demanding what you want?

Assessment

- Were the students able to formulate I-statements using three components?
- Were the students able to explain why I-statements work better than You-statements in resolving conflicts?

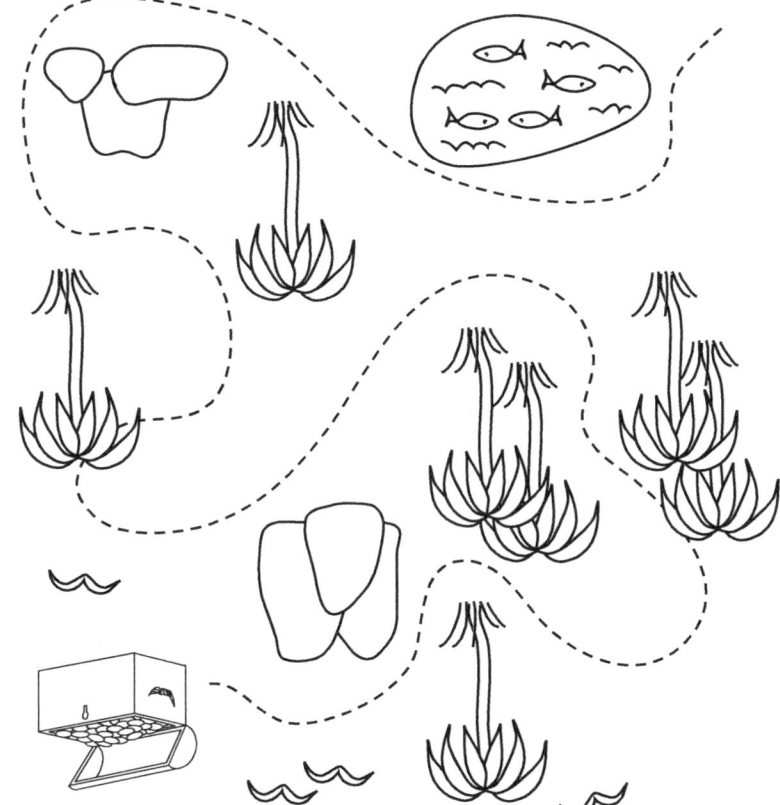

I-Statements in Action

Read the following situations and practice writing I-statements using the three necessary components.

1. At recess there is a line for the water fountain and you are really thirsty. Someone cuts in front of you.

    The problem: _____

    Your feelings: _____

    Your need: _____

2. Your little sister wore your favorite sweater to school without asking your permission.

    The problem: _____

    Your feelings: _____

    Your need: _____

3. Your best friend borrowed your favorite jacket and returned it with a big hole in it.

    The problem: _____

    Your feelings: _____

    Your need: _____

4. You have friends over and your little brother keeps coming into your room uninvited.

    The problem: _____

    Your feelings: _____

    Your need: _____

5. You are talking to your friend and your little sister keeps trying to get your attention to play.

    The problem: _____

    Your feelings: _____

    Your need: _____

6. Your neighbor borrowed your bike and left it out in the rain.

    The problem: _____

    Your feelings: _____

    Your need: _____

Life Skills

Life Skills

Negative Comments Are Downers

Objectives

The students will:
- Understand that put-downs and negative statements can damage the feelings, ideas, and enthusiasm of others.
- Explain how put-downs and negative statements block communication.
- Describe alternatives to put-downs.

ASCA Standards

PS:A1.6   Distinguish between appropriate and inappropriate behavior
PS:A2.6   Use effective communication skills
PS:C1.11   Learn coping skills for managing life events

Materials

One copy of the experience sheet, *Put-Down Add-Up*, for each student

Procedure

Lead a discussion about the derogatory ways in which we sometimes respond to the ideas, accomplishments, and feelings of others. In your own words, say:

Have you ever come up with a great idea that you couldn't wait to share with someone? But when you described your idea, the person you told made fun of it or put you down in some way? Have you ever been afraid to share your strong feelings about something because you were certain no one would understand or, worse, you'd be ridiculed for your feelings? We can easily destroy a person's enthusiasm just by the things we say. We may not mean to do it, but we can kill their ideas and make them feel foolish for feeling the way they do.

Life Skills

Life Skills

Ask the students to help you brainstorm a list of statements that can hurt communication and damage the feelings, ideas, and enthusiasm of others. Write their ideas on the board. Include statements such as:

Can't you see I'm busy?
Not bad for a girl.
Are you kidding me?
You can't be serious!
Who asked for your opinion?
What a stupid idea! Just like a guy.
That's a silly question.
You shouldn't feel that way.
Don't be such a wimp.

Have pairs of volunteers role-play some of the items from the list. Instruct one person to initiate an interaction and the other to respond using the put-down. After each role-play, invite the actors to describe their thoughts and feelings during the exchange. Then ask the group to think of at least two alternative positive statements that could be substituted in that situation. Role-play and debrief those as well.

Distribute the experience sheets and go over the directions. Point out that the sheet asks for "what," "when," and "where," but not "who" made each statement. Stress the importance of anonymity.

Establish a time period for the experiment, such as three days or until the next meeting. Encourage the students to stay alert to what's going on around them so that they can hear and record numerous examples of put-downs.

At the conclusion of the experiment, ask the students to share some of the statements they recorded. Generate discussion about positive alternatives that could have been used by the people involved.

Discussion Questions

1. Why do we respond to others with put-downs and other types of negative statements?
2. Where do you think we learn this type of communication?
3. If you know someone who frequently makes these kinds of statements to you and others, what can you do about it?
4. What can you do when someone puts you down?
5. What can you do when you hear someone put down another person?
6. How can you change your own bad communication habits?

Assessment

- Were the students able to identify a variety of put-down statements?
- Did the students describe the negative effects of put-downs on the people receiving them?
- Were the students able to formulate positive statements that could be substituted for put-downs in various situations?

Put-Down Add-Up

Directions: Record put-downs and negative statements that you hear people say to each other at school, home, and play.

Date/Time	Location	What You Heard

Life Skills

Being in Control

Objectives

The students will:
- Identify different kinds of self-control and self-management.
- Demonstrate behaviors associated with self-control in a variety of situations.
- Assess their own levels of self-control.

ASCA Standards

PS:A1.8   Understand the need for self-control and how to practice it

Materials

none

Procedure

Begin the session by asking the students what the term *self-control* means. Help to clarify the students' responses. In the process, establish that having self-control means being able to restrain and regulate one's own behavior.

Ask the students to think of a time when their emotions were so strong that they couldn't control themselves. Maybe they didn't want to cry or yell or laugh, but the feelings were overpowering.

Invite volunteers to tell the class about their experiences. Ask one or two to act out their incidents, demonstrating exactly what happened.

Next, whisper one of the following situations to a volunteer and have that student act out the situation in pantomime (nonverbally). Have the class guess what is happening and identify the emotion that the student is trying to control.

- You just crashed your skateboard, banging your leg badly, in front of several older kids.
- You get a low grade on a math test for which you studied very hard.
- You open your backpack and a big spider crawls out.
- Your friend passes you a very funny cartoon during quiet time and you try not to laugh.
- Your teacher refers you to the principal for something you didn't do.
- The boy or girl you like just phoned and invited you to a party.

Life Skills

Repeat this process with the remainder of the situations and a new volunteer each time. After each pantomime, talk about methods typically used to control reactions to strong emotions (biting tongue, clenching fists, taking deep breaths, blinking, stiffening muscles, looking away, etc.)

Draw a long horizontal line across the board. At one end write "Explosive Evan." At the other end write "Corked-up Corrine." Explain to the students that the line is a self-control continuum and Evan and Corrine represent the extreme endpoints. Ask the students to help you describe Evan and Corrine. Have fun with this and encourage the students to exaggerate their descriptions. For example:

Explosive Evan blows up all the time. At the slightest provocation, his nostrils flare, tears cloud his eyes and agonizing, earth shaking sounds emerge from his throat. Evan was once able to control himself for 20 seconds and that was when a bee landed on his nose.

Corked-up Corrine is as stiff as a store mannequin. Her expression almost never changes and her movements are rigid and controlled. People have exhausted themselves trying to make Corrine laugh or blink or get angry. But Corrine thinks she's cool and would rather die than lose control.

Ask two or three students at a time to write their names somewhere on the continuum. Explain that before they do this they must decide how much self-control they have. Are they closer to Evan's end of the continuum or Corrine's? Give all of the students an opportunity place themselves on the line.

Lead a culminating class discussion focusing on the concepts of self-control and self-management. Then, with the last few minutes remaining, play a little game with the students. Tell them to sit absolutely still without fidgeting, talking, or blinking. Explain that the last student to move is the winner. Time the students and proclaim the winner, "Self-control King" or "Self-control Queen" for the day.

Discussion Questions

1. Why is it important to learn self-control?
2. What would school be like if students and teachers never made any effort to manage their feelings or behavior?
3. What does self-management have to do with responsibility?
4. What do your parents mean when they tell you to "be on your best behavior"?
5. How do you feel when you successfully control yourself?

Variation

Ask the students to draw a picture of themselves demonstrating self-control in a recent situation. Remind them of all the examples that have been discussed and acted out. Have them share their drawings in small groups, explaining the incidents and the feelings they were able to control.

Assessment

- Did the students demonstrate understanding of the behaviors involved in self-control?
- Were the students realistic in assessing their own levels of self-control?

Passive - Aggressive - Assertive

Objectives

The students will:
- Demonstrate assertive, aggressive, and passive response styles.
- Explain why assertiveness is the most effective and positive response style.

ASCA Standards

PS:A1.6   Distinguish between appropriate and inappropriate behaviors

PS:C1.11   Learn coping skills for managing life events

Materials

One copy of the experience sheet, *Passive, Aggressive, or Assertive?*, for each student

Procedure

Write the words "Passive," "Aggressive," and "Assertive" on the board. Explain to the students that these labels represent styles of responding to people and events. Two of the styles tend to create problems. The third style is usually very effective. Using the following information, explain the styles, giving an example of each.

Aggressive

An aggressive person acts like a bully and pushes others around—physically, verbally, or both. He or she responds to situations by speaking loudly, acting or sounding angry, and using threats, accusations, and name-calling. An aggressive person doesn't respect the rights of others and can make you feel angry, hurt, or scared.

Passive

A passive person is what you might call wishy-washy. He or she speaks very softly, slumps, doesn't look at you, and may even appear scared or nervous. Passive people feel unsure. They usually let others make the decisions and then go along with those decisions, even when they are dangerous or wrong.

Assertive

Assertive people usually stand up for what they want while respecting the rights of others. They look directly at others without staring in a threatening way, and they speak up confidently without yelling. They don't always do what the crowd does. They follow through on their responsibilities to other people.

Life Skills

Read the situations below and ask volunteers to demonstrate how a person might respond using each of the three response styles:

1. The class is on the basketball court and is choosing teams for a game. You want to play center, but so do two other students.

2. You are at a birthday party. The kids start talking about playing a mean trick on a friend of yours who is not there.

3. You've been told by your mom to go straight home after school, but two friends ask you to go with them to the park. You want to obey your mom, but your friends make it hard for you. They insist that she won't find out.

Distribute the experience sheets and go over the instructions. Allow the students time to complete the sheets individually. Then ask them to form groups of four or five. Direct the groups to dramatize the three situations described on the experience sheet, taking turns playing the aggressive, passive, and assertive roles. Circulate and assist. If time permits, ask some of the groups to repeat their dramatizations for the entire class.

Discussion Questions

1. What are the main differences between the response styles?
2. Which response style is the most effective? Why?
3. How can a passive person become more assertive?
4. How can an aggressive person become more assertive?

Assessment

- Were the students able to demonstrate assertive, aggressive, and passive behaviors?
- Did the students recognize the differences between the three kinds of behavior?
- Did the students explain why assertive behavior works better than aggressive or passive in most instances?

Life Skills

Passive, Aggressive, or Assertive?

Read the stories below. Decide which response is passive (P), which is aggressive (AG), and which is assertive (AS). Write your answers next to each response.

1. The teacher tells John that he must redo his homework assignment because it wasn't done right. John responds:

    ___ You can't make me do it again! No way. It's not my fault.
    ___ What difference does it make? You'll give me a bad grade anyway.
    ___ Okay, but first I need you to tell me what I did wrong.

2. Esther asks her friend Mary to help her carry some things to the auditorium after school. Mary responds:

    ___ I can't help you right now, Esther. My mom's waiting out front.
    ___ Oh, gee, if you insist. But Mom's waiting and she'll be mad if I'm late.
    ___ If you can't carry the stuff, why did you volunteer? I'm busy.

3. When she gets home from work, Pete's mother brings his bike in out of the rain. When Pete thanks her, she says:

    ___ If you weren't such a moron, you wouldn't have left it out in the rain in the first place.
    ___ You're welcome. Maybe you can return the favor someday.
    ___ That's me, always picking up after everyone.

Life Skills

What's Your Idea?

Objectives

The students will:
- Experience the power of focused critical thinking.
- Understand that problems often have multiple solutions, and goals can be reached in many ways.

ASCA Standards

PS:B1.2 Learn and apply critical thinking skills

Materials

Timer or clock/watch with a second hand; list of topics (see below) written on the board prior to the session; writing materials

Procedure

Tell the students that you want their help in doing some critical thinking. Ask the students how many know what brainstorming is. Listen to the comments of those who have participated in brainstorming sessions before and clarify that brainstorming is a process in which many ideas or solutions are generated for solving a problem or handling a situation. In your own words, explain:

Imagine that you and a friend want to surprise another friend by doing something special on his or her birthday. There are many possible things that you could do, but until you think of them you can't do them. The more ideas you come up with, the better your chances of choosing the perfect surprise. You decide to hold a brainstorming session. You spend 5 minutes listing as many ideas as you can think of. You write them all down and you don't stop to discuss any of them until the 5 minutes are up. You just keep thinking and throwing out ideas. Afterwards you go back and talk about each idea and then agree on the best one.

Ask the students if they can help you make a list of rules for brainstorming based on the process you just described. You should end up with these rules on the board:

1. Suggest as many ideas as you can think of. Don't worry about details, just be creative.
2. Write down every idea.
3. Don't reject, put down, evaluate, or discuss any idea during the brainstorming process.

Have the students form small groups of four or five and choose a recorder. Make sure that the recorders have paper and pencils. Then, in your own words, explain the assignment.

Life Skills

Pick a topic from the list on the board. I will give you the signal to start brainstorming. You will have 3 minutes to come up with as many ideas as you can think of. Write them all down and be sure to follow the rules. At the end of 3 minutes, I'll give you the signal to stop.

Circulate and observe the groups. Call time at the end of 3 minutes. Do a quick check of each group, commenting on the number of ideas generated and reinforcing the students for their creativity. Review any rules that the students had difficulty with.

If possible, have the groups repeat the process several more times, using new topics during each round. Do not evaluate (or allow the students to evaluate) any suggested ideas. Focus entirely on gaining practice in brainstorming. Reserve about 20 minutes for a culminating discussion.

Topics

- What can you do to help out at home?
- How can you surprise your parent on her/his birthday?
- How can you make your room a better place to study?
- What can you do to have fun on a rainy Saturday?
- What can you do if you get lost?
- What can you do if you think someone is following you?
- How can we rearrange the classroom to make it better?
- What kind of class party shall we have for the holidays?
- How can we show our thanks as a class on Thanksgiving?
- How can we make the school more attractive?
- How can you meet and make new friends?
- How can we decide who goes first in a game?
- How can we design a better playground?

Discussion Questions

1. What was easiest about brainstorming? What was hardest?
2. How did you feel and what did you do when someone suggested a wild or crazy idea?
3. Why is it important to think of many different possibilities when you are trying to solve a problem?
4. Why not just do the first thing that pops into your head?
5. Once you have a long list of ideas, what do you do next?

Variation

When working with younger students, conduct the brainstorming sessions with the total group, writing ideas on the board.

Assessment

- Were the students able to envision many possibilities in each situation?
- Did the students demonstrate understanding of the value of having choices?

Life Skills

Current Events Research

Objectives

The students will:
- Summarize a current events article on an important issue or event.
- Generate solutions to a current events problem presented by the teacher.
- Generate and choose solutions to a problem.

ASCA Standards

PS:B1.1   Use a decision-making and problem-solving model
PS:B1.3   Identify alternative solutions to a problem
PS:A1.9   Demonstrate cooperative behavior in groups
PS:A2.2   Respect alternative points of view

Materials

Current events articles obtained by you and the students prior to class

Procedure

Ask the students to obtain a current events article from a newspaper, news magazine, or reputable online news site. Have them bring a hard copy of the article to school on the day of the activity. Require that the articles deal with an issue or event of some importance. Bring an article of your own dealing with a problem for which creative solutions are obviously needed.

Talk to the students about the importance of being well-informed. Explain that the world is shaped by the interest and participation of individuals working together to build, produce, feed, govern, and educate. In the process they create conflicts and problems that must be solved. Ask the students what kinds of issues, events, and problems they discovered while reading news articles. Ask two or three volunteers to briefly tell the class what they learned.

Have the students form dyads and take turns sharing their articles. Allow about 5 minutes for this. Then read your article aloud to the class. Define terms used in the article and discuss the problem. Ask these questions:

- What is the problem?
- Whose problem is it?

Announce that through group discussion the students are going to come up with solutions to the problem described in the article.

Have the students form groups of three to five. Have each group choose a leader and a recorder. Then announce that the groups will have 20 minutes to brainstorm solutions to the problem. Review the rules for brainstorming and post them in a location visible to everyone.

Rules for Brainstorming

1. Think of as many possible solutions as you can in the allotted time.
2. Use your imagination and be creative.
3. Do not question, criticize, or evaluate any suggestion during the brainstorming process.
4. After the brainstorming period is closed, go back and evaluate and discuss the suggestions.
5. As a group, agree on the best solution.

Call time after 10 minutes to close the brainstorming. Then have the groups discuss and evaluate their suggestions for 10 additional minutes. Their task is to choose one solution to present to the class. Suggest that they answer these questions:
- Will this solution solve the problem?
- Can this solution actually be done?
- Will combining any suggestions make a better solution?

Allow a few more minutes for discussion. Have the group leaders report to the class.

Discussion Questions

1. What was the hardest part about finding a solution to this problem?
2. If your group was not able to come to a decision, why not?
3. How were disagreements or conflicts handled in your group?
4. How will learning to solve problems here in the classroom help prepare us to solve them in the outside world?

Assessment

- Did the students choose appropriate current events articles?
- Were students able to accurately summarize the problem they chose?
- Were the solutions that the students chose realistic? Were they creative?

A Team Problem-Solving Activity

Objectives

The students will:

- Generate ideas for solving a problem.
- Evaluate and test possible solutions.
- Demonstrate a final solution to the problem.

ASCA Standards

PS:A3.5   Share knowledge
PS:B1.1   Use a decision-making and problem-solving model
PS:B1.3   Identify alternative solutions to a problem

Materials

Egg timer or hourglass (or picture of either), two identical glass jars, wide masking tape, large container of salt, one piece of heavy paper (and a couple more in reserve), a nail, a pencil, and scissors

Procedure

Tell the students that you are going to test their problem-solving skills. Explain that problem solving is a lot like decision making. First you have to figure out what your alternatives are (different ways you might be able to solve the problem). Then you have to decide which one will work (or work best). Point out that there are different kinds of problems. In some problems, like math problems, you are trying to find a correct answer or solution. In other problems, like a jigsaw puzzle, you know what the solution is, but you have to figure out how to get there. Ask the students if they can think of other kinds of problems.

Show the students the egg timer/hourglass and demonstrate how it works (or show them the picture and tell them how it works). Then set the rest of the materials on a table in the front of the room. Announce the problem:

Figure out how to make a timer out of these materials.

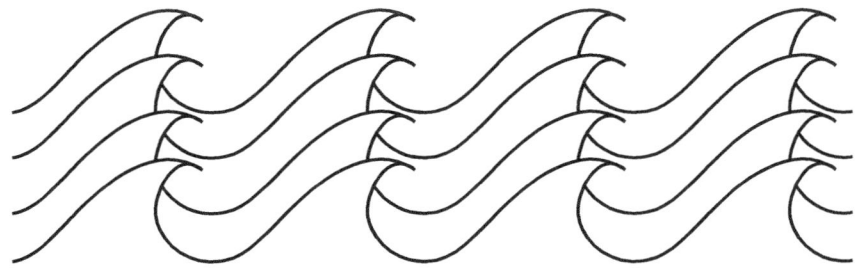

Life Skills

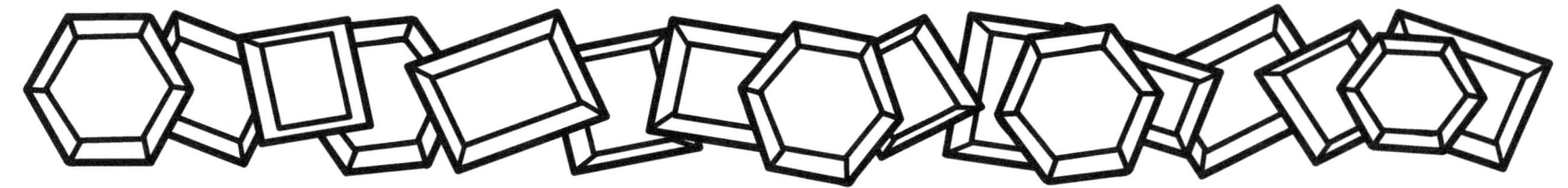

Allow a few students at a time to come to the table and examine the materials, including the egg timer/hourglass. Then ask the students how they think you should proceed. Write their suggestions on the board under the heading, "Possible Solutions." Don't start evaluating ideas until the students have run out of ideas. Keep in mind that the ideas will probably describe single steps, not the entire solution.

When the brainstorming is over, take one idea at a time and discuss what would happen if you used that idea. Manipulate the materials (or allow volunteers to manipulate them) to see if the idea might work. When the students think that an idea will work (such as taping the mouths of the two jars together), try it. Then say, "That seems to work, but how can we get the salt inside and control its flow from one jar to the other?"

If the students get stuck, don't solve the problem for them. Set it aside and return to it later, or the next meeting.

When the problem has been solved and the timer completed, conclude the activity with a discussion focusing on the problem-solving process.

Discussion Questions

1. What was it like to solve this problem?
2. What process did we use to come up with ideas?
3. What process did we use to evaluate the ideas?
4. If we had some other kinds of materials, could we have solved the problem another way?
5. What could we use instead of paper? Instead of tape? Instead of salt?
6. What should you do if a solution doesn't work?

Variation

Assemble multiple sets of materials and challenge the students to solve the problem in small groups. Have each group show its solution to the class and describe how it worked together to solve the problem.

Assessment

- Were the students able to describe solutions (or partial solutions) using the materials provided?
- Did the students persist, even when their ideas failed?

What Shall We Do?

Objectives

The students will:
- Make a group choice from among alternatives.
- Use communication and negotiation skills to reach a group decision.

ASCA Standards

PS:A1.4   Learn how to interact and work cooperatively in teams
PS:A1.5   Learn to make decisions
PS:A1.9   Demonstrate cooperative behavior in groups
PS:A2.2   Respect alternative points of view

Materials

One copy of the following list of "Choices" for each group

Procedure

Have the students form small groups of four to six. Announce that the members of each group are going to work together to make a decision. In your own words, elaborate:

I want you to pretend that you are the student council for our school. This is an exciting time for you because you have an important decision to make. The council has been given $10,000 by an anonymous donor. You must decide how to spend the money. However, the donor has narrowed your range of choices. You must decide from among six alternatives.

Give each group a copy of the list of choices. Read through the list with the students.

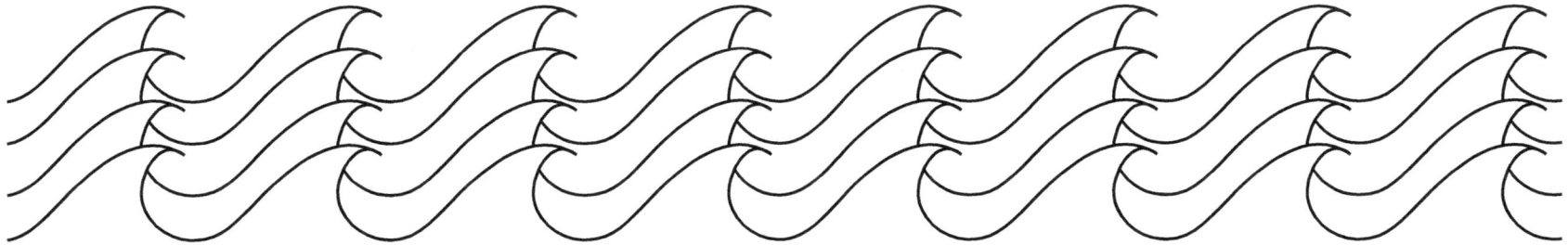

Life Skills

Choices

1. Take the student council (your group) to Disney World.
2. Donate the money to a local children's hospital to be used to help with the treatment of a child from an uninsured family.
3. Host a big party, fair, or festival for the entire school.
4. Donate the money to a homeless shelter.
5. Fund badly needed playground or athletic equipment for the school.
6. Put the money in a savings account for the student council.

Explain to the students that they will have 20 minutes to reach a decision. List the following rules for interaction on the board and discuss as needed:

- One person speaks at a time, with no interruptions.
- Listen to and consider the ideas and opinions of all members.
- Consider the benefits and drawbacks of each alternative.
- Agree on one choice that is acceptable to all members of the group.

After calling time, give the groups an additional 5 minutes to discuss their behavior during the decision-making process. Then gather the entire group together for a culminating discussion.

Ask each group to share what their decision was and how they reached it.

Discussion Questions

1. What kind of communication took place in your group?
2. What were the major disagreements or conflicts in your group?
3. What did you do to resolve disagreements?
4. How easy or difficult was it for your group to come to a decision?
5. What did you learn about group decision making?

Variations

Have the groups achieve consensus on a first and second choice; on first, second, and third choices; or on a rank ordering of all alternatives.

Assessment

- Were most of the groups able to reach consensus on a choice?
- Did the students complete the decision making process with minimal adult assistance?

Learning Strategies

Lerning Strategies

Tips for Improving Study Habits

Objectives

The students will:
- Learn and practice effective study habits.
- Develop and implement plans for self-improvement.

ASCA Standards

A:A1.2   Display a positive interest in learning

A:B1.3   Apply the study skills necessary for academic success at each level

A:A1.5   Identify attitudes and behaviors leading to successful learning

Materials

One copy of the experience sheet, *Identifying Time-Wasters*, for each student

Procedure

Begin by asking the students where and how they study. Call on volunteers to share their study strategies. List particularly helpful or innovative ideas on the board. Tell the students that you are going to describe additional study tips. Explain that if they are willing to incorporate these suggestions, they will soon be more successful students.

Have the students take notes as you present the following ideas. Write key words on the board to make it easier for the students to understand each point.

1. **Plan a specific time to study for each class.** Most students making the transition from elementary to middle school and from middle to high school fail to recognize that more is expected of them. Most teachers at these levels assign homework on a daily basis.

2. **Study the difficult subjects first.** The difficult classes demand more energy than the easier ones so save the "light" subjects for last.

Learning Strategies

3. **Schedule short, frequent breaks during study or homework sessions.** Whenever possible, study for approximately 20 minutes and take a 5-minute break. Then study again for 20 minutes and take another 5-minute break. We tend to remember better what we learn at the beginning and end of each study period, so create more beginnings and endings. Give your brain a break.

4. **Study at your best time of the day.** Some of us are morning people and function most effectively during the early morning hours. Others of us are most productive in the afternoon or evening. Study your most difficult subjects during your optimum time period.

5. **Establish a special study area.** Select a place that you can use only for study. This should not be on your bed or near a television. Your body and mind are trained to respond to their environment. Your body has learned that a bed is a place for sleep; your mind knows that the TV is a tool for relaxation and entertainment. Study at a desk or table. Give your body the signal that it is time to study.

6. **Study in a quiet place.** Don't study in front of a television or near a loud stereo. The majority of research clearly shows that the optimum way to study is in silence or with soft music, not to the accompaniment of TV, loud music, or other distractions.

7. **Avoid using the phone during scheduled study time.** If someone else can answer the phone, have that person take messages. Then return your calls later. If you have a cell phone, turn it off. If you are the only one at home, let an answering machine or voicemail take messages.

8. **Make good use of the scheduled study time.** If you haven't accomplished what you planned, review your actions and notice the ways in which you wasted time. Since we are creatures of habit, we tend to waste time the same ways again and again.

9. **Pretend you are a "paid" student.** If you were employed as a student, would you be earning your wages? If your breaks were longer than your study sessions, you would probably have your pay docked or lose your job.

10. **Push yourself to finish assignments.** Sometimes we let ourselves get close, but decide that we are too tired or busy to finish an assignment. If you can press yourself to finish, you will establish a habit of accomplishing what you set out to do.

Distribute the experience sheets and go over the directions. Give the students a few minutes to complete them. Then have the students form dyads or triads and share their findings and conclusions.

Finally, bring the group back together for a summary discussion.

Discussion Questions

1. What are some of your biggest time-wasters?
2. Which ones are the most difficult to give up?
3. How can you improve your study habits?
4. Which study tips do you plan to try?
5. Who will you ask for help or support in order to carry out your improved study plan?

Assessment

- Did the students identify time-wasters?
- Did the students describe specific ways of eliminating or reducing time-wasters?
- Did the students express understanding of the study tips?

* For additional information and strategies on study skills, see *Studying, Test-Taking, and Getting Good Grades* by Susanna Palomares and Dianne Schilling, Innerchoice Publishing, 2006.

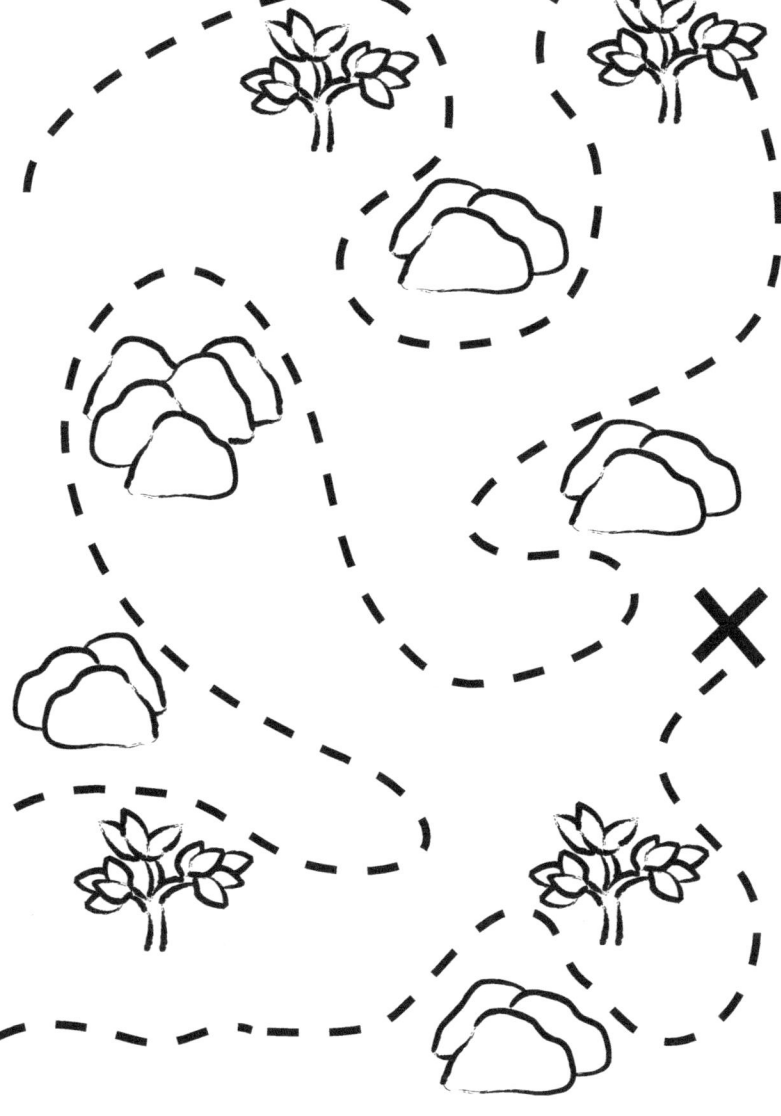

Learning Strategies

Identifying Time-Wasters

Some of the biggest roadblocks to effective study are time-wasters like cell phone calls, e-mail, and video games. What are your biggest time-wasters?

List all the ways you waste time when you should be studying. _____

_____

_____

Now go back and put checkmarks next to your two biggest time-wasters.

Why are these time-wasters so attractive to you? What are you getting out of them? _____

_____

_____

What are these time-wasters costing you? What price are you paying? _____

_____

_____

Now pick three time-wasters from your list that you are willing to reduce or eliminate. Write them below and describe how you plan to control them.

Time-Waster	How I Plan to Reduce or Eliminate
1. _____	_____
	_____
2. _____	_____
	_____
3. _____	_____
	_____

Lerning Strategies

What's Your Style?

Objectives

The students will:
- Assess their preferred learning styles.
- Use learning-style information to enhance performance.

ASCA Standards

A:A2.4 Apply knowledge and learning styles to positively influence school performance

A:B1.6 Use knowledge of learning styles to positively influence school performance

Materials

One copy of the experience sheet, *What Style Are You?* for each student; optional pre-made chart of learning strategies (see below)

Procedure

Begin by informally polling the students regarding their preferred ways of learning. Ask for a show of hands from those who learn best by seeing written words, pictures, graphs, maps, and charts. Then ask for a show of hands from those who learn best by hearing spoken directions, lectures, stories, and examples. Finally ask which students learn best by handling objects, taking things apart and putting them back together, acting things out, and conducting experiments.

Explain that the three main ways of learning are visually (seeing), auditorily (hearing), and kinesthetically (doing). Share your own learning style and explain to the students how you use your style to learn more effectively. Be sure to stress that there is no best way to learn and that exposing yourself to a variety of approaches can be very helpful.

Distribute the experience sheets. Explain that the self-assessment will give the students a clearer picture of which learning style they prefer. Allow a few minutes to complete the assessment.

Learning Strategies

Direct the students to add up the number of eye, ear, and hand answers they chose. Take a second show of hands and compare it to the first. Ask how many students arrived at a different conclusion after completing the assessment. Call on volunteers to describe the differences.

On the board, or a pre-made chart, list the following tips for each learning style. (Next to the three headings, draw symbols of an eye, an ear, and a hand.) Explain that these are specific behaviors that will help the students learn more effectively.

Visual Learner

- Sit near the front of the class where you can see well.
- Draw pictures and charts as you read about or study a subject.
- Create and use flash cards.
- Study for tests by rereading source materials.

Auditory Learner

- Sit where you can hear well.
- Read study notes and written materials aloud to yourself.
- Use a recorder to tape lectures, stories, and directions.
- Create rhymes, raps, and dialogues of study materials.

Kinesthetic Learner

- Physically follow directions as you read or hear them.
- Draw pictures and charts to involve muscle movement.
- Develop skits and plays of things you are learning.
- Stand or walk around while studying or practicing from memory.

Discussion Questions

1. Which strategies do you already use when studying?
2. Which new ideas are you going to try?
3. What other strategies do you use that are not listed?
4. What can we do here in class to help you learn better?
5. What should you do if you have more than one learning style?

Assessment

- Did the students accurately identify their preferred learning styles?
- Did the students identify strategies that will help them learn more effectively?

What Style Are You?

Circle one answer to each question. When you have finished, add up your visual (eyes), auditory (ears), and kinesthetic (hands) answers.

1. If you could only have one of these when you study, which would you choose?
   - 👁 A neat, organized work area.
   - 👂 A totally quiet room.
   - ✋ A comfortable place to sit.

2. Which assignment would you like best?
   - 👁 Read a story.
   - 👂 Give an oral report.
   - ✋ Create a project.

3. Which would you rather do?
   - 👁 Write a story.
   - 👂 Tell a story.
   - ✋ Act out a story.

4. When you have free time, which do you prefer to do?
   - 👁 Watch a movie or read a book.
   - 👂 Listen to music or talk with a friend.
   - ✋ Play a game or sport.

5. Which would you rather join?
   - 👁 An art class.
   - 👂 A musical group.
   - ✋ A sports team.

6. When you are going to read a book for fun, which do you choose?
   - 👁 A book with lots of pictures.
   - 👂 A book with lots of dialogue.
   - ✋ A story with lots of action, or a book with puzzles and games.

7. When you are standing and waiting in line, what do you usually do?
   - 👁 Look around and try to find something interesting to watch or read.
   - 👂 Talk to the people around you.
   - ✋ Move around as much as possible—pace, stretch, or fidget.

8. When you use new software, program a cell phone, or build a model, how do you start?
   - 👁 Read the directions and study the diagrams.
   - 👂 Talk to someone who can tell you how to do it.
   - ✋ Start working and figure it out as you go along.

9. How would you choose to study for a test?
   - 👁 Read notes and headings and look at pictures and diagrams.
   - 👂 Read out loud and have someone ask you questions.
   - ✋ Make a diagram or model of the material, or make up a sample test.

10. If you don't know how to spell a word, what do you usually do?
    - 👁 Write it out so you can see how it looks.
    - 👂 Spell it out loud or sound it out loud.
    - ✋ Go ask someone or check in an online dictionary.

Learning Strategies

Tips for Working with Study Groups

Objectives

The students will:
- Demonstrate cooperative learning strategies.
- Learn and practice effective study habits.

ASCA Standards

A:A1.2   Display a positive interest in learning
A:A3.2   Demonstrate the ability to work independently as well as the ability to work cooperatively with other students
A:A3.5   Share knowledge
C:A2.4   Learn how to interact and work cooperatively in teams

Materials

One copy of the experience sheet, *Tips for Study Groups*, for each student

Procedure

Begin by pointing out that education sometimes becomes highly competitive as students compete for good grades. Yet everyone's job is easier when the teacher and students pull together to try to ensure that school is a "win-win" situation—one in which all students succeed. Point out that people are social beings and generally enjoy and draw power from working cooperatively in groups.

Ask the students to help you brainstorm some of the benefits of working cooperatively. Quickly list their comments on the board. Be sure to include these benefits:

- camaraderie and fun
- support and encouragement
- extra brainpower
- incentive to stick to scheduled study times
- strength and energy when you're tired or discouraged
- a chance to build rewarding relationships

Learning Strategies

Make these points about studying with a buddy or in groups:
- Studying with friends is okay if joking around, playing music, etc., does not interfere with the real purpose of getting together, which is to study.
- Study groups should be limited to four or five people.
- If possible, rotate the location of study groups from home to home. Study outdoors occasionally if the weather permits. If possible, have the host student provide water or juice.
- At the end of each meeting, clarify the location of the next meeting, the subject to be studied, and the materials needed. Hold each member accountable for arriving with appropriate materials, ready to contribute to a productive session.

Distribute the experience sheets and read through the suggestions together.
(The explanatory paragraphs below may be used as a script. The same information is abbreviated on the student experience sheet.)

1. Test each other by asking questions about material from lectures, reading assignments, and notes. For example, have each group member write four or five test questions to bring to each study session. Compile the questions and have everyone take the test as a way of reviewing, and of identifying areas where study is needed.

2. Practice teaching each other the material. One of the best ways to learn something is to teach it. Divide up the material and have members take turns instructing the rest of the group on the main points related to their portion.

3. Compare and contrast notes. Have everyone contribute his or her notes from lectures or reading assignments or both. Compare the notes and use this as a gauge in deciding which material is most important. If everyone wrote it down, consider it significant. Ask questions about anything that is confusing.

4. Brainstorm test questions as a group. After teaching each other and comparing notes as a group, spend 5 to 10 minutes brainstorming possible test questions. Compile a list (along with those questions created individually) in a special section of your notebook.

Announce that you are going to conduct an experiment in group study by having the students prepare for a test in groups.

Randomly divide the class into groups of four or five. Working individually, have the students each develop four test questions related to a recent class assignment. Tell them to take turns asking their group the questions as a kind of pretest to determine where the group needs to concentrate its study efforts.

Then have the group divide up the information to be learned and assign each individual a section to teach the group at the following meeting. End the second session with a 5- to 10-minute brainstorm of test questions covering the entire assignment.

Test the class on the assigned material and grade the tests in your usual manner.

Discussion Questions

1. How did you do on the test?
2. How does studying with a group compare to studying alone?
3. What is the most difficult part of studying with a group? What is the easiest part? The best part?
4. What else have you learned about the dynamics of studying with a group?

Assessment

- Did students' scores on the experimental test exceed those of previous tests?
- Did the majority of students participate actively in the experimental study groups?
- Did the students demonstrate effective study skills?

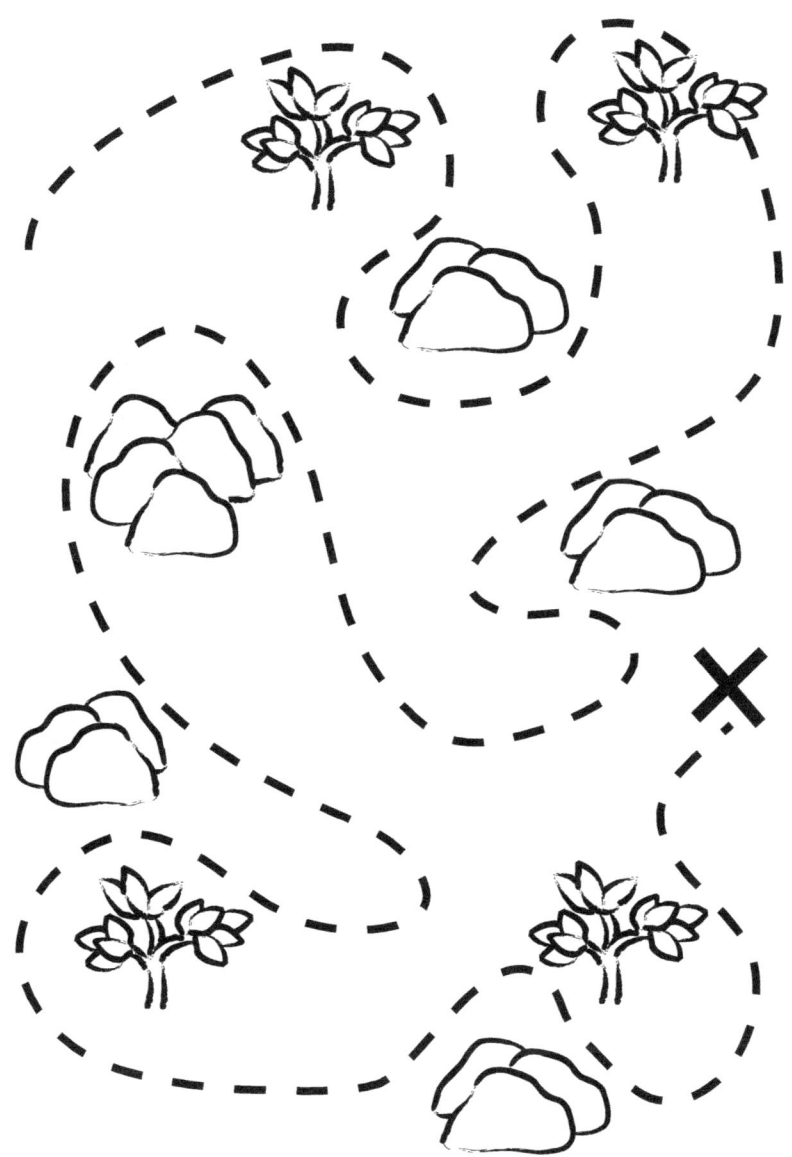

Learning Strategies

Tips for Study Groups

Here are four great ways to study with a group or a study buddy. Keep this list as a reminder.

Test each other by asking questions about material from lectures, reading assignments, and notes.

1. Have each person write four or five test questions.
2. Combine the questions to make a test.
3. Take the test.
4. Score the test.
5. Study the things you missed.

Teach each other the material.

1. Divide up the material.
2. Study your part.
3. Take a turn teaching the main points of your part to the rest of the group.

Compare and contrast notes.

1. Have everyone contribute his or her notes from lectures or reading assignments or both.
2. Compare the notes and pick the most important points. If everyone wrote it down, consider it important.
3. Ask questions about anything that is confusing.

Brainstorm test questions as a group.

1. Teach each other or compare notes (your choice).
2. Brainstorm test questions for 5 to 10 minutes.
3. Compile a list.
4. Keep it in your notebook.

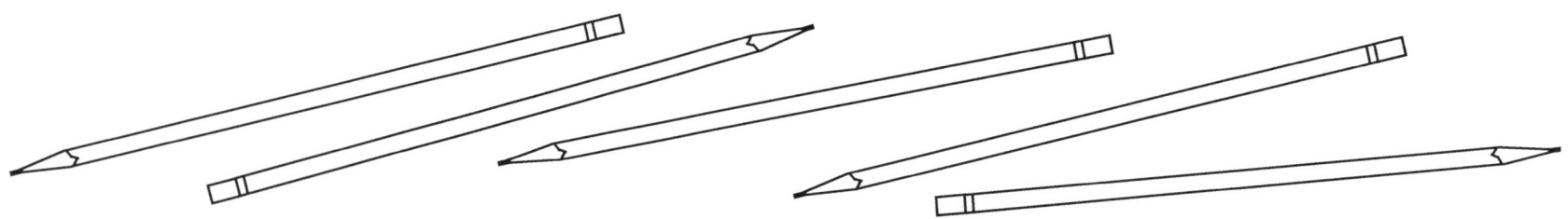

Lerning Strategies

Making To-Do Lists

Objectives

The students will:
- Experience the value of keeping a daily to-do list.
- Explain how to-do lists can increase school and general success.

ASCA Standards

A:A2.1   Apply time-management and task-management skills
C:A1.7   Understand the importance of planning
C:A1.10   Balance between work and leisure time

Materials

One copy of the experience sheet, *My To-Do List*, for each student

Procedure

Begin by discussing the value of to-do lists. Explain that creating a daily list of homework assignments, appointments, meetings, and other activities:
- Increases the chances of achieving each day's objectives.
- Reduces the number of things you have to remember.
- Prioritizes tasks so the most important things can be done first.
- Increases your reliability.
- Encourages other good self-management habits.

Announce that the students are going to make and use a practice to-do list.

Distribute the experience sheets and go over the directions. If it is late in the day, have the students complete the sheet for the following school day. Allow sufficient time for them to recall and list all of their assignments, activities, chores, appointments, and meetings.

At a follow-up session, give the students an opportunity to discuss the experience.

Learning Strategies

Extension

Make additional copies of the experience sheet available for students who wish to continue using to-do lists. Then repeat this activity occasionally (monthly or bi-monthly) to help the students internalize the habit.

Discussion Questions

1. How much and in what ways did the to-do list help you?
2. What was the hardest thing about using a to-do list?
3. What would you change about the to-do list if you could design a new one?
4. How can keeping a to-do list increase your reliability?
5. How can a to-do list make you more relaxed and confident?
6. When is the best time to write down a task on your to-do list? (as soon as you know about it)

Assessment

- Did the majority of students make and follow a to-do list?
- Did the students report greater productivity using to-do lists?
- Did the students indicate a desire to continue using to-do lists?

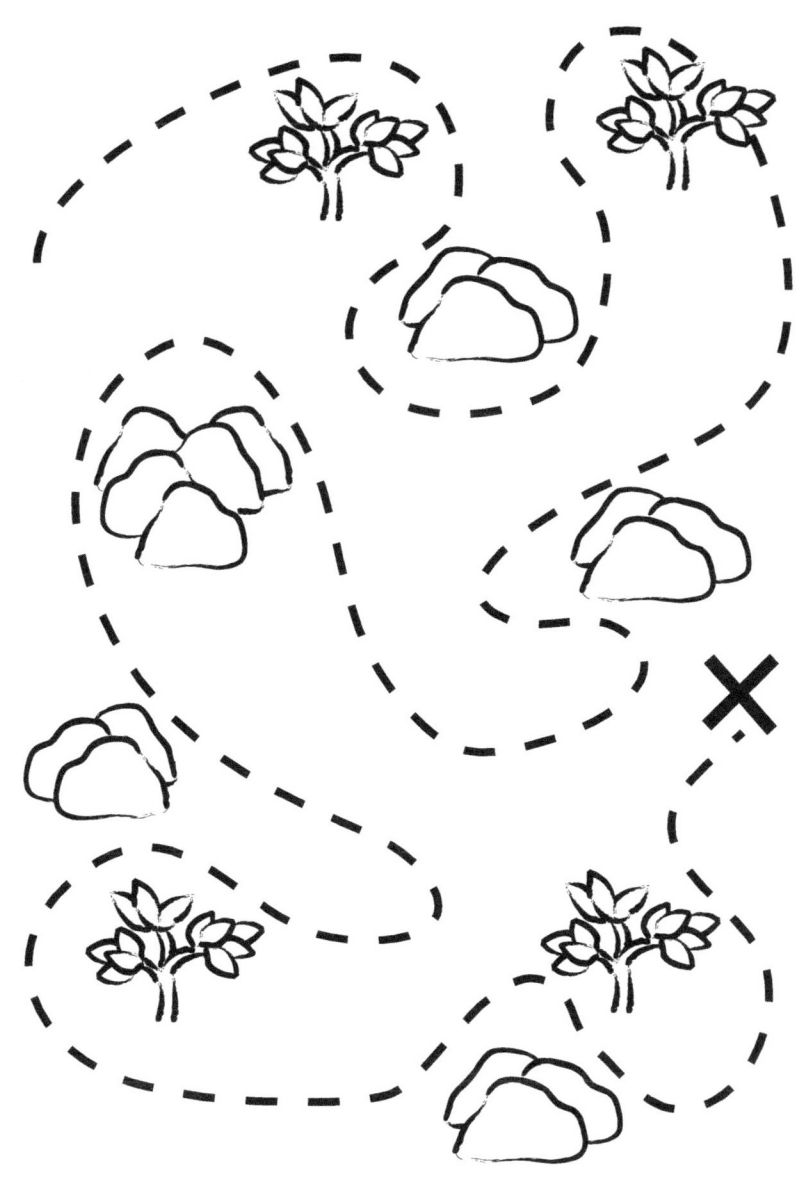

My To-Do List

Directions

1. List all of the separate tasks that you plan to complete today, and estimate how long it will take to complete each one.
2. Mark either A, B, or C for each task. A is "*must do.*" B is "*nice to do.*" C is "*can wait.*"
3. Prioritize your "A" tasks (#1 is most important).
4. Complete the "A" tasks in their order of importance.
5. Prioritize the "B" tasks.
6. Do as many "B" tasks as you can, in order of importance.
7. When you have finished a task, put a check mark in the last column.

Keep your to-do list with you throughout the day.

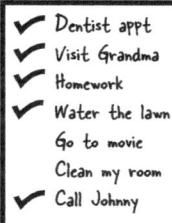

Today's Date	Task	Time Estimate	A	B	C	√

Learning Strategies

Music, Mood, and Mental Performance

Objectives

The students will:
- Understand the effects of music on mood and emotion.
- Learn to use music as a study tool.

ASCA Standards

A:A1.2   Display a positive interest in learning
A:A1.5   Identify attitudes and behaviors leading to successful learning

Materials

a variety of musical selections (see procedure)

Procedure

Have the students bring their favorite songs to class on CDs or digital devices (e.g., iPods). Have the students take turns telling the class the name of their choice and the reason they like it. Tell them they will have a chance to play their selections later in the session.

Next, ask the students to listen to several pieces of music that you have chosen to illustrate the power of music.

Play excerpts from the following types of music in the order shown: First, heavy metal or rap; second, classic rock or rhythm and blues; third, a piano sonata or concerto; fourth, country; and finally, baroque music from such composers as Vivaldi, Telemann, Corelli, or Handel.

Play about two minutes of each selection. Ask the students to notice how their mood shifts in response to the changes in music. Allow no comments until all of the selections have been played. Then ask volunteers to describe how they felt while each type of music was playing. Record key words on the board.

Learning Strategies

Explain that music is an extremely powerful way of evoking emotions and mood changes. Different types of music can cause people to feel joyful, romantic, patriotic, melancholy, energetic, calm, and many other sensations and emotions. Composers know how to manipulate melody, instrumentation, tempo, rhythm, and other musical elements to elicit particular responses. For example, research has shown that baroque music slows both pulse and breathing and relaxes the brain. This type of music is conducive to studying and learning. Fast paced, rap or heavymetal tends to do the opposite and probably interferes with studying and learning for most people.

Play additional musical selections, stopping after each one to ask the students how the music makes them feel. For example, play a romantic orchestral piece, a lively show tune, a march, and a cello concerto. Finally, allow the students to play the music they brought. However, first stipulate that the music may not contain obscene lyrics or lyrics that glorify violence, suicide, sex, or racism.

Conclude the activity with a discussion.

Discussion Questions

1. How did you feel as the music changed?
2. What kind of music, if any, do you usually study to?
3. What kind of music is good to play if you are feeling stressed and would like to relax?
4. What kind of music can cheer you up when you feel down?
5. Have you ever exercised to music? What kind?
6. What is your favorite movie or TV theme music? What do you like about it?

Assessment

- Were the students open and attentive to a variety of musical selections?
- Did the students describe appropriate mood changes in response to the music?

Eating for Brain Power

Objectives

The students will:
- Understand the importance of healthy eating.
- Assess their eating habits.
- Plan healthful menus.
- Monitor the effects of improved eating habits on school performance.

ASCA Standards

PS:C1.7 Apply effective problem-solving and decision-making skills to make safe and healthy choices

Materials

One copy of each of the experience sheets, *Pyramid Menu Planning* and *A Healthy Food Pyramid*, for each student

Procedure

Part 1

Begin by asking the students what they have eaten today. List their responses on the board.

Next, pass out the experience sheet *A Healthy Food Pyramid*. Talk about the types of foods in each group and the recommended daily amounts in cups or ounces. Give some concrete examples, such as combinations of fruits that add up to two cups; or bread, pasta, and cereal servings that add up to six ounces.

Next, guide the students to categorize the foods they listed on the board into the five groups:

1. Grains
2. Vegetables
3. Fruits
4. Milk
5. Meat and Beans

Notice where the preponderance of foods fall. If the students list numerous sweets, such as candy, cookies, donuts, and soft drinks, or fatty-salty snacks like chips, talk about the importance of limiting saturated fats, sugars, and sodium.

Learning Strategies 87

Explain that good health relies on a balanced diet. Students need to eat foods that provide them with a variety of nutrients, including proteins, carbohydrates, fats, minerals, vitamins, and water. When students deprive their bodies of basic nourishment, they run the risk of becoming deficient in essential nutrients and more vulnerable to stress and illness.

Point out that food is the fuel of the body, and exercise generates energy from that fuel. Ideally, food and exercise constitute a balanced system of energy intake and output. If intake exceeds output, the extra fuel is converted to fat and causes weight gain. If output exceeds intake, the body uses stored fat for fuel, which results in weight loss.

Stress that a balanced diet is central to healthy living and promotes peak physical and mental performance. This includes school performance—the ability to concentrate, reason, recall, create, compute, and calculate.

Part 2
Have the students pair up. Distribute the experience sheet, *Pyramid Menu Planning*, and go over the directions. Tell the students to work together to plan a carefully balanced menu for one day. Urge them to identify foods they enjoy that satisfy the recommendations of the food pyramid. Circulate and offer assistance.

When the students have completed their menus, invite volunteers to tell the class about their favorite meal (from the menu).

Part 3
Ask the students to keep a seven-day log of the foods they eat and the amount of water they drink. Allow the pairs to continue working together on this assignment. Urge them to drink six to eight glasses of water a day and to make a serious effort to eliminate junk foods (sweets, salty snacks, high-fat fast foods). Ask the students to monitor their moods, energy levels, academic performance, and athletic performance during this time.

At the end of the week, invite the students to compare their results. Notice increases in energy, ability to focus in the classroom, and/or feelings of well-being.

Conclude the activity with further discussion.

Lerning Strategies

Discussion Questions

1. What changes did you make in your diet as a result of this activity?
2. How did those changes seem to affect your school performance?
3. What was the hardest part about menu planning?
4. What is the hardest part about eating a healthful diet?
5. How can we help each other improve our eating habits?
6. What is meant by the term "empty calories?" What kinds of foods give you empty calories?
7. Why would you want to feed the only body you'll ever have a steady diet of empty calories?

Assessment

- Did the students demonstrate understanding of the food pyramid?
- Did the majority of students create healthful menus?
- Did the students make a serious effort to modify their eating behaviors throughout the activity?

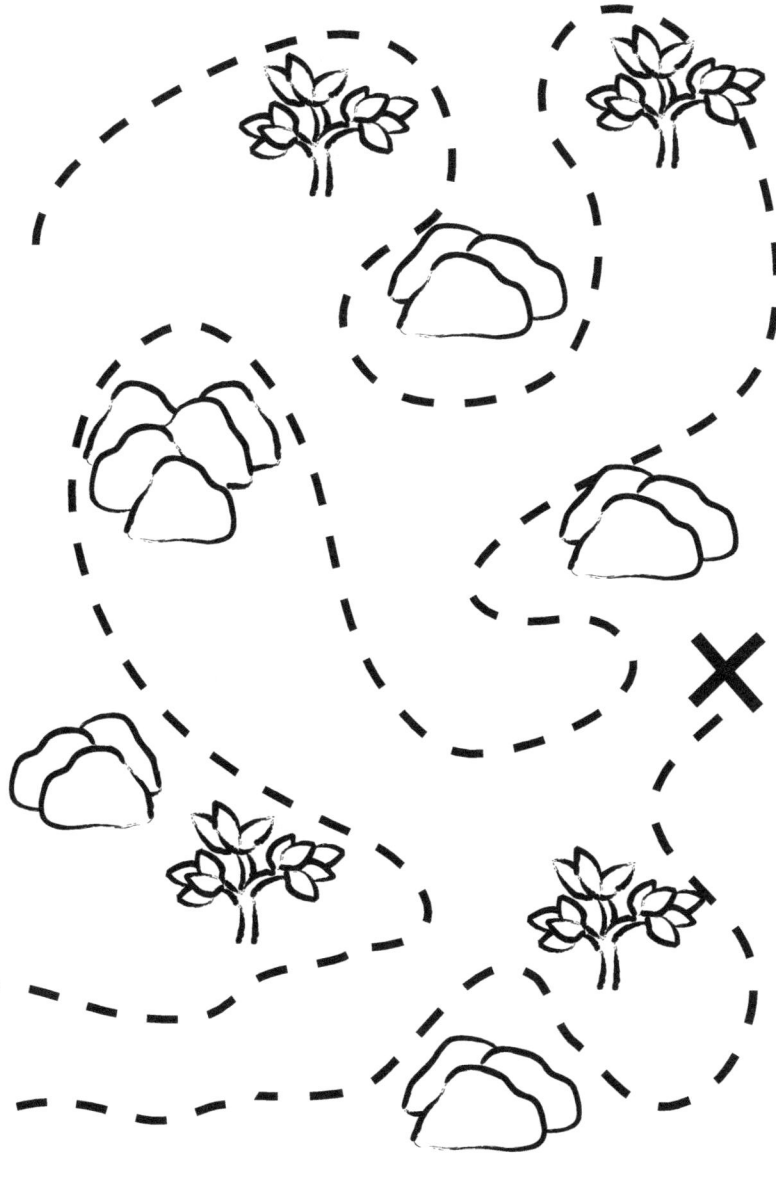

Learning Strategies

Pyramid Menu Planning

Directions

Plan all of your meals and snacks for one day. Include servings from each of the five food groups. You'll find the information on the Food Pyramid.

Breakfast	1. Grains _____ 2. Vegetables _____ 3. Fruits _____ 4. Milk _____ 5. Meat and Beans _____
Snack	1. Grains _____ 2. Vegetables _____ 3. Fruits _____ 4. Milk _____ 5. Meat and Beans _____
Lunch	1. Grains _____ 2. Vegetables _____ 3. Fruits _____ 4. Milk _____ 5. Meat and Beans _____
Snack	1. Grains _____ 2. Vegetables _____ 3. Fruits _____ 4. Milk _____ 5. Meat and Beans _____
Dinner	1. Grains _____ 2. Vegetables _____ 3. Fruits _____ 4. Milk _____ 5. Meat and Beans _____

Lerning Strategies

A Healthy Food Pyramid

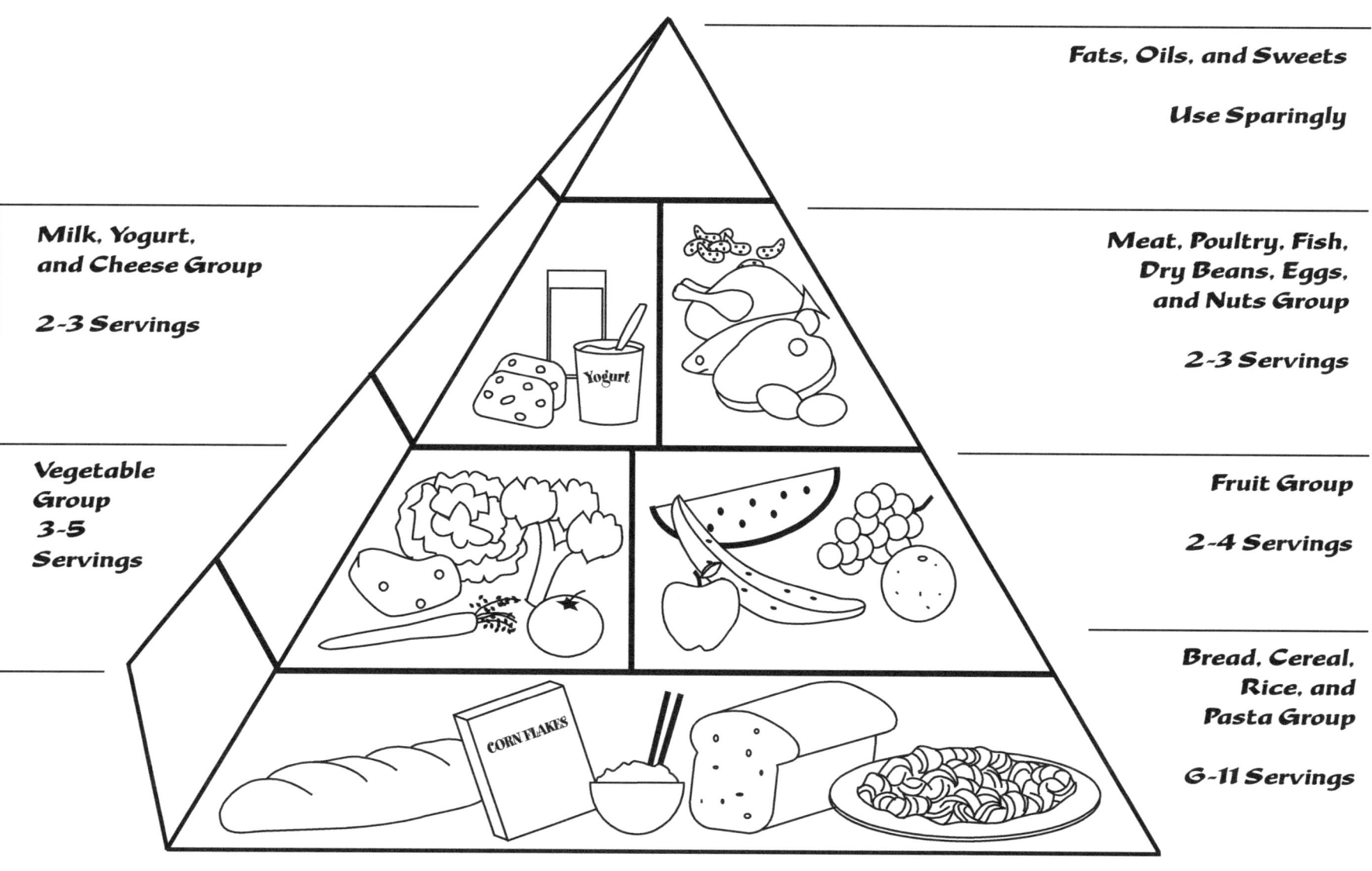

Health and Wellness

Identifying Stress

Objectives

The students will:
- Define stress.
- Identify and describe stressful events in their own lives.
- Demonstrate appropriate ways of dealing with stress.

ASCA Standards

PS:B1.4   Develop effective coping skills for dealing with problems

PS:C1.10   Learn techniques for managing stress and conflict

PS:C1.11   Learn coping skills for managing life events

Materials

Large sheets of newsprint or poster paper and colored markers; one copy of the experience sheet, *Visualize a Relaxing Place*, for each student

Procedure

Divide the students into groups of four or five. Give each group a large sheet of newsprint and one or more markers. Suggest that the groups each choose a recorder.

Write "Stress is…" on the board. Ask the groups to brainstorm specific examples of stressful events or conditions. Suggest that they try to recall times when they were anxious or upset about something. Examples might be:

- Forgetting your permission slip on the day of a field trip
- Striking out in the seventh inning
- Failing a math test
- Being pressured by a friend who wants to copy your homework

Have the groups take turns reading their lists to the rest of the class. Pick two or three good (possibly less obvious) examples and ask the students why these events are stressful. Have them describe how they feel, physically and emotionally, when such events occur.

Health and Wellness

With the entire class, brainstorm a list of activities that can be used to relieve stress. Some possibilities are:

- Take some slow, deep breaths.
- Run around the block or track.
- Play with a pet.
- Talk to a friend.
- Take a bike ride.
- Read a favorite book.
- Play a computer game
- Do some slow stretches.
- Apologize (if you did something hurtful or wrong).
- Ask for a hug.
- Discuss the situation.
- Solve the problem.

Have each group choose one stressful situation from their list and develop a role play showing how the event can be handled. Allow the groups approximately 15 minutes to plan and rehearse their role-plays.

Have the groups perform their role-plays. At the end of each performance, asks the audience to describe the technique(s) used to manage the stressful situation. Ask what other techniques or skills could have been used. Thank and applaud each group.

Distribute the experience sheets and go over the directions, explaining that the technique of visualization can be especially effective at reducing stress. Give the students a few minutes to complete the sheet.

Lead a culminating discussion.

Discussion Questions

1. How does visualizing a favorite place help to reduce stress?
2. What did the other techniques we discussed have in common?
3. Why is it a good idea to relax your mind and body when faced with a problem?

Assessment

- Did the students give appropriate examples of stressful events?
- Did the students describe a variety of stress-relieving techniques?
- Did the students effectively demonstrate stress-relieving techniques in their role plays?

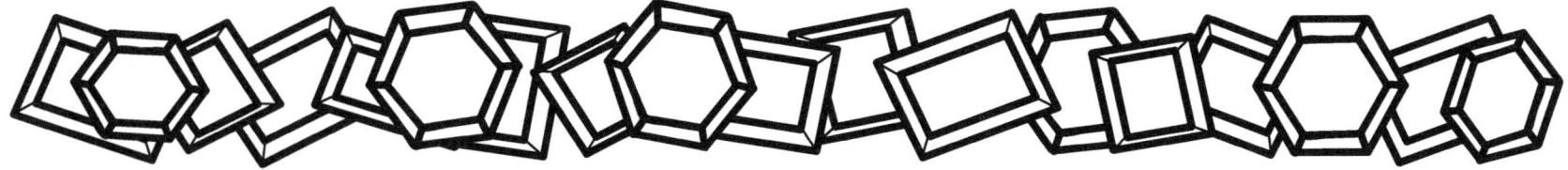

Visualize a Relaxing Place

My Special Place

When you feel upset or stressed out, if you find yourself going over and over the problem in your head without coming to a solution, take a break. Try to relax for a while so that you can think more clearly later on.

If you learn to relax your mind, your body will relax, too. One way to relax is to visualize yourself in a favorite place. Here's how to get started:

In the space to the right and on the back of this sheet, write about a special place where you feel safe, comfortable, and peaceful. It can be a real place or one that you make up in your mind. Include lots of details as you describe how this special place looks, sounds, smells, and feels. Have fun and be sure to relax while you are writing.

Here's the best part: Return to this special place whenever you want to relax. It will help you to cope with problems and stressful events.

Health and Wellness

Being in Balance

Objectives

The students will:
- Identify stressful situations.
- Describe stress-reduction techniques.
- Experience simple meditation exercises that can be used to relieve stress and regain emotional balance.

ASCA Standards

PS:B1.4   Develop effective coping skills for dealing with problems

PS:C1.10   Learn techniques for managing stress and conflict

PS:C1.11   Learn coping skills for managing life events

Materials

Classical or other relaxing music; one copy of the experience sheet, *Staying Balanced*, for each student

Procedure

Begin by talking with the students about what it means to be out of balance. Start with bodily examples, which the students will relate to immediately, then move the discussion to emotions. For example, ask, *"How many of you have ever lost your balance?"*

Ask two or three volunteers to demonstrate what happened when they lost their balance. Establish the concept of a center around which weight is distributed evenly when we are in balance, and that getting off balance usually means that too much weight has shifted to one side or another.

Then, in your own words explain:

Losing your balance in gymnastics, walking along a wall, riding a bike, or skating are examples that occur with your body. But you can get out of balance inside, too. One way is from strong negative emotions. If you get very nervous or angry or afraid, you start to feel and act out of control or unbalanced. Can you think of a time when you were out of balance because of negative feelings?

Health and Wellness

Invite several students to share experiences in which they felt controlled by negative emotions. List the emotions they mention on the board. Then explain further:

To get back in balance, we have to become centered again. Being centered inside means being quiet, calm, relaxed, and alert.

Distribute the experience sheets and go over the directions. Tell the students to list situations and events that have made them feel out of balance, and then to list the things they have done to get back into balance—to feel calm, relaxed, and alert.

When the students have finished writing, ask volunteers to share their stressful events and techniques for regaining balance.

Finally, lead the students in one or more of the meditation exercises. When you have finished, facilitate a summary discussion. Encourage the students to practice centering exercises whenever they feel stressed or out of balance.

Discussion Questions

1. How did you feel when you were doing these relaxation exercises?
2. Why is it important to stay in balance, or get back in balance when you are stressed?
3. When you feel stressed or upset, what happens to your ability to study and learn?
4. How might you use exercises like this on your own, at school or at home?

Assessment

- Did the students verbalize understanding of the concept of emotional balance?
- Did the majority of students name effective ways of regaining emotional balance?
- Did the students participate fully in the meditation exercises?

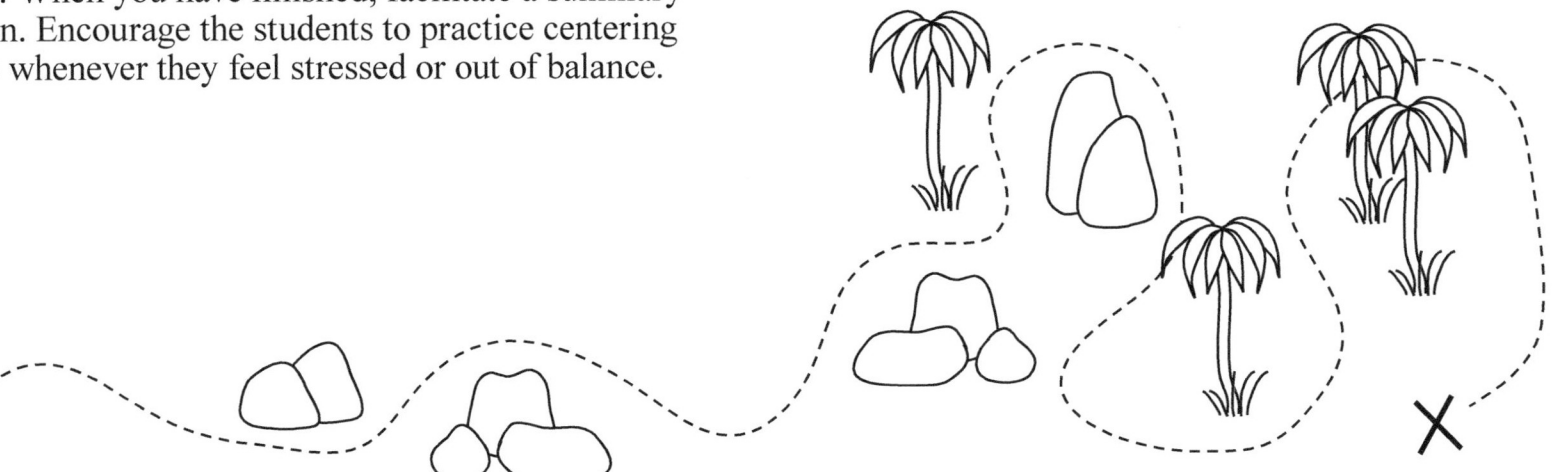

Health and Wellness

Simple Meditation

Tell the students to sit comfortably and close their eyes. Then, slowly read this centering exercise in a soothing tone:

Take several deep breaths. . . Feel your body begin to relax . . . Breathe in and hold it . . . breathe out . . . Breathe in and hold it . . . breathe out. . . Focus your attention on your feet . . . Breathe in so deeply that you can feel the air move through your body . . . all the way to your toes . . . Do that again . . . This time feel the air sweeping all the tension and negative feelings with it . . . Breathe out . . . releasing the tension . . . pushing out the negative feelings . . . Feel your body relax more and more with each breath . . . Feel your stomach relax . . . your heart . . . your chest . . . your shoulders . . . Keep breathing . . . deeply . . . until all of the tension has left your body . . . Then, when you are ready, bring your awareness back to this room and open your eyes.

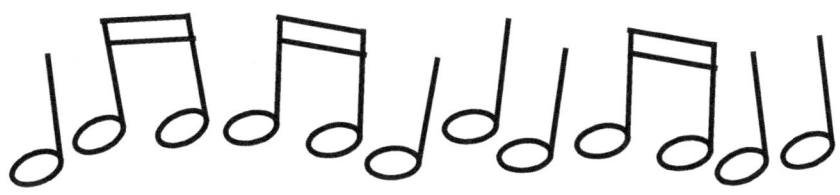

Visual Meditation

Ask the students to pick out an object somewhere in the room and go sit near it. (It's okay if several students pick the same object, just as long as they can all gather around it without crowding one another.) Explain that the object can be a book, ball, picture, flower, light fixture, etc. When all of the students have picked an object and are settled, say to them:

Focus all of your attention on the object . . . Fix your eyes on it . . . Without looking away, begin to breathe deeply and slowly . . . slowly and deeply . . . Let your body relax . . . Let your arms relax . . . Let your shoulders relax . . . Let your legs and feet relax . . . As you look at this object begin to feel its energy . . . the energy that gives it shape . . . and color . . . the energy that attracted you to it . . . Let yourself connect with the energy in this object . . . Let any tension or negative feelings that you have flow out of you . . . and into this object . . . Keep breathing deeply . . . while you watch the tension leave you . . . and flow in a stream . . . across space . . . and into the object . . . Send all of it there . . . and relax . . . relax . . . relax . . . When you are completely relaxed, look away from the object and bring your attention back to this room.

Health and Wellness

Music Meditation

Tell the students to sit comfortably and close their eyes. Begin playing the relaxing music at a low volume while you give these directions:

Take several deep breaths . . . and, as you listen to the music . . . begin to relax your body . . . Relax your feet and legs . . . Relax your stomach and back . . . Relax your chest . . . Relax your arms and shoulders . . . Relax your neck . . . and relax all the features of your face . . . Now, breathe deeply . . . and imagine that you are breathing in the music . . . breathing it into your lungs . . . where it enters your blood . . . carried by millions of molecules of oxygen . . . to all parts of your body . . . Feel the music as it flows through your arms . . . and hands . . . to the tips of your fingers . . . Feel it flow through your heart . . . your stomach . . . into your legs . . . and your feet . . . all the way to your toes . . . Let the music wash away any last bit of tension left in your body . . . Feel it swirl over and around any negative feelings . . . and carry them away . . . Negative feelings have no power against this music . . . They simply disappear . . . So let them go . . . and when they are all gone . . . open your eyes . . . and bring your awareness back to this room.

Health and Wellness

Staying Balanced

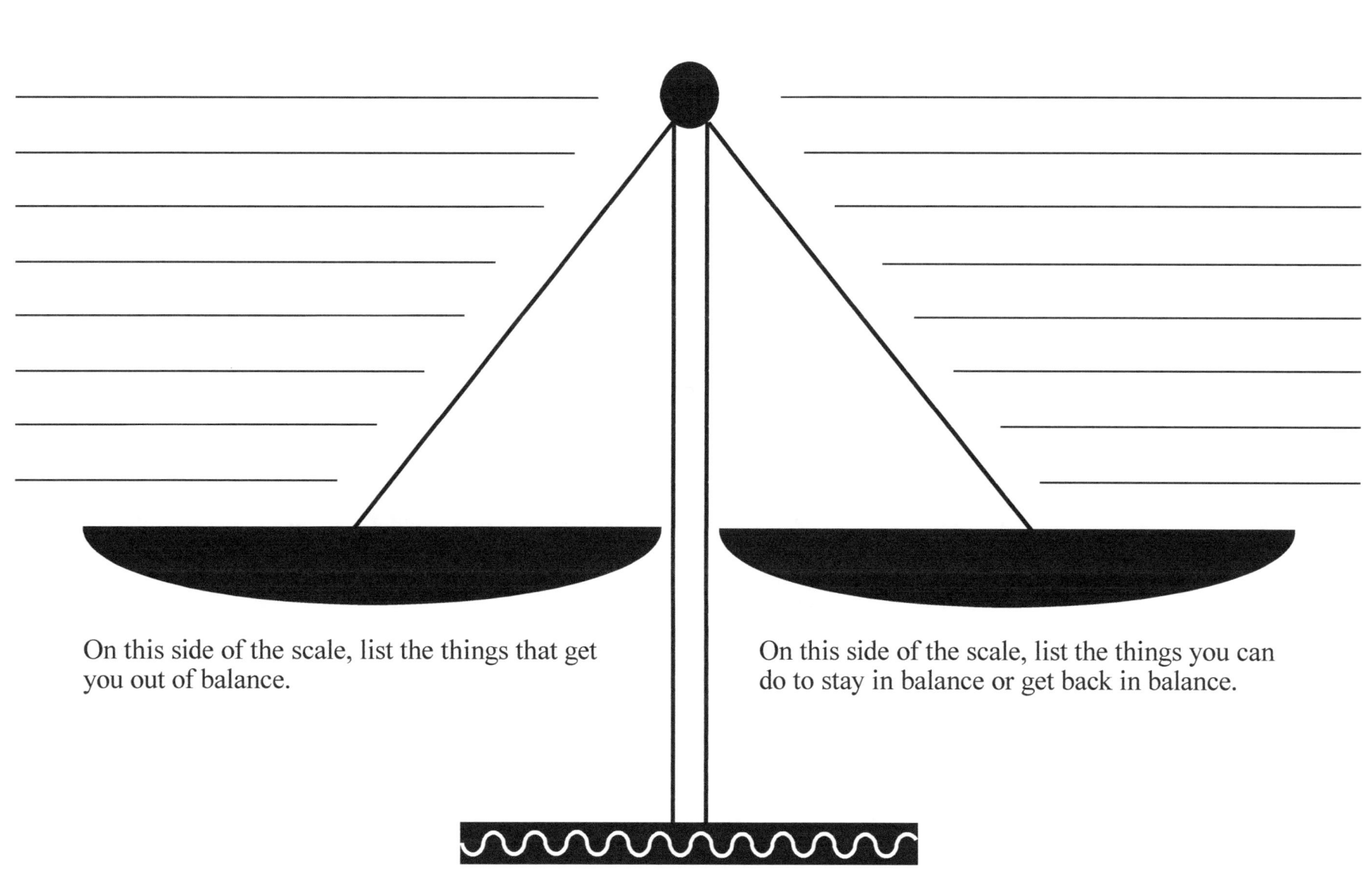

On this side of the scale, list the things that get you out of balance.

On this side of the scale, list the things you can do to stay in balance or get back in balance.

Health and Wellness

A Roll of the Cube

Objectives

The students will:
- Identify strategies for dealing with stress.
- Explain how specific strategies can be used to relieve stress.

ASCA Standards

PS:B1.4   Develop effective coping skills for dealing with problems

PS:C1.10   Learn techniques for managing stress and conflict

PS:C1.11   Learn coping skills for managing life events

Materials

Chart paper and markers; scissors, tape, pencils, crayons, and colored markers; one copy of the experience sheet, *My Calming Cube,* for each student

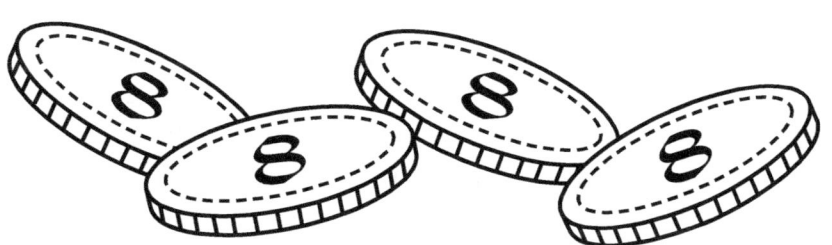

Procedure

Ask the students to think about a time when they were really upset and yet were able to calm down and get their feelings under control. Ask, *"What helped you to calm down when you felt stressed?"*

List the calming strategies that the students name. For example:
- Take several deep breaths.
- Talk to a friend or adult you trust.
- Do something active, such as jog, skip rope or shoot baskets.
- Write the problem down and think it through.
- Imagine a peaceful place.
- Count to 10.
- Do something distracting, like watch a movie or play a video game.

Distribute the experience sheets and go over the directions. Suggest that the students pick their top six strategies from the list on the board.

Health and Wellness

When the Calming Cubes have been illustrated and constructed, allow the students to take turns rolling their cubes like dice and explaining or demonstrating to the group how the featured strategy helps to reduce stress.

Conclude the activity with a discussion.

Discussion Questions

1. Why is it important to know how to calm yourself when you feel stressed?
2. How does stress affect your health? …your relationships? …your schoolwork?
3. How will you use the Calming Cube to help control stress?

Assessment

- Did the students identify a variety of stress-reducing strategies?
- Did the students demonstrate their understanding of those strategies in their cube illustrations?

Health and Wellness

My Calming Cube

Directions

In the three squares across, and in the three squares down, write and illustrate six strategies for calming down when you are stressed. Cut along the dotted lines. Fold along the solid lines to make a cube. Secure the sides with tape.

When you feel stressed, roll the cube and pick a calming strategy.

Health and Wellness

Up in Smoke

Objectives

The students will:
- Describe how tobacco affects the body.
- Identify nicotine as the addictive drug in tobacco.
- Identify tar and other gases as poisons found in tobacco smoke.
- Describe negative effects of smoking.

ASCA Standards

PS:C1.8   Learn about the emotional and physical dangers of substance use and abuse

PS:C1.7   Apply effective problem-solving and decision-making skills to make safe and healthy choices

Materials

Room freshener, an onion or lemon, a sharp knife, a stick of incense, matches, several sheets of large chart paper and colored markers or poster paints

Procedure

In your own words, present the following information on tobacco and tobacco smoke. Write key words and phrases on the board.

- Tobacco is a plant whose shredded leaves are smoked in pipes, cigars and cigarettes.
- Nicotine is the main drug in tobacco.
- Smokers can become very dependent on nicotine. That's why smokers find it hard to stop smoking.
- The best way to avoid dependency is never to start smoking. Most people do not smoke.
- Tobacco changes the way the body works. It makes the heart beat faster and the body work harder.
- Tar is a dark brown, sticky substance in tobacco smoke. Tar is a poison. It coats the lining of the lungs and windpipe, and clogs the passageways so that air cannot pass freely in and out of the lungs.
- The harmful gases in tobacco smoke take up some of the space that oxygen would normally have in the body, so smokers often feel tired.
- Smoking damages a person's sense of smell and taste.

Health and Wellness

- Smoking causes diseases like cancer and emphysema.
- The smoke given off by a burning cigar, pipe, or cigarette causes nonsmokers to experience some of the same poor health effects as smokers. This is called passive smoking.
- Passive smoking can cause nonsmokers to cough, feel tired, experience a burning sensation in the eyes, headaches, stuffy nose and sore throat. Over a long period of time, passive smokers can get the same serious diseases as smokers get.

Tell the students that you are going to conduct an experiment. Ask them to close their eyes and to raise their hands when they smell an odor. Open the air freshener. Then, slice the lemon or onion. Finally, light a stick of incense. Point out that those closest to the source of the odor noticed the smell first. Note how fumes travel through the air and reach the nose even though they are invisible. Explain that tobacco smoke is more visible, but travels in the same patterns, leaving its poisons behind.

Have the students create posters depicting some of the negative effects of smoking. Divide the class into small groups. Tape large sheets of chart paper around the room, one sheet per group. Give each group a set of colored markers or paints. Encourage the groups to include both illustrations and slogans in their posters.

Lead a culminating discussion.

Discussion Questions

1. What are some of the dangers of smoking?
2. What is passive smoking and how does it work?
3. Why are the dangers of passive smoking as great as smoking?
4. What are some of the poisons in tobacco?
5. What is the best way to avoid becoming dependent on tobacco?

Extension

For additional activities, see *Don't Get Hooked: Tobacco Awareness and Prevention Activities* by David Cowan and Susanna Palomares, Innerchoice Publishing, 2005.

Assessment

- Did the majority of posters illustrate student understanding of tobacco facts and the dangers of smoking?
- In discussion, did the students describe a variety of reasons why tobacco should be avoided?

Welcome and Unwelcome Touching

Objectives

The students will:
- Differentiate between appropriate and inappropriate touching.
- Learn alternative ways of responding to inappropriate behavior.

ASCA Standards

PS:B1.3   Identify alternative solutions to a problem

PS:C1.3   Learn about the differences between appropriate and inappropriate physical contact

PS:C1.5   Differentiate between situations requiring peer support and situations requiring adult professional help

PS:A1.7   Recognize personal boundaries, rights, and privacy needs

Materials

One copy of the experience sheet, *How to Handle Unwelcome Touching*, for each student; drawing paper, crayons, or colored markers

Procedure

In your own words, explain:

Your body belongs to you. You have the right to say what happens to it and who touches it. Welcome touches, such as hugs from friends and family members, feel good. They make you feel loved and cared for.

Unwelcome touches usually don't feel good. They are given against our wishes. An unwelcome touch can be anything from a forced hug or kiss to the fondling of your private parts. Unwelcome touches can make you feel uncomfortable, scared, confused, and angry. Unwanted conversation about something very private and inappropriate intimate glances fall into the same category as unwelcome touching.

Distribute the experience sheets. Read aloud the *Things to Remember* and have a brief discussion about the meaning of each item.

Have the students draw a picture of safe touches. Invite volunteers to show their drawings to the class. Use the drawings to draw comparisons between the features of safe and welcome touches and touches that are unwelcome and unsafe.

Discussion Questions

1. What should you do if someone tries to force his or her attentions or affection on you?
2. How can you tell the difference between a hug that is warm and friendly and a hug that is threatening or aggressive?
3. If someone reaches out to touch you and you don't want to be touched, what should you say or do?
4. Who is in charge of your body?

Assessment

- Did the majority of students differentiate between appropriate and inappropriate touching?
- Did the students describe appropriate responses to unwelcome touching?

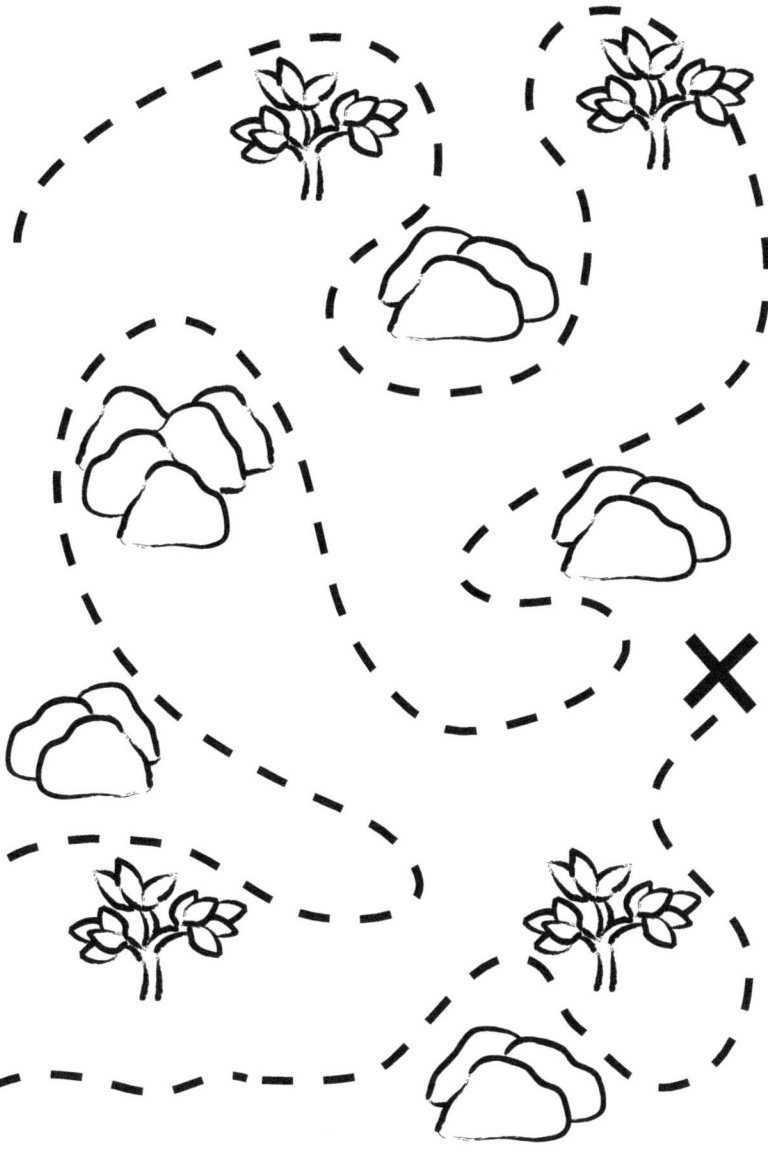

How to Handle Unwelcome Touching

Things to Remember

If you or someone you know has been receiving unwelcome touches, remember these important suggestions:

1. Talk with a trusted adult about what has been happening.

2. Don't be afraid of hurting someone's feelings or causing a scene.

3. Don't worry about what might happen to the person who is bothering you.

4. What is happening is not your fault. You are not responsible for other people's behavior.

5. You have the right to be safe and to decide who touches you.

6. Tell someone what is happening, now.

Health and Wellness

Say No and Mean It

Objectives

The students will:
- Define sources and effects of peer pressure.
- Learn and practice four ways of saying no to peer pressure.

ASCA Standards

PS:B1.8   Know when peer pressure is influencing a decision
PS:C1.7   Apply effective problem-solving and decision-making skills to make safe and healthy choices
PS:C1.9   Learn how to cope with peer pressure

Materials

One copy of the experience sheet, *Four Ways to Say No*, for each student; colored markers, pencils and/or crayons

Procedure

Write the term "peer pressure" on the board and ask the students to help you define it. For example, say: *If someone in this class tries to get you to do something that you don't want to do, that's an example of peer pressure. If your friend tries to get you to do something you might want to do, but aren't sure about, that too is peer pressure. Sometimes peer pressure is good and sometimes it's harmful. Peer pressure is good when it makes you consider things that are good for you, like being friendly or playing fair. Peer pressure is harmful when it tries to get you to do something that is wrong or unhealthy.*

Ask the students to help you brainstorm examples of both kinds of peer pressure. List them on the board. Pick one of the examples, or use this one:

Monica pressures Lu to go with her to the mall after school, even though Lu is expected to go straight home and do homework.

Health and Wellness

Ask two students to come forward and play the parts of Monica and Lu. Direct "Monica" to urge "Lu" to go with her to the mall. Tell Lu to simply say, "No.'" On the board, write in large letters:

Say NO.

Allow a few more moments of role-playing, then stop the action again. Tell Monica to keep up the pressure, and direct Lu to say, "No," and give a reason, such as "We have a rule about doing homework first." On the board, write the words:

Say NO and give a reason.

Allow the students to act out the situation for a few moments, then stop the action again. Tell Monica not to take no for an answer. Direct her to keep pressuring Lu. This time, tell Lu to say, "No," and suggest that they do something else, such as, "go to the mall together on Saturday." On the board, write the words:

Say NO and suggest something else to do.

Allow the students to act out this exchange before stopping the action once more. Tell Monica not to give up, but this time tell Lu to say, "No," and walk away. On the board, write:

Say NO and leave.

Have the students act out the fourth and final strategy, which will end the role play.

Review the strategies. Add this heading to the sentences on the board: "Four Ways to Say No."

Ask the students to read the four strategies with you. Explain that in harmful peer pressure situations, they should remember these four strategies. Tell them: *If the first doesn't work, use the second. If the second doesn't work, use the third. If the third doesn't work, use the fourth—leave the situation.*

Distribute the experience sheets and drawing materials. Go over the directions. Give the students several minutes to complete their drawings.

Have the students role play additional examples of harmful peer pressure. Observe and coach each set of actors. Encourage the students to suggest situations and strategies from their drawings. Give as many students as possible an opportunity to practice the four strategies. Following each dramatization, ask questions to generate discussion.

Discussion Questions

1. How did you feel when you said no?
2. What strategy was easiest? Why?
3. What strategy was hardest? Why?
4. What strategy worked best?
5. Why do kids pressure each other?
6. Why is it important to practice resisting peer pressure?

Assessment

- Did the students explain how peer pressure can be harmful?
- Did the students demonstrate understanding of the four strategies?

Four Ways to Say No

Directions

Draw a picture showing each way to say no.

Say NO.	Say NO and give a reason.	Say NO and suggest something else to do.	Say NO and leave.

Health and Wellness

A Safe Place

Objectives

The students will:
- Identify neighborhood signs, safe areas, and people from whom they can seek help.
- Recognize potential hazards in the community.

ASCA Standards

PS:B1.5   Demonstrate when, where, and how to seek help for solving problems and making decisions

PS:C1.6   Identify resource people in the community and school, and know how to seek help

Materials

Large sheets of art paper (one per group), scrap paper for planning and practice and colored marking pens

Procedure

A good way to begin this activity is to take the students on a walk through the neighborhood around the school. Point out signs, intersections, traffic lights, busy driveways—anything that is either potentially hazardous or increases safety.

When you return to the classroom, form small groups and ask the students to work together to develop a map of the neighborhood they just visited. To help the students get started, draw a simple map showing the school and surrounding streets on the board. Spend some time reminding the students about the buildings and other features that surround the school.

Distribute the scrap paper, art paper and colored marking pens. Suggest that the students work individually at first, on scrap paper, and then combine their impressions and ideas to create the final map. Circulate and assist. Help the students properly label structures and streets.

Ask each group to come forward and show its finished map to the class. Point to first one spot on the map and then another, each time asking the group to trace a route from that point to a safe location nearby. Ask questions, such as:

- If you were here and something happened, where could you go to find an adult to help you?
- What helpers (police, crossing guards, storekeepers, etc.) might you find in this area?
- Why did you choose this route instead of that route?

Health and Wellness

After every group has had an opportunity to share their map, display all of the maps around the room. Facilitate a summary discussion.

Discussion Questions

1. What makes a place safe or unsafe?
2. What are some unsafe things that kids sometimes do going to and from school?
3. What safety cautions should you remember on rainy days?
4. What kinds of areas should you stay away from?
5. Why is it better to walk or ride your bike in the company of friends?
6. What should you do if someone frightens or threatens you?

Variations

After the map sharing and discussion about safe routes, give the students some additional time to add these routes to their maps. Suggest that they draw stick figures and print captions explaining their safety people and routes.

Assessment

- Did the students demonstrate familiarity with their neighborhood?
- Did the students explain safe steps to take in various situations and places around the school?

Health and Wellness

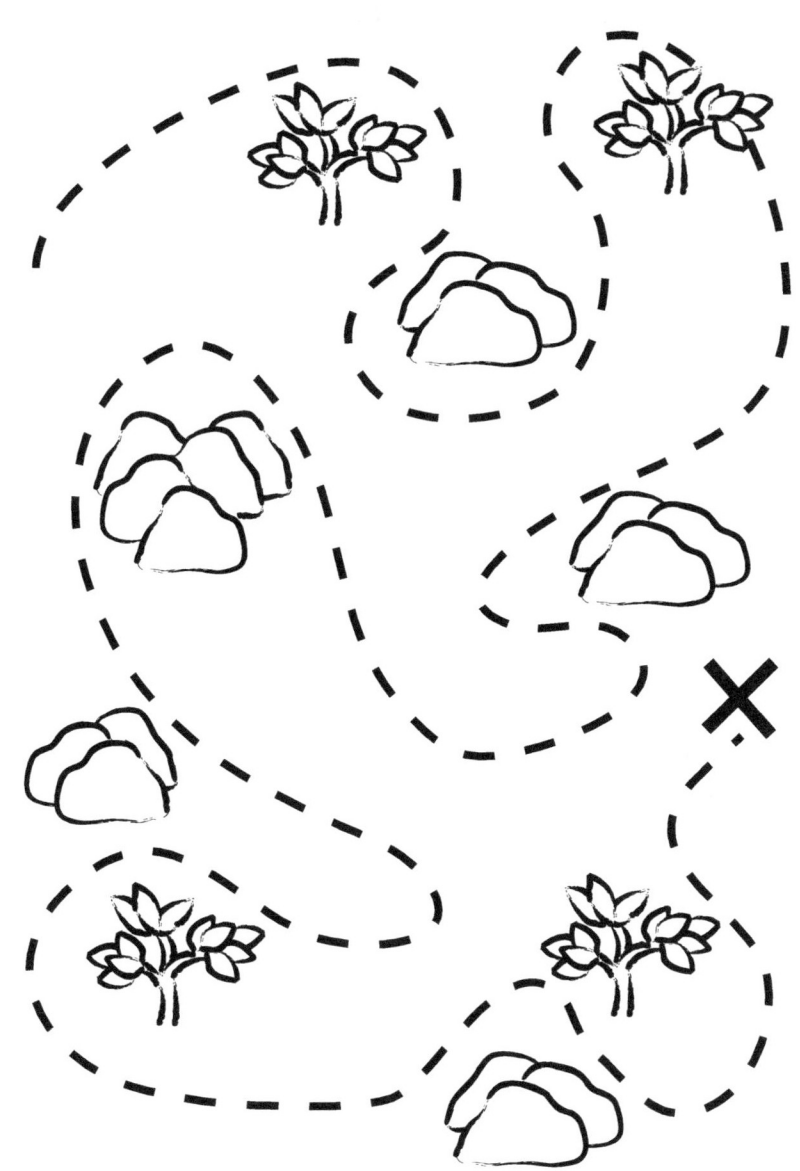

What Would You Do?

Objectives

The students will:
- Become aware of potentially unsafe situations.
- Test their knowledge of safety-conscious behaviors.

ASCA Standards

PS:C1.6   Identify resource people in the school and community, and know how to seek help

PS:C1.7   Apply effective problem-solving and decision-making skills to make safe and healthy choices

Materials

One copy of the experience sheet, *What Would You Do?*, for each student; writing materials

Procedure

Tell the students that the subject of this activity is safety. Explain that they are going to have an opportunity to see how much they already know about being safe at home, at school, in their neighborhoods, and when going to and from places.

Distribute the experience sheets and review the directions. Assure the students that they will not be graded on the quiz, that it is intended to give them information about how their decisions and actions affect their safety. Urge the students to think carefully about what they would do in each situation described.

Allow the students plenty of time to complete the quiz. When they have finished, go over the answers one at a time, discussing each situation. Welcome any ideas that the students present and encourage them to consider various alternatives and consequences. Stress that these are the best answers given the amount of information conveyed, but that other actions might be even better depending on what else is actually going on in the situation.

Answers:

1. (B)	6. (J)	11. (L)
2. (F)	7. (K)	12. (C)
3. (N)	8. (E)	13. (I)
4. (G)	9. (H)	14. (D)
5. (O)	10. (M)	15. (A)

Conclude the activity with a discussion.

Health and Wellness

Discussion Questions

1. What information should you give your parents before you go anywhere?
2. What is the buddy system and how does it help keep you safe?
3. What are some situations in which you should firmly say no?
4. What are some situations in which your first action should be to leave?
5. What kinds of situations should you report to a parent, teacher, or other trusted adult?
6. How does talking about safety like this help you?
7. Who deserves to be safe?

Variations

With lower-grade students, don't necessarily omit the experience sheet. Consider sending it home to parents. In class, describe each situation and two or three alternative actions. Ask the students, "Which is best?" Then discuss the reasons why certain behaviors create more safety than others.

Ask groups of students to role play situations from the experience sheet. The dramatizations can be as elaborate or as simple as you and the class want to make them. Coach the actors through each performance, inviting the audience to suggest alternative actions and trying them out as well. Focus on the possible consequences of each action.

Assessment

- Did the students verbalize understanding of safety conscious behaviors?
- Did the majority of students choose correct answers on the quiz?

Health and Wellness

What Would You Do?

You make decisions every day. Some decisions involve your safety. The numbered items below describe situations that you might face. The lettered items describe actions you could take to deal with those situations. Read each situation and pick the best action. Write the letter of that action on the line.

____ 1. You are on your way to a friend's house and you think a car is following you.

____ 2. You see a friend hitching a ride.

____ 3. You ride your bike to the store.

____ 4. You received money for your birthday and want to spend it at the mall.

____ 5. You are at the book store and your friend wants to shoplift a book.

____ 6. You must take your house key to school.

____ 7. A stranger tells you that he or she has been sent to take you home from school.

____ 8. You are playing in your yard when a neighbor asks, "Can you help me with these groceries?"

____ 9. Your bike has been stolen.

____ 10. You are walking down the street. A car pulls up beside you and the driver says, "My dog is lost. If you'll help me find her, I'll pay you."

____ 11. A stranger bothers you in a movie.

____ 12. You have just witnessed a robbery.

____ 13. You are home alone and the doorbell rings. A voice from outside says, "Is anyone home? I need to check your phone."

____ 14. You need to call for help and there is no telephone directory.

____ 15. You put on the new jacket you got for your birthday.

A. Mark it with your name and address before you wear it.
B. If it is nearby, go immediately to your friend's house; if not, run in the opposite direction. Tell an adult what happened.
C. Remember what you saw and report it to the police.
D. Dial 911.
E. Say that you have to ask your parent first. Don't go inside anyone's home without your parent's approval.
F. Copy down the license number and call the police.
G. Go shopping with a friend or parent. If a friend, ask your parent to drop you off and pick you up.
H. You are the victim and should call the police.
I. Keep the door closed and locked. Call a neighbor and describe what happened.
J. Carry it inside your clothing.
K. Call your parent(s) to make sure.
L. Move and tell an usher.
M. Stay away from the car. Go tell an adult what happened.
N. Lock it well.
O. Try to talk your friend out of it. If you can't, leave the store.

Health and Wellness

Taming the TV Habit

Objectives

The students will:
- Develop awareness of alternatives to watching TV and video games.
- Understand some of the effects that watching TV has on the brain.
- Substitute other activities for TV each day for one week.

ASCA Standards

PS:A2.1   Apply time-management and task-management skills

PS:A3.3   Develop a broad range of interests and abilities

PS:B1.2   Understand consequences of decisions and choices

Materials

One copy of the experience sheet, *Better Than TV Any Day!* for each student

Procedure

Begin by asking the students how many hours of TV they watch each weekday and on weekends. Call on volunteers. Widen the discussion to include the shows that the students prefer, and the types of monitoring and restrictions imposed by their parents.

In your own words, explain how TV viewing affects the brain. Make these points:

- Your brain is constantly growing and changing based on your activities and the things you learn.
- Brain cell growth continues into your teens and beyond.
- Passive TV viewing slows down the brain. Instead of creating lots of mental activity, TV causes your brain to go into "neutral."
- When you watch TV, your brain receives less oxygen than when you are active, which can further dull your thinking and reactions.

Brainstorm activities that the students can substitute for TV—activities that require active mental and/or physical involvement. Write ideas on the board.

Health and Wellness

Distribute the experience sheets. Have the students choose seven activities from the list on the board and write them in the columns of the experience sheet. Challenge the students to do at least one activity each day for the rest of the week during a time period when they would normally be watching TV. Have them record the day/date and length of time spent doing each substitute activity, and to describe how well they liked the activity.

When the students bring back the experience sheet to the next meeting, have them share their results in small groups. Lead a culminating discussion.

Discussion Questions

1. How do you feel after watching several hours of TV?
2. How did you feel after doing one of the substitute activities you selected?
3. Which activities did you enjoy as much as watching TV?
4. Why is it healthy to limit TV and video viewing?
5. How can you use TV, movies, video, or computer games to learn new things?

Assessment

- Did the majority of students describe appropriate activities to substitute for TV?
- Did the student logs indicate time spent each day experimenting with substitute activities?

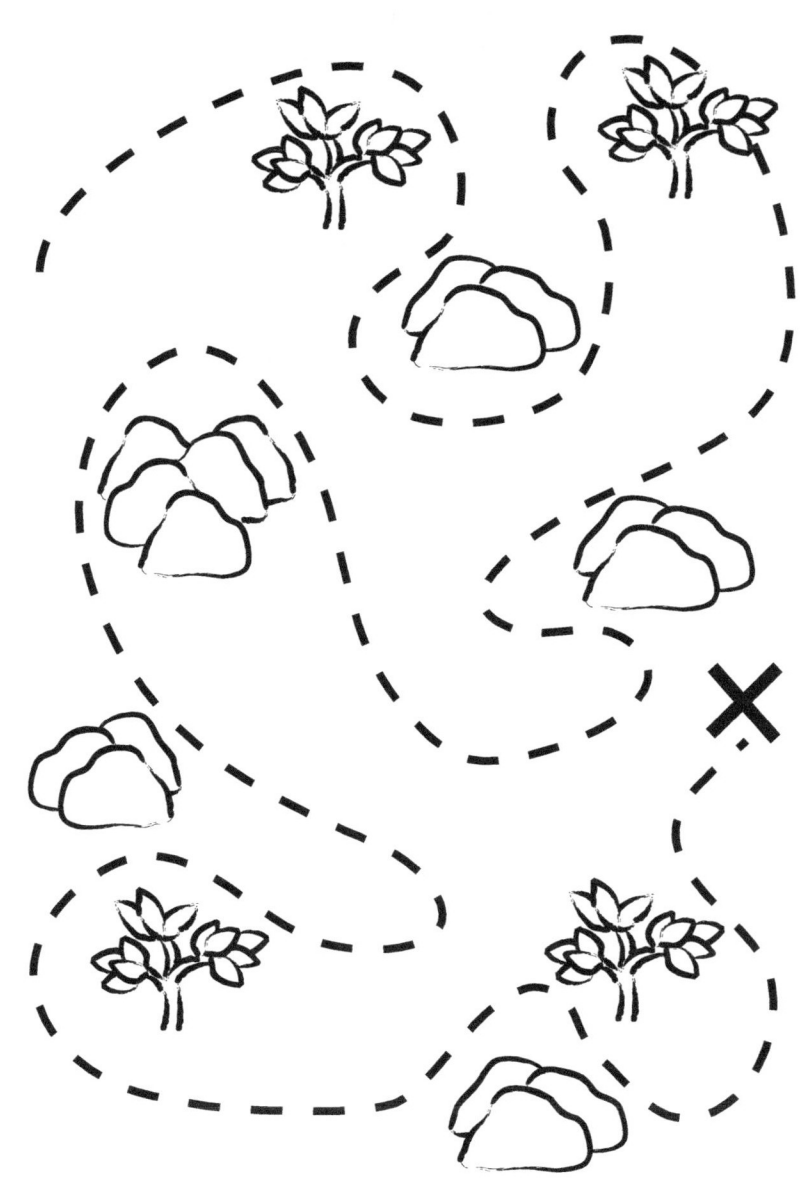

Health and Wellness

Better Than TV Any Day

Activity Name	Day and Date of Activity	How Much Time Spent on Activity?	How Well Did I Like the Activity?

Health and Wellness

Living a Healthy Life

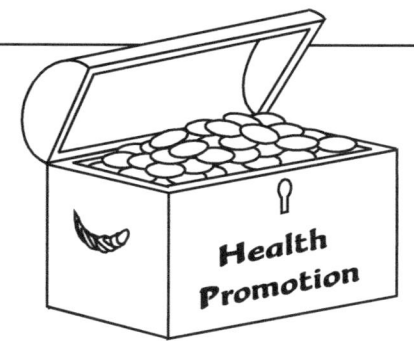

Objectives

The students will:
- Identify specific activities that contribute to personal health and vitality.
- Commit to practicing specific healthful activities for one month.

ASCA Standards

PS:B1.2   Understand consequences of decisions and choices

PS:C1.7   Apply effective problem-solving and decision-making skills to make safe and healthy choices

Materials

One copy of the experience sheet, *A Month of Vitality*, for each student

Procedure

Write the heading *Vitality* on the board. Brainstorm current synonyms for vitality in the youth vernacular (punch, dash, hustle, zip, etc.) Talk to the students about what it means to have vitality: to stay healthy, to have lots of energy, to feel good. Help the students realize that they have the power to either build or destroy their own vitality through the things they do and think every day.

Ask the students to help you brainstorm areas of life that can affect vitality. Quickly list them on the board. Here are some possibilities:

- Sleep
- Diet
- Exercise
- Leisure activities
- Cleanliness/grooming
- Wellness
- Learning
- Attitude/thoughts
- Character
- Friends
- Family
- Pets

Health and Wellness

Ask the students to help you list specific activities in several of the listed areas. For example:

Diet
> Eat a good breakfast.
> Have a fresh fruit snack instead of candy.
> Try a new vegetable.

Wellness
> Get 8 to 10 hours of sleep every night.
> Have regular medical and dental checkups.
> Say no to alcohol and other drugs.

Learning
> Read a book.
> Look up a new word.
> Ask a question.
> Find out how something works.

Attitude/thoughts
> Say something positive to yourself.
> Learn from a mistake.
> Appreciate positive qualities in other people.

Character
> Tell the truth.
> Keep your promises.
> Be kind to others.

When you list an activity, ask the students to describe how it builds vitality. Point out that each activity adds to the reserves of vitality from which they draw when they need extra energy or when they are under stress.

Distribute the experience sheets. Go over the instructions and encourage the students to write down at least one activity for each day of the month.

Extension

If the students complete their vitality calendars in class, ask them to share their calendars in groups of three. Urge them to contract with the members of their triad to complete every activity they have listed.

Discussion Questions

1. What kinds of foods should you eat to produce high levels of vitality or energy?
2. How is your schoolwork affected when your vitality is low?
3. Who is responsible for safeguarding your well-being and vitality?
4. What do you usually do when you feel yourself dragging?

Assessment

- Did the students describe habits and behaviors that contribute to vitality?
- Did most student calendars list a variety of practical ways to build vitality?

A Month of Vitality

Having vitality means staying healthy, having more energy and feeling good. Increase your vitality this month by writing a daily suggestion to yourself on this calendar. Include all areas of your life that contribute to your own vitality—personal care, nutrition, friendships, positive thoughts, and healthy ways to cheer yourself up. Make sure to include activities like exercise, listening to music, running, relaxing with a book, hugs instead of drugs, and eating fresh fruit. Then tape the calendar to your mirror at home, or put it in a place where you will see it every day. If you find that it increases your vitality, make a calendar for next month and each of the following months.

Sunday	Monday	Tuesday	Wednesday	Thursday	Friday	Saturday

Health and Wellness

Remembering a Loved One

Objectives

The students will:
- Recall a happy memory involving a person they have lost.
- Express feelings and thoughts in a letter to the person they lost.

ASCA Standards

PS:B1.4 Develop effective coping skills for dealing with problems

PS:C1.11 Learn coping skills for managing life events

Materials

Writing paper; relaxing music (optional)

Procedure

Have the students close their eyes and take a comfortable position. If you have music, begin to play it at a low volume. In a gentle yet audible voice, read the following guided imagery exercise, pausing for at least five seconds between phrases.

Take a deep breath and let it out slowly . . . Begin to relax your body and your mind . . . Keep breathing deeply . . . Feel the tension leave each part of your body . . . Relax your feet and ankles . . . your calves and thighs . . . your hips, stomach, and chest . . . your hands and arms . . . your back, shoulders, and neck . . . your face . . . While you are relaxing, begin to think about a person you have lost . . . See the person exactly the way you like to remember him or her . . . Picture everything in detail . . . And with this image in your mind, begin to recall a happy memory that you shared with the person . . . a vacation, a job that you did together, a meal . . . Remember it in detail . . . Recall the surroundings . . . what you said . . . how you felt . . . Keep breathing deeply while you relive completely that happy memory (pause 15 seconds) . . . Now, think of something that you would like to say to the person you lost . . . If you could communicate with this person right now, what would your message be? . . . Would you tell the person what you appreciated about him or her? . . . Would you share the memory you just recalled? . . . Would you ask a question? . . . See yourself speaking to the person now (pause 15 seconds) . . . When you are finished, say good-by to the person . . . Take your time . . . Know that you can revisit this person in your mind whenever you wish . . . When you are ready, open your eyes and return to the group.

Health and Wellness

Give the students a few moments to readjust, quietly accepting any tears or other expressions of sadness.

Distribute the writing paper. Tell the students that you would like them to write down some of their thoughts and feelings in the form of a letter to the person they lost. In your own words, explain:

You don't need to show this letter to anyone, so say whatever you want to say. Perhaps you want to write down the same words you said to the person in your imagination, or maybe you want to say something entirely different. It's up to you. Begin your letter with "Dear..." and the name you always used to address the person. Then, simply write. You'll have 15 minutes to complete your letter.

When the students have finished writing, facilitate a summary discussion.

Discussion Questions

1. How has your life changed since you lost this person?
2. What is hardest about dealing with the loss right now?
3. What did you learn from the things we did here today?

Assessment

- Did the students respond appropriately during the guided imagery?
- Did students describe ways of dealing with loss during discussion?

Health and Wellness

Five Stages of Grief

Objectives

The students will:
- Describe a personal loss.
- Discuss the five stages of dealing with loss.

ASCA Standards

PS:B1.4 Develop effective coping skills for dealing with problems
PS:C1.11 Learn coping skills for managing life events

Materials

Colored markers, pencils and/or crayons and drawing paper

Procedure

Begin by introducing students to the topic of loss. For example, you might say the following:

We experience many kinds of loss in our lives: the death of a family member or friend, the loss of a parent through divorce, friends moving away, a pet dying, a relationship breaking up.

When something like this happens, our strong feelings can make it very difficult to cope. It helps to know that other people experience losses and get through them. It also helps to understand the stages our feelings go through as we adjust to the loss.

Ask the students to think of a loss they have experienced. Invite them to tell the group:

- The nature of the loss (death, divorce, etc.)
- When it happened
- How they are feeling about it now
- Any other details they would like to mention

As the students share, model attentive listening and facilitate discussion.

Next, introduce the five stages of loss first described by Elisabeth Kübler-Ross in her book, *On Death and Dying*. As you explain each stage, write key words on the board (suggested explanations appear in italics, below). Invite the students to add observations from their own experiences. Taking the time to elicit student contributions will enrich the discussion.

Health and Wellness

Stages of Loss

1. Denial

   When we know we are about to lose someone, or something that we value, the first reaction is disbelief. For example, we tell ourselves, "No, this can't be happening," "Everything will be okay tomorrow," or "This is just a bad dream. I'll wake up soon."

2. Anger

   When we can no longer deny the loss, we experience frustration and anger. We think, "What did I do to deserve this?" "How can s/he do that to me?" or "This could only happen in an unfair, stupid world."

3. Bargaining

   After we express our anger, we may begin to feel hopeful again. We think, "Maybe if I'm a better person, Dad will stay," or "If I promise to help take care of her, maybe God will let Grandma live," or "I'll change all of my bad habits and she will like me again."

4. Grieving

   At this stage, we allow ourselves to feel the pain and hurt. We may cry a lot and feel very depressed and hopeless. Difficult as it is, this is a very important stage. A person can't fully recover from a loss without grieving.

5. Acceptance

   Finally, we start to feel okay again. We may still be sad sometimes, but life returns to normal and we no longer think constantly about the person or condition we lost.

Note: From *On Death and Dying (pp. 34-121)*, by Dr. E. Kübler-Ross, 1997. New York, NY: Macmillan Publishing Co., Inc. Used with permission

Point out that people don't always go through the stages in sequence. Sometimes they bounce back and forth between two or more stages for a long time. In some cases, completing the cycle can take many months. Friends, relatives, and teachers who don't realize how long it can take may wonder why the person hasn't snapped out of it.

Distribute the drawing materials. Ask the students to think about a recent loss and to draw a picture of themselves (or someone else) experiencing one of the stages. Suggest that they use cartoon bubbles to show what they are thinking or saying to others. When they have finished, ask volunteers to show their drawings to the class and describe what it depicts.

Discussion Questions

1. Which of the stages do you remember going through after a recent loss?
2. How did you feel at each stage and how did you behave?
3. How will knowing the stages help you cope with loss in the future?
4. Many people who want to help simply don't know what to do or say. What would you like them to do or say?
5. What have you learned from this activity?

Assessment

- Did the students describe appropriate examples of loss?
- Did the majority of students demonstrate understanding of various feelings associated with loss?

Everybody Is Afraid of Something

Objectives

The students will:

- Express anxieties and fears that they have experienced.
- Explore alternative ways of coping with fears.

ASCA Standards

PS:B1.4 Develop effective coping skills for dealing with problems

PS:C1.11 Learn coping skills for managing life events

Materials

Writing materials, a copy of the experience sheet, *We All Have Fears,* for each student

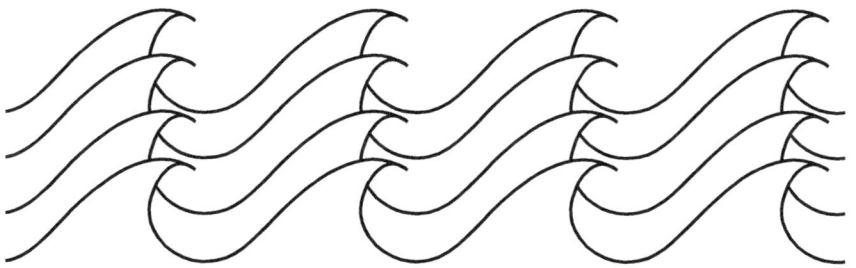

Procedure

Distribute the experience sheets and go over the directions. Give the students a few minutes to complete the self-assessment. Pick several of the items on the assessment and ask for a show of hands to indicate the various levels of fear (1 through 5). Ask volunteers to describe suggested techniques for lessening the fear. Use the results of the assessment to initiate a discussion about situations that create fear.

Tell the students that you would like them to write down in detail one of the scariest things that has ever happened to them. As an example, describe one or two scary things that have happened to you or to someone you know. Have the students entitle their story, One of the Scariest Things That Ever Happened to Me.

As a pre-writing activity (optional), ask volunteers to tell the class about their scary experience.

On a subsequent day, have the students read their stories to the class. Allow enough time for everyone to share. Ask questions to obtain additional details.

Health and Wellness

Divide the class into groups of six to eight. Have each group select one story (from the group) to role play.

Instruct the groups to fictionalize their selected story. Write the following steps on the board:
1. Make up names for the characters.
2. Describe what the characters look like, their ages, how they talk, and any other important descriptive information.
3. Decide from what point of view to tell the story.
4. Describe the setting in detail.
5. Explore plot alternatives and embellish the story.
6. Explore different resolutions to the problem and choose the best solution to role play.

Provide time for planning and rehearsals. Then have each group perform for the rest of the class.

Discussion Questions

1. Do you think that sometimes a fear can be caused more by our perception of something than by the thing itself? Explain.
2. How did it feel to talk about a scary experience?
3. What similarities did you notice about the scary things we shared? What differences?
4. What are some things we can do to overcome fears?
5. Why does it help to talk about things we are afraid of?

Assessment

- Did the majority of students assess their fear responses realistically?
- Did the students describe helpful techniques for controlling fear?
- Did the role plays demonstrate thoughtful management of fearful situations?

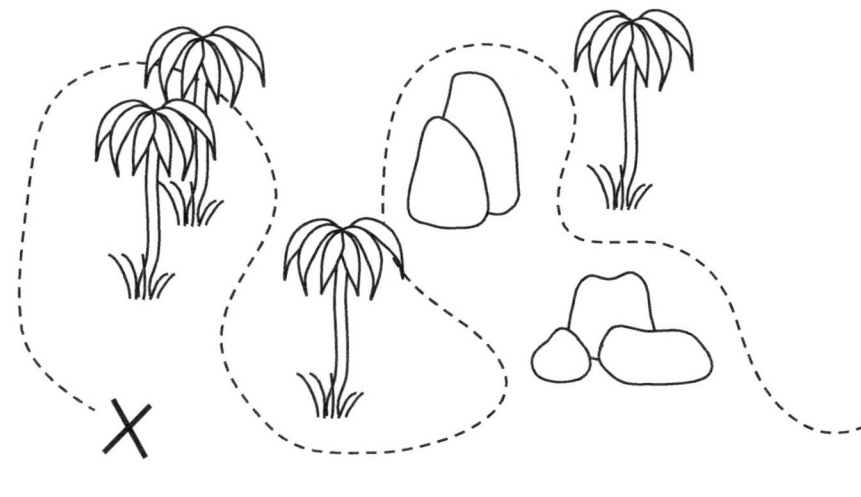

Health and Wellness

We All Have Fears

All people have fears of one type or another. Some people are afraid of high places, others of being embarrassed. Some are afraid of death, or the dark.

Below is a list of things that often scare people. Look at each item in the left-hand column and circle the number that best describes how you feel.

In the right-hand column, write a suggestion to yourself about what you can do to be less afraid.

1 = not afraid 2 = somewhat afraid 3 = afraid 4 = very afraid 5 = extremely afraid

How afraid am I?

1. afraid of the dark — 1 2 3 4 5
2. afraid of speaking in front of a group — 1 2 3 4 5
3. afraid of being alone — 1 2 3 4 5
4. afraid of strangers — 1 2 3 4 5
5. afraid of getting poor grades — 1 2 3 4 5
6. afraid of high places — 1 2 3 4 5
7. afraid of the dentist — 1 2 3 4 5
8. afraid of doing something wrong — 1 2 3 4 5
9. afraid of parents getting divorced — 1 2 3 4 5
10. afraid of horror movies — 1 2 3 4 5
11. afraid of being laughed at — 1 2 3 4 5
12. afraid of being beat up — 1 2 3 4 5
13. afraid of fire — 1 2 3 4 5
14. afraid of being yelled at — 1 2 3 4 5
15. afraid of being hurt — 1 2 3 4 5
16. afraid of big dogs — 1 2 3 4 5

Things I can do to be less afraid

1. _____
2. _____
3. _____
4. _____
5. _____
6. _____
7. _____
8. _____
9. _____
10. _____
11. _____
12. _____
13. _____
14. _____
15. _____
16. _____

Health and Wellness

Logical and Illogical Fears

Objectives

The students will:
- Describe some of their fears.
- Distinguish between tenable and untenable fears.

ASCA Standards

PS:B1.4 Develop effective coping skills for dealing with problems
PS:C1.11 Learn coping skills for managing life events

Materials

One copy of the experience sheet, *Managing Your Fears*, for each student

Procedure

Ask the students to take a few minutes to think about some of their fears. Explain that fear is an emotion that causes anxiety and a sense of dread, and that everyone is afraid of something. As an example, tell the students about one or two things that you are afraid of.

Next, ask the students to write down four or five of their fears. After everyone has finished, ask volunteers to share some of their fears. Be accepting of all contributions and don't allow any put-downs or laughing as the students share.

Explain to the students that people are wise to have some fears. Logical fears protect us from harm. The fear of big dogs is a logical fear, because poorly trained and uncontrolled dogs have been known to attack people. The fear of deep water is a logical fear if you don't know how to swim.

However, some fears are illogical. They provide no self-protection and serve no useful purpose. In fact, these fears sometimes keep people from enjoying life fully and from doing things they would otherwise like to do. Fears of the dark and ghosts are examples of illogical fears.

Make two columns on the board with the headings, "Logical Fears" and "Illogical Fears." Collect the students' papers and read aloud several fears. As you read each fear, have the students decide if it is logical or illogical. If they can't decide, ask questions to help them reason it through. Record the fear in the appropriate column.

Health and Wellness

Ask for suggestions on how to deal with some of the illogical fears listed.

Distribute the experience sheets and give the students a few minutes to complete them. Conclude the activity with further discussion clarifying the difference between logical and illogical fears.

Discussion Questions

1. How do we learn to be afraid of something?
2. What are some fears that you would like to overcome?
3. Has a fear ever prevented you from having fun? Explain.
4. What steps have you taken to overcome your fears?

Assessment

- Did the students readily distinguish between logical and illogical fears?
- Did the students describe ways of overcoming illogical fears?

Health and Wellness

Managing Your Fears

Think about times when you were afraid of someone or something, but everything turned out okay. Just as monsters are not real, most of the time our fears are not real either.

In the left-hand column, describe illogical fears that you have had. In the right-hand column, describe what actually happened.

What I Feared Would Happen	What Actually Happened

Here are four things you can do to get over illogical fears:

1. Admit the fear to yourself.
2. Research the thing you fear at the library or on the internet. Learn as much as you can. Knowledge is power!
3. Talk with a trusted teacher or counselor about your fear.
4. Write about your fear in a journal or diary. Explore your feelings and the causes of your fear.

Learning, talking, and writing about your fears can help you get over them. But remember, changing your feelings takes time and patience.

Health and Wellness

Working Through Crises

Objectives

The students will:

- Illustrate feelings and thoughts related to a personal crisis.
- Learn ways to better cope with crisis situations.

ASCA Standards

PS:B1.5   Demonstrate when, where, and how to seek help for solving problems and making decisions

PS:C1.11   Learn coping skills for managing life events

Materials

Drawing paper; colored markers and/or crayons; other art materials

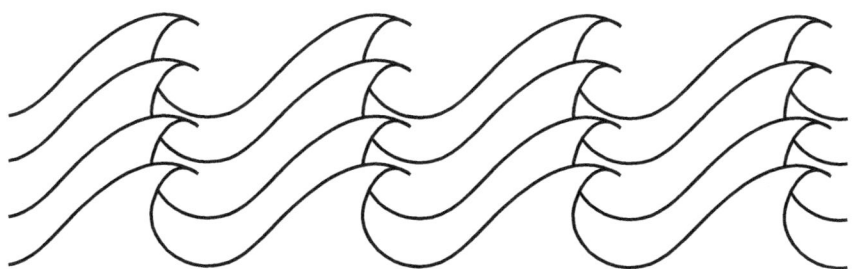

Procedure

Ask the students if they know what the word "crisis" means. Listen to and clarify the responses of volunteers. Explain that a crisis is a time when a big change occurs in a person's life, often caused by a loss of some kind, and always accompanied by strong emotions. Give several examples of personal crises and ask the students to think of others. Write them on the board. Your list should include:

- Death of a relative
- Death of a friend or pet
- Divorce or separation of parents
- Job loss by parent
- Moving away and leaving friends
- Family illness or accident
- Being hurt or abused

Distribute the art materials and ask the students to draw a picture of a personal crisis that they have experienced. Allow at least 15 minutes for this process. Then ask volunteers to share their drawing with the class, explaining details of the event and how they felt.

Health and Wellness

Facilitate discussion after each sharing. Talk in general about the thoughts and feelings people typically experience in connection with each crisis shared. In the process, make these points:

- Every crisis eventually passes.
- Powerful, hurt feelings are gradually replaced by more positive feelings.
- Family events, such as divorce, are never the child's fault.
- There are people in the community who are willing and able to help.

Discussion Questions

1. What kinds of thoughts did you have during your crisis?
2. Which thoughts were helpful? Which were unhelpful?
3. What feelings are common during a crisis?
4. To whom can you go for help during a crisis?
5. What can you do to help yourself?
6. Why do we have a tendency to feel guilty when we lose a person or a pet we love?

Variations:

In a second phase of the activity, allow students who have experienced similar crises to meet in small groups for sharing and further discussion. Suggest that they respond to the topic, "How I Survived My Crisis."

Instead of drawing, older students may prefer to write fictionalized accounts of their crises in the form of short stories or plays. After the stories/plays have been written, facilitate peer critiquing sessions, editing and rewriting. Allow students to share their finished work. Those who write plays should be given an opportunity to cast, rehearse, and perform them.

Assessment

- Did the students describe and/or illustrate common reactions to crises?
- Did the students describe ways of coping effectively with crises?

How to Ask for Help

Objectives

The students will:

- Describe when help is needed.
- Identify, contrast, and discuss effective and ineffective ways of seeking help.

ASCA Standards

PS:C1.6   Identify resource people in the school and community, and know how to seek help

PS:C1.7   Apply effective problem-solving and decision-making skills to make safe and healthy choices

Materials

One copy of the experience sheet, *Many Ways to Ask for Help*, for each student

Procedure

Get the students' attention by writing the exclamation, **HELP!** in large letters on the board. Wait a few moments to pique their curiosity and then ask them: What is "help?"

Listen to their ideas. When everyone seems to agree on a definition, say, "Give me some examples of times when you or I might need help."

List their suggestions on the board. Include examples such as:

- When you feel sick.
- When you injure yourself.
- When you don't understand an assignment.
- When you can't solve a math problem.
- When someone threatens to hurt you.
- When someone tries to give or sell you drugs.
- When you witness an accident, crime, or fight.
- When you can't study at home.
- When you are not getting your schoolwork done and you don't know why.
- When you keep getting low grades no matter how hard you try.
- When you feel so worried or depressed about something that you can't concentrate.

Health and Wellness

As you record the students' suggestions, express empathy for the feelings they might have under those circumstances, e.g., "Yes, Mat, and you'd probably be feeling pretty scared if that happened," or "No matter how hard you try, Sue, when you feel worried, it's awfully hard to think about social studies or spelling words."

Draw a line down the middle of the board and write the headings, "Effective" and "Ineffective," on either side of the line. Next, select one situation and develop a brief scenario around it so that the students can imagine themselves in the situation. For example, say: *You're sitting there and all the other kids have started working. You see them getting out paper and books. Some are starting to move around the room and some are writing. It hits you that you have absolutely no idea what you are supposed to be doing.*

- *What are some ineffective ways of asking for help in this situation?*
- *What are some effective ways?*

Record suggestions under the appropriate heading, discussing each one briefly. For example, yelling across the room to a friend would be ineffective because it would irritate the teacher and disrupt the class. Going up to the teacher and explaining your confusion (without interrupting) would probably be effective.

Follow the same procedure with other examples from the list.

Distribute the experience sheets and go over the directions. Give the students a few minutes to complete the sheet.

Ask several volunteers to share their methods (from the sheet) for telling a person that they need to talk. Transcribe particularly effective ideas on the board. If time permits, have pairs of students role play several of the suggested methods.

Discussion Questions

1. How do you feel when you get help that you need?
2. How do you feel when someone insists on helping you, even though you don't want help?
3. What are some reasons that you might hesitate to ask for help?
4. In what kinds of situations should you always ask for help?
5. What can you do if you need help and no one is around to ask?

Assessment

- Did the students name a variety of situations in which asking for help is necessary and appropriate?
- Did the students distinguish between effective and ineffective ways of asking for help?

Many Ways to Ask for Help

Think of two people you would feel comfortable talking to if you needed help. Write their names here:

1. _____

2. _____

To let someone know you'd like to talk about a problem:

- First, check to make sure the person isn't busy.
- Then, say something like, "Can I talk to you about something?" or "I've got a problem that is bothering me. Could I talk to you in private?"

Think of two other ways to tell a person that you'd like to talk to them. Write them here:

1. _____
   _____

2. _____
   _____

If the person you've asked is not available, or is unhelpful for any reason, pick someone else. Don't stop asking for help until you get it. Don't count on others to know when you are in trouble. Adults can't always tell.

If you need help, ask for it.

Another way to get help is to write a note or send an email to the person you'd like to talk with. Tell him or her what is happening and how you are feeling. Make sure the person understands what is bothering you. Say what it is you want. Send the email or give the note to the person and ask for a response.

Health and Wellness

Emotional Intelligence

Emotion Pantomime

Objectives

The students will:
- Demonstrate nonverbal behaviors.
- Correctly identify feelings based on nonverbal behaviors.

ASCA Standards

PS:A1.5   Identify and express feelings
PS:A2.7   Know that communication involves speaking, listening, and nonverbal behavior

Materials

A box or bag containing the 18 emotions listed on the "Emotion List," cut into separate slips; one copy of the experience sheet, *Take a Close Look*, for each student

Procedure

Ask the students to pair up. Have each pair draw one slip of paper with an emotion written on it. Direct the pairs to go to a private place for five minutes and plan a short pantomime of the emotion.

Explain that the students are to act only with their faces and bodies. They may neither say words, nor make vocal noises. The object is to do such a good job of acting that the class will be able to guess how the actors are feeling in their roles.

When the students have finished planning, have them take turns performing their pantomimes.

After each pantomime, ask the class to tell the actors how they appeared to be feeling. Finally, ask the actors to reveal the emotion they were acting out.

Distribute the experience sheets and go over the directions. Instruct the students to complete the sheet as homework. Assign a due date.

At a follow-up session, have the students share what they observed in small groups. Then invite several volunteers to come to the front of the class and mimic what they observed for each of the three emotions. Facilitate discussion.

Emotional Intelligence

Discussion Questions

1. What did you learn about body language through this activity?

2. What role did empathy play in identifying emotions? What enabled you to feel empathy?

3. How do your friends reveal their emotions—mostly through words, or mostly through facial expressions and body language?

4. Which emotions were the toughest to identify?

5. What were some of the main indicators of anger? ...of fear? ...of sadness? ...of happiness? ...of tiredness?

6. Why is it important to understand how someone is feeling?

Assessment

- Did the students act out emotions appropriately?
- Did the students correctly identify emotions from body language cues?

Emotional Intelligence

Emotion List

Happy	**Curious**	**Sad**
Excited	**Angry**	**Afraid**
Confused	**Guilty**	**Playful**
Comfortable	**Nervous**	**Confident**
Bored	**Suspicious**	**Brave**
Jealous	**Shy**	**Uncertain**

Emotional Intelligence

Take a Close Look

If you look closely you can tell how people feel by the expressions on their faces and the way they move their bodies.

Go to a busy place where you can sit down and watch lots of people go by. Look closely and write down what you see.

2. Describe an angry person.

Head: _____

Eyes: _____

Mouth: _____

Shoulders/arms: _____

Posture: _____

Legs/feet: _____

Draw a picture here.

1. Describe a happy person.

Head: _____

Eyes: _____

Mouth: _____

Shoulders/arms: _____

Posture: _____

Legs/feet: _____

Draw a picture here.

3. Describe a tired person.

Head: _____

Eyes: _____

Mouth: _____

Shoulders/arms: _____

Posture: _____

Legs/feet: _____

Draw a picture here.

Emotional Intelligence

Things I Appreciate

Objectives

The students will:
- Identify specific things in their lives that they appreciate.
- Express appreciation for advantages and beneficial life conditions.

ASCA Standards

PS:A1.2   Identify values, attitudes, and beliefs
PS:A1.5   Identify and express feelings

Materials

9" by 12" drawing paper (two pieces per student); colored pencils, markers, or crayons; tape

Procedure

Ask the students to name specific people, things or conditions in their lives that they appreciate. Explain that to appreciate something means to fully recognize its worth, quality, and importance, and to be thankful or grateful for it.

Write all responses on the board. The list should include items such as:
- parents and other family members
- friends
- pets
- good health
- TV, movies, video games, phones, etc.
- sports teams, clubs and organizations
- home, bedroom, bed, pool, and other household amenities
- neighborhood, community, nation
- specific foods
- play equipment and toys
- clothing
- education, school, library, computer, books, etc.
- freedom of speech, religion, assembly, etc.
- democracy, the right to vote
- money, allowance

Explain that you want every student to select 12 things that they really appreciate having in their lives and illustrate them on a poster.

Emotional Intelligence

Distribute two sheets of drawing paper to each student. Have the students divide each sheet into six equal parts by folding the long side into thirds and the short side in half. Demonstrate this process.

Direct the students to illustrate one appreciated item in each of the 12 resulting spaces. Suggest that they give their poster a title, such as "Things I Appreciate" or "The Top Twelve." When they have finished all 12 illustrations, the two sheets can be taped together along either the long or short edges to form a single large poster.

Have the students take turns sharing their posters with the group, describing each of the twelve things they appreciate. Display all the posters around the room.

Discussion Questions

1. What does it mean to take something for granted?

2. What kinds of advantages do we have in this country that people in many other countries don't enjoy?

3. Why is it important to take time to appreciate the good things we have in our lives?

4. What are some other ways to show your appreciation?

Assessment

- Did the students name a variety of specific assets, advantages, and beneficial conditions?
- Did the students express appreciation for the things they have?

The Trouble with Cliques

Objectives

The students will:
- Identify ways to make friends.
- Discuss effects of cliques.
- Practice inclusive behavior in peer interactions.

ASCA Standards

PS:A2.8   Learn how to make and keep friends
PS:B1.8   Know when peer pressure is influencing a decision
PS:C1.9   Learn how to cope with peer pressure

Materials

One copy of the experience sheet, *The Cost of Fitting In*, for each student

Procedure

Have the students form two teams. Give the teams 10 to 15 minutes to brainstorm ways of making new friends. At the end of the allotted time, reconvene the class and ask the groups to share their lists.

Possible ideas include:
- Sit beside someone different in the cafeteria and say hello.
- Offer to show someone new around the school.
- Join a school organization.
- Offer to help someone carry a heavy load.
- Team up with someone you don't know very well to work on a class project.
- Run an ad in the school paper asking for a companion for specific activities, like hiking or bicycling.
- Ask someone you know to introduce you to new people.
- Go to the gym or track after school and say hello to the kids who are practicing.

Write the word "Clique" on the board and ask the students to help you define it. Two possible definitions are:

    A small, exclusive group of friends or associates.

    An "in" group of kids that define itself as much by who is excluded as by who is included.

Emotional Intelligence

Discuss how a clique's policy of exclusion causes members to have difficulty making new friends, and can completely frustrate the efforts of someone who is not in the clique to become friends with someone who is. Stress that kids often want to be part of a clique so that they will be liked by "important'" people and feel important themselves. Point out that cliques generally consist of people from the same cultural, ethnic or racial backgrounds. They usually exclude anyone "different."

Distribute the experience sheets. Allow the students about 10 minutes to complete the sheet. Then ask them to rejoin their teams and share their answers to the questions.

Encourage the students to commit to making one new friend in the next week, or including one new person in their existing group of friends. Explain that this assignment carries one important restriction: the person they befriend or include in their group should be different from them or the group in some way.

Stipulate that before they can claim to have complete the assignment, the students must do something tangible with the new friend, such as sit together at an assembly, eat lunch together, go jogging or bicycling together, visit each other's home, see a movie together, or play video games after school. Ask the students to pay particular attention to the "clique phenomenon" and avoid doing anything that causes another person to feel left out. Conclude the activity with a discussion.

Discussion Questions

1. In what ways do you think cliques are good?

2. In what ways do you think cliques are harmful?

3. In what ways do the members of a clique miss out when they exclude others?

4. Of what value to a group is having varied membership?

5. Have you ever wanted to belong to a clique? If so, why was it important?

6. What would happen if there were no cliques at school?

7. What kinds of cliques do adults have?

Assessment

- Did the students generate a variety of strategies for making new friends?
- Did the students identify several disadvantages of cliques?
- Did the majority of students commit to practicing inclusive behavior?

Emotional Intelligence

The Cost of Fitting In

Is it worth it to be in? What have you done to be included in a group?

I have…(answer Yes or No)

_____ Risked losing friends.

_____ Hurt people who thought they were my friends by making them feel left out.

_____ Done something I thought was not right.

_____ Done something I knew was against the law.

_____ Used alcohol or drugs.

_____ Done something that might have harmed me physically.

_____ Done something that cost me a lot of money.

_____ Done something that interfered with my schoolwork.

_____ Done something my parents would have objected to if they had known.

_____ Done whatever was necessary as long as it didn't harm anyone else.

_____ Done something that was against my religion.

_____ Done whatever was necessary.

Can you remember a time when you were pressured to exclude someone from an activity?

_____

How did you feel? _____

_____

What did you do? _____

_____

If this ever happens again, what do you think you will do?

_____

_____

Emotional Intelligence

Our Powerful Thoughts

Objectives

The students will:
- Experience the power of thoughts to produce sensory reactions.
- Compare the physical and emotional effects of positive and negative thoughts.

ASCA Standards

PS:C1.11 Learn coping skills for managing life events
A:A1.5 Identify attitudes and behaviors leading to successful learning
A:A2.2 Demonstrate how effort and persistence positively affect learning

Materials

none

Procedure

Begin by asking the students if they would like to learn one way of becoming healthier, happier, and more successful in school.

Ask the students to close their eyes while read them the following visualization exercise:

Imagine a bright yellow lemon. Now imagine yourself cutting the lemon in half ... See yourself picking up half of the lemon and squeezing it ... Watch the juice ooze out ... Now take the lemon half and hold it up to your nose and smell the tangy aroma of the lemon ... Imagine putting the lemon to your mouth and tasting it.

After a few seconds, tell the students to open their eyes.

Ask: *What did you feel or experience during this visualization?* (Some people experience a sour taste, salivate and wrinkle their noses when they imagine smelling and tasting the lemon.)

To encourage discussion, ask:

- Was there a lemon in the room?
- Why did some of us physically react as though we were actually smelling and tasting a lemon?
- What does this tell you about the power of thoughts?

Explain that thoughts can also create emotions. Positive thoughts can make us feel happy, while negative thoughts can make us feel depressed.

Emotional Intelligence

Scientists have also demonstrated that emotions strengthen our immune system, which helps us resist illness and fight infections.

Ask the students to brainstorm a list of negative statements that kids often say to themselves. Write them on the board. Include such items as:
- I'm no good at this.
- Nobody likes me.
- They're picking on me.
- I'm stupid in math.
- I'll never make the team.

Now ask the students to brainstorm an equal or greater number of positive statements. Make a second list of these.

Use the familiar "muscle testing" exercise to demonstrate how thoughts can influence bodily reactions. Demonstrate the process with a volunteer. First, have the volunteer extend his or her dominant arm straight out to the side. Second, have the volunteer choose a negative message from the list. Third, tell the volunteer to simultaneously think the words and say them out loud *with conviction* while you press down on his or her arm with two fingers of one hand. Tell the volunteer to resist the pressure as you press and to notice how it feels. Tell the class to watch for movement.

Then have the volunteer choose a positive message from the board and repeat the exercise. Ask the volunteer to describe any differences in his or her sensation of strength and ability to resist the pressure. Ask the class to comment on differences in perceived movement.

Have the students choose partners and do the same exercise, with each person taking a turn in both roles. Circulate and offer assistance, as needed. Lead a follow-up discussion.

Discussion Questions

1. When did your arm feel stronger, while making the positive statement or the negative statement? Why do you think that happened?

2. How did you feel while making the positive statement?

3. How did you feel while making the negative statement?

4. Can you think of a recent time when your thoughts produced fearful, angry, or jealous feelings?

5. What does the expression, "She worried herself sick," mean?

6. Can you think of a recent time when your thoughts produced happy, excited, or loving feelings?

7. How can you use positive thoughts to improve your school performance? …athletic performance? …social life?

Assessment

- Did the majority of students describe how thoughts produce physical and emotional reactions?
- Did the students state that positive thoughts affect performance positively?

The Real Me

Objectives

The students will:
- Identify their positive inner and outer qualities.
- Recognize the strengths and positive traits of others.

ASCA Standards

PS:A1.1   Develop positive attitudes toward self as a unique and worthy person

PS:A1.10   Identify personal strengths and assets

Materials

Large cans with lids (such as coffee cans) or shoe boxes with lids; several magazines; colored paper, yarn, ribbons, scraps of cloth, crayons, or magic markers and other decorative materials; scissors and white glue

Procedure

Place the materials on large tables or designated work areas. Give each student a container.

Have the students decorate their containers on the inside and outside to reflect their own positive inner and outer qualities. Suggest that they cut and paste pictures from magazines to symbolize specific traits or qualities. For example, a picture of flowers on the inside of the container could represent a cheerful attitude, and a picture of baseball on the outside could represent a love of sports.

Suggest that the students further embellish the containers with pieces of colored fabric, ribbons, yarn, and drawings. As the students work, decorate a container yourself.

Facilitate creativity by talking with the group about specific positive qualities. Develop a long list of qualities on the board and brainstorm ways of symbolizing them.

Have the students take turns sharing their finished containers with the group. Facilitate discussion throughout the sharing session.

Discussion Questions

1. What are three inner qualities depicted in your container? What are three outer qualities?

2. What did you learn about yourself while decorating your container?

3. What similarities did you notice among our containers? What differences?

Assessment

- Did the students identify and describe specific positive qualities?
- Did the students show acceptance and appreciation for the self-proclaimed qualities of others?

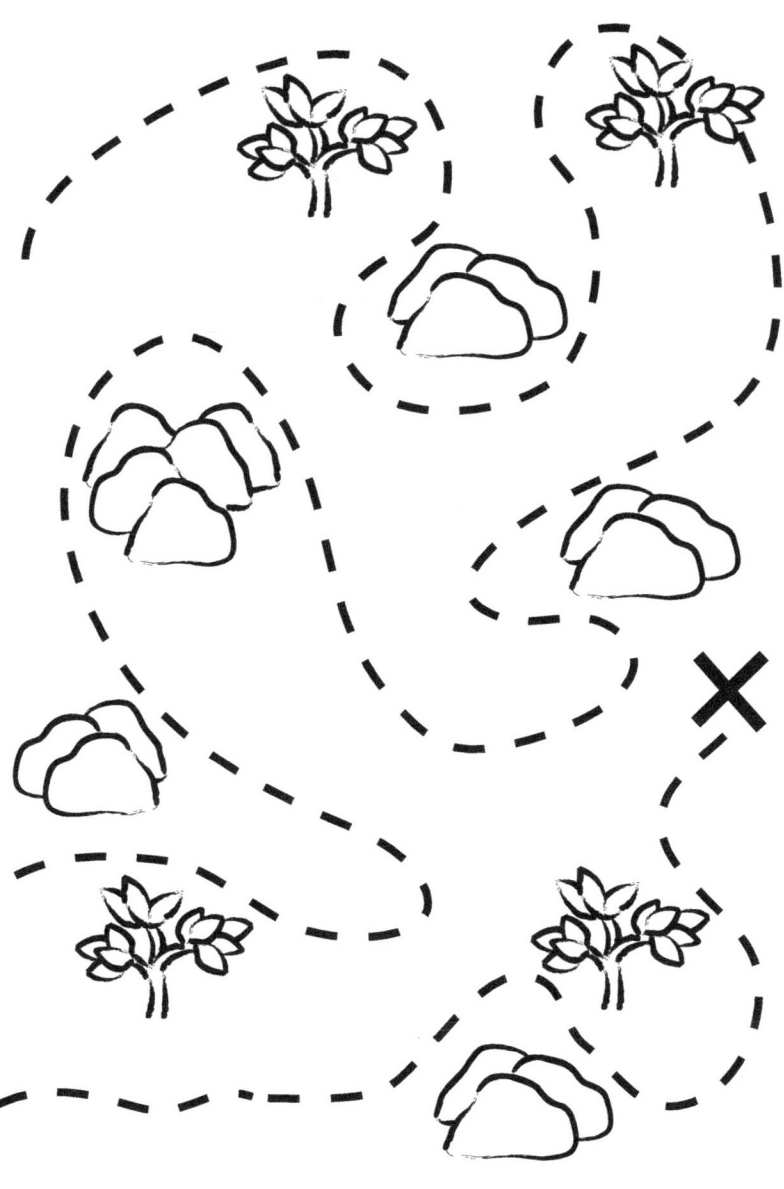

Emotional Intelligence

Writing Haiku Poetry

Objectives

The students will:
- Practice creative writing.
- Express positive and negative feelings in poetry.

ASCA Standards

PS:A1.2   Identify values, attitudes, and beliefs
PS:A1.5   Identify and express feelings

Materials

Pencils, paper, and several poetry books containing haiku poetry

Procedure

Ask the students if they have ever tried to express strong feelings, such as anger or happiness, in writing. Perhaps they described their emotions in a letter to a friend, or in a diary. Allow volunteers to share their experiences with the group. Explain that one way to express feelings productively is to write about them poetically. Inform the students that haiku is a type of Japanese poetry that can express feelings very directly and simply.

Share several haiku poems with the students and ask them to identify the feelings expressed in the poems. Write one or two on the board. Here are two:

Snow falls quietly
Covering the city,
Loneliness returns.

Ripe watermelon
Hidden under leaves and dirt,
My birthday surprise!

Explain that in Haiku the writer expresses a mood, often through something in nature. The writer captures things like loneliness, sadness, beauty, and peace in just three lines. Most haiku is written with 5 syllables in the first line, 7 syllables in the second and 5 in the third.

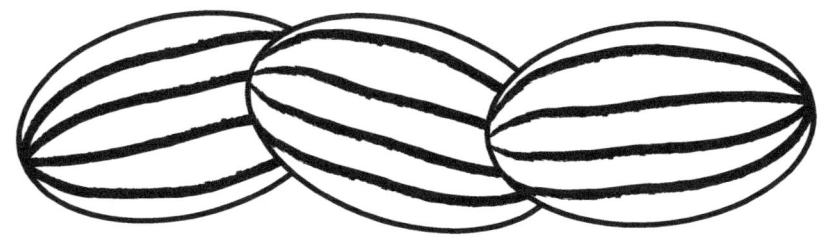

Emotional Intelligence

Spend a few minutes brainstorming feeling words. List these on the board in one column. Then ask the class to think of something in nature that could be used to represent each feeling. List the item in a second column, next to the word it symbolizes. For example, an electrical storm could represent anger, with thunder and lightning expressing explosive inner conflicts. Spring, new grass, buds on the trees and flowers could symbolize feelings of happiness and warmth. Fear could be a tiger, or some other wild animal. Sadness might be the death of an animal due to starvation.

Have every student choose a familiar feeling and write a three-line haiku poem about it. Suggest that the students use the 5-7-5 syllable pattern, and include references to nature. Remind them that the poem does not have to rhyme, and that its lines need not be complete sentences. Encourage the students to use descriptive words, making use of dictionaries and thesauruses. Write a haiku poem yourself to model the process. Share it with the class.

Conclude the activity by having the students share their poems first with a partner and then in small groups. Finally, invite volunteers to read their poems to the entire class. Publish poems in a "Haiku Feelings" book or online format, or post them on a bulletin board.

Discussion Questions

1. Why are feelings sometimes hard to express?

2. Why is it important to learn positive ways of expressing your emotions?

3. What are some other ways to express feelings productively?

Extension

Let the students set their poems to music, transforming them into short songs. An easy way to do this is to compose one melody for the first and third lines and a contrasting melody for the second.

Assessment

- Did the students identify and express a variety of feelings?
- Did the student poems demonstrate an understanding of feelings?

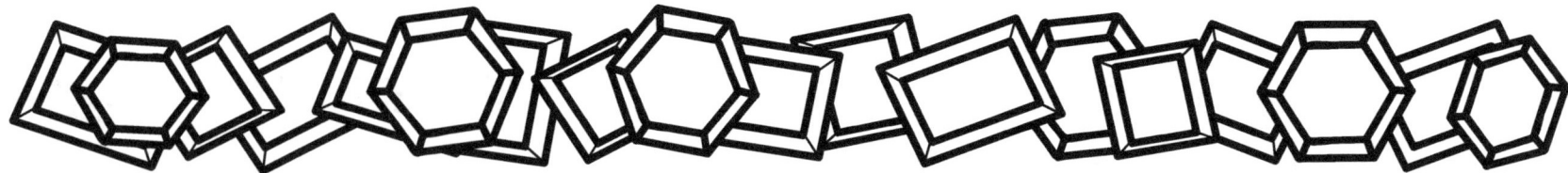

Emotional Intelligence

A Picture of Me

Objectives

The students will:
- Identify positive traits in themselves.
- Discover the positive traits of classmates.

ASCA Standards

PS:A1.1   Develop positive attitudes toward self as a unique and worthy person

PS:A1.1   Identify personal strengths and assets

Materials

For each puzzle: one sheet of 8.5" X 11" tag or poster board, crayons or colored markers, scissors, a pencil, and a small envelope. Several flat boxes approximately 9 inches by 12 inches

Procedure

Give each student a piece of tag or poster board and crayons or markers. Ask the students to take a few moments to think of a very positive image of themselves. For example, hitting a home run, helping to fix dinner, or getting a good grade on a paper. Then have them draw and color that image on the tag board, filling the sheet from edge to edge with color.

Next, tell the students to turn the picture over and write a secret message on the other side about a positive trait, special interest, hobby, or goal. The message can be related to the picture, or it can be about something else. Tell the students to include their names in the messages.

Distribute scissors and envelopes. Have the students cut their pictures into large puzzle pieces. Demonstrate this process for older students. For younger students, either provide assistance or collect the pictures and make the puzzles yourself, later. Have each student store his or her puzzle pieces in the envelope provided.

Emotional Intelligence

Have the students form groups of three or four. Give each group a flat box. Tell the groups to take one puzzle at a time and assemble it in the bottom of the box, put the lid on the box, turn the box over and remove the lid to read the secret message. If they can't read the message, they will have to reassemble the puzzle until the pieces fit together correctly.

Finally, reconvene the class and ask group members to describe each other's positive traits as stated in the secret messages. Encourage discussion about various traits and about positive self-image in general.

Before collecting the puzzles, have the students print their names on the envelopes. Store the puzzles in their envelopes at a learning center or special interest area so that the students may rework them.

Discussion Questions

1. Why is it important to recognize our own and each other's positive traits?

2. What new information did you learn about a classmate?

3. What other positive messages could you have written about yourself?

Assessment

- Did the students identify and describe positive traits?
- Did the students accept and appreciate the positive traits of others?

Emotional Intelligence

The Power of Words

Objectives

The students will:
- Identify typical positive and negative phrases they say to themselves and each other.
- Experience the effects of positive and negative self-talk.

ASCA Standards

PS:A1.1   Articulate feelings of competence and confidence as learners

PS:A1.5   Identify attitudes and behaviors leading to successful learning

PS:A1.1   Develop positive attitudes toward self as a unique and worthy person

Materials

none

Procedure

Ask the students what they need in order to grow. They will probably answer *food, water, air, oxygen, love,* etc. Accept and acknowledge these answers. Then tell the students that you have in mind something else that makes people grow—words.

Explain:

Positive words actually make us get bigger. We stand straighter, look taller, feel better, and act older when we hear positive words about ourselves. It doesn't matter if someone else says the words to us, or we say them to ourselves. The effect is the same. Of course, the opposite is also true. Negative words make us smaller. When people say negative things to us—or we say them to ourselves—we slump, look shorter, feel worse, and often act younger. Can you believe that words do all that?

Ask the students to brainstorm two lists: one made up of positive things people say and the other made up of negative things. Get the process going by suggesting some phrases yourself and writing them on the board under the headings, "Growing" and "Shrinking." Accept contributions from the students and build lists that include the phrases on the next page.

Emotional Intelligence

Growing	Shrinking
• That's great!	• That's awful
• Good work!	• Poor work!
• I like that!	• I hate this.
• You can do it.	• You're doing a lousy job.
• You're doing a good job.	• This is a drag.
• This is fun to learn.	• This is too hard.
• That's easy.	• I don't want to.
• I'll try it.	• This is boring.
• This is interesting.	

Next, have some fun by demonstrating how the words and phrases work. Ask a student to read through the negative list, saying the phrases directly to you. As the student reads, start to "shrink." Visibly get smaller with each phrase, until (if willing) you are on the floor. Then (looking up from the floor) ask the student to read the list of positive words to you. Start to "grow" and get taller with each phrase. Finally, stand on a chair and make yourself as tall as possible. Ham it up. Let your facial expressions and posture reflect increasing negative/positive effects.

Have the students form dyads and take turns doing the same exercise.

When the mirth has subsided, point out that most of the negative things people hear actually come from themselves, not from others. Ask the students: How many of you say negative things like these to yourselves?

Explain that the things we say to ourselves make up our "self-talk." We need to replace negative self-talk with positive self-talk in order to grow.

Go around the room and have every student make a positive statement about himself or herself, starting with the word "I." Model the process. If a student can't think of something to say, point to the board and help the student pick a phrase from the "Growing" list.

Conclude the activity with a discussion.

Discussion Questions

1. How do you feel when someone makes a "growing" statement to you?

2. How do you feel when someone makes a "shrinking" statement to you?

3. Which is easier — saying negative things to ourselves or saying positive things? Why?

4. How do we learn our self-talk habits?

5. How can we help each other use positive self-talk?

Assessment

- Did the students state a variety of self-talk examples?
- Did the students demonstrate the effects of positive and negative self-talk?

My Success Inventory

Objectives

The students will:
- Recognize and describe achievements and successes.
- Identify strengths and talents in themselves and others.
- Practice positive self-talk.

ASCA Standards

PS:A1.1   Develop positive attitudes toward self as a unique and worthy person
PS:A1.2   Identify values, attitudes, and beliefs
PS:A1.10 Identify personal strengths and assets

Materials

One copy of the experience sheet, *My Success Inventory*, 12 small self-adhesive labels, and a *Target Worksheet* for each student

Procedure

Begin by talking with the students about the many things they have accomplished so far in life. Describe a variety of examples, such as learning to walk, talk, dress, dance, play, sing, count, problem-solve, read, write, ride a bike, skateboard, roller-blade, ski, play softball, volleyball, soccer, basketball, cook, play an instrument, use a computer, be a friend, join an organization, earn a merit badge, award, or certificate; learn to type, paint, build things, baby-sit, care for a pet.

Distribute the experience sheets and go over the directions. Allow about 15 minutes for writing.

Ask the students to form groups of four or five. Give 12 small, self-adhesive labels and a *Target Worksheet* to each student.

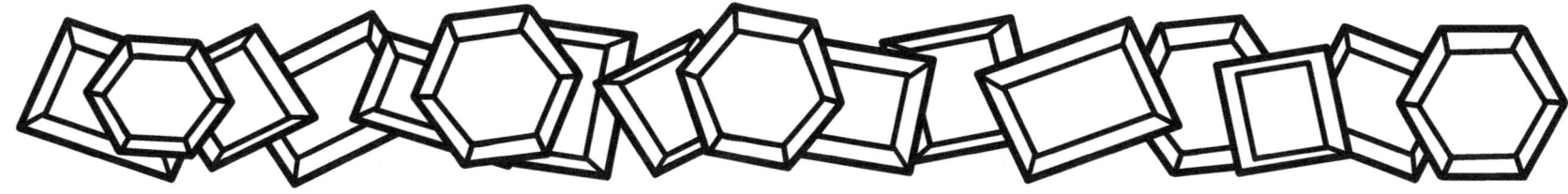

Emotional Intelligence

Direct the students to take turns describing their accomplishments to the other members of their group. In your own words, explain:

Tell the group why you picked those particular successes. Explain how you felt about them at the time they occurred and why they are particularly meaningful to you now.

Immediately after you share, the other members of your group will each make three labels that describe positive things about you based on the successes you shared. For example, the first person's labels might say, "energetic," "musically talented,"' and "good friend." Then while you hold up your target, that person will look directly at you, tell you what he or she has written on each label and stick the labels on your target.

The other members of your group will then take a turn giving you their labels in the same manner. If there are three other people in your group, you will end up with nine labels on your target. A second person in the group will then take a turn reading his or her successes and being labeled. Then a third person will be the target and so on.

Circulate and assist the groups, as needed. Ensure that the students do not engage in any kind of teasing or put-downs. If you observe a student using the third person ("She is energetic.") when labeling a target, stop the person and help him or her rephrase the statement in the second person ("You are energetic.") Lead a follow-up discussion.

Discussion Questions

1. How did you feel after doing this exercise?

2. What did you learn about yourself? ...about other members of your group?

3. How did you decide which accomplishments to include on your list?

4. Why do we spend so much time thinking about our failures and weaknesses when we have all accomplished so much?

5. Where can you put your target so that it will continue to remind you of your successes?

Assessment

- Were the majority of students able to name a variety of accomplishments?
- Did all students receive sincere positive feedback from their peers?

Emotional Intelligence

My Success Inventory

Your life is full of successes, one after another, year after year. The things you've accomplished could fill a book. Look back now at the child you were and the young adult you are becoming. Recall some of the many things you've learned and achieved and write the most memorable here:

Five skills I mastered before the age of ____ .

1. _____
2. _____
3. _____
4. _____
5. _____

Four skills I accomplished between the ages of ___ and ___ .

1. _____
2. _____
3. _____
4. _____

Four of my achievements between the ages of ___ and ___ .

1. _____
2. _____
3. _____
4. _____

Five major things I accomplished between the ages of ___ and ___ .

1. _____
2. _____
3. _____
4. _____
5. _____

Emotional Intelligence

Target Worksheet

Emotional Intelligence

The Value of Validations

Objectives

The students will:
- Make positive statements about classmates.
- Explain the meaning and importance of validations.

ASCA Standards

PS:A1.1 Develop positive attitudes toward self as a unique and worthy person

PS:A2.3 Recognize, accept, respect, and appreciate individual differences

Materials

8.5" X 11" blank paper, fine-point marking pens in dark colors (one per student), and masking tape

Procedure

Ask if anyone knows what a validation is, or what it means to validate someone. Listen to all responses. If you like, jot ideas on the board. Explain that a validation is an expression of approval, and that to validate someone means to say something positive that lets the person know you respect and appreciate him or her.

Make these additional points about validations:

- A validation is similar to a compliment. "I like the way you fixed your hair today," and "I think you are nice to help me with my math problem," are validations.
- Receiving validations from others feels good and builds self-esteem.
- Giving a validation is like giving a gift, and it doesn't cost a penny.
- Validations should always be sincere. Usually people can tell when we say something we don't really believe.
- At first it may feel strange to give validations, but with practice anyone can do it.
- A validation expresses what you are thinking and feeling, so try starting it with the word, "I" (I think…, I feel…, I appreciate…).
- Be as clear and specific as you can. Describe what you like or appreciate in the other person. If you say, "You're fun," or, "You look nice," the person won't understand nearly as well as if you say, "I love the clever things you say," or "I really like you in that red shirt."

Emotional Intelligence

Ask the students to help you formulate different kinds of validations. Keep coming up with examples until you are reasonably sure the students have a good grasp of the concept.

Give each student a sheet of paper, a marking pen and a couple of pieces of masking tape. Have the students help each other tape the papers to their backs. Then, in your own words, give these directions:

We're going to practice giving each other validations. I want everyone to get up and start walking around the room. Think of something positive and sincere about each person you meet. But instead of saying the words, use your pen to write the words on the person's back. Keep it brief and write in small letters, because I want each of you to write something on the back of every person in the room.

Circulate and monitor the students to ensure they write only positive statements. When they have finished, give the students a minute or two to remove the papers from their backs and read the comments that people have written. Then lead a brief discussion.

Discussion Questions

1. How does it feel to validate others?

2. How does it feel to be validated?

3. Which of the comments on your sheet surprised you?

4. What are some other ways to show people that you appreciate them?

Assessment

- Did the students make sincere positive comments about each other?
- Did the majority of students find something positive to say about every member of the class?

Emotional Intelligence

Diversity

Diversity

Where We Came From

Objectives

The students will:
- Identify countries of family origin.
- Research and share cultural information.
- Recognize and appreciate diverse cultural backgrounds.

ASCA Standards

PS:B1.7   Demonstrate a respect and appreciation for individual and cultural differences

PS:A1.1   Develop positive attitudes toward self as a unique and worthy person

PS:A2.4   Recognize, accept and appreciate ethnic and cultural diversity

Materials

U.S. and world maps; colored pins, flags, or other map markers; one copy of the experience sheet, *My Family Roots*, for each student

Procedure

Introduce this activity by explaining that the United States is a land of many different peoples, all of whom have the right to share in its benefits and freedoms. Point out that no one ethnic group "owns" the U.S. because all of its citizens (other than Native Americans) or their ancestors came from other lands.

Share with the students a bit about your own ethnic background and the lands from which your ancestors immigrated.

Next, tell the students they are going to do some individual research to find out about the lands from which they, their parents, grandparents, or earlier ancestors came. They will also learn some interesting things about the perceptions and experiences of these family members.

Distribute the experience sheets. Go over the directions and questions to make sure that the students understand them. Illustrate by answering some of the questions relative to your own family history.

Diversity

When the students have completed their questionnaires, have them report orally to the class. Allow plenty of time for reactions and discussion. On U.S. and world maps, using colored pins or flags, mark the various places the students and their families have lived. (For example, use one color to show countries of ancestral origin and a different color to mark places where the students have lived.)

Discussion Questions

1. How many different countries are represented in our class?
2. Why is it important to take pride in and share our family and ethnic backgrounds?
3. What would school be like if all of us had exactly the same background and experience?
4. How does knowledge of our different ethnic backgrounds help promote cooperation and understanding?
5. How did you feel when you were interviewing your family member? What new information did you learn?
6. Why is it important to know your cultural roots?
7. How do we all benefit from the cultural diversity in the classroom?
8. What can we do to help others appreciate diversity?

Assessment

- Did the majority of students learn and share information about their family origins?
- Did the students demonstrate acceptance and respect for the diverse backgrounds reported by their classmates?

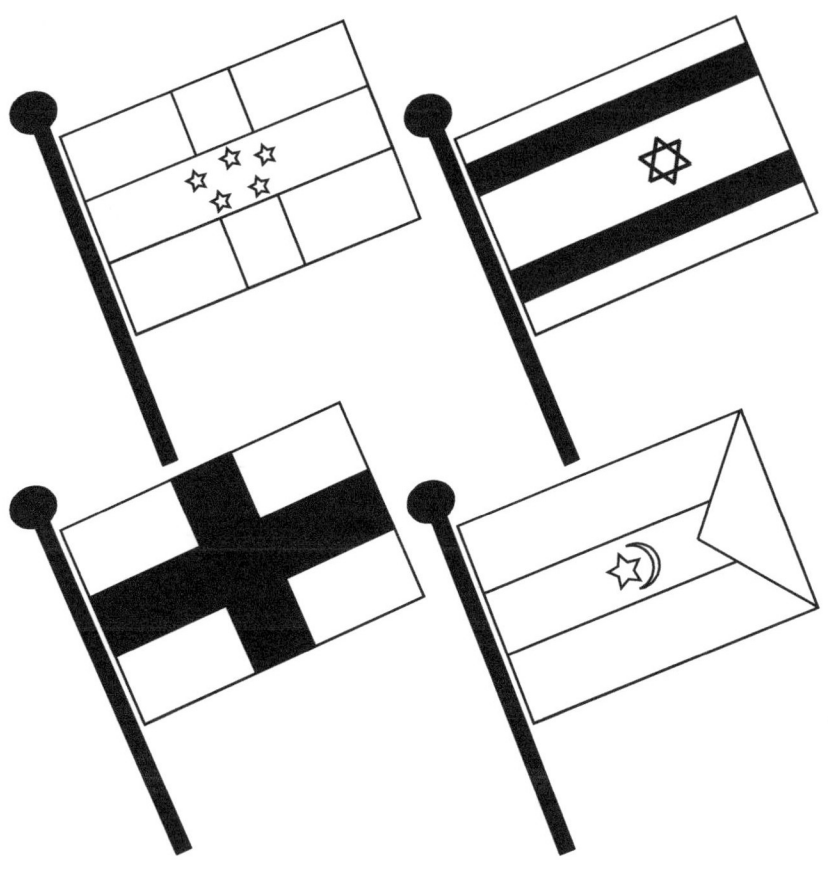

My Family Roots

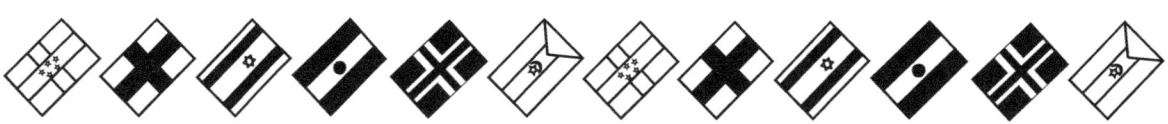

All of us have family roots. If we trace our families back far enough, we can learn about our ancestors. Talk to a parent or other family member. Write down his or her answers to the questions below.

1. What is our family's first language? _____

2. In what countries did our ancestors live? _____

3. What kind of work did family members do in their country of origin? _____

4. Where did they go to school and what was school like? _____

5. When did our family first come to the United States? _____

6. Why did they come to the United States? _____

7. What was it like to leave home and go where they didn't know anyone or what to expect? _____

8. What problems did they or you encounter moving to the U.S.? _____

9. What facts or stories can you tell me about our family origins or traditions? _____

10. What else can you tell me about my family roots? _____

Bring this completed experience sheet to class and share what you learned.

Diversity

Diversity

Diversity "R" Us

Objectives

The students will:
- Develop awareness and appreciation of other cultures.
- Learn about each other's cultural backgrounds.

ASCA Standards

PS:B1.7   Demonstrate a respect and appreciation for individual and cultural differences

PS:A1.1   Develop positive attitudes toward self as a unique and worthy person

PS:A2.4   Recognize, accept, and appreciate ethnic and cultural diversity

Materials

One copy of the experience sheet, *Cultural Background Interviews*, for each student

Procedure

Begin the activity by having the students think about what they learned from the student reports in the previous activity, "Where We Came From." Ask, *"Which countries and cultures that you heard about particularly interest you?"* Facilitate sharing.

Next, pair the students so that each student has a partner from a different country (or region) of origin. Explain that the pairs will interview each other to learn information about their partner's culture and country of origin.

Distribute the experience sheets and go over the questions. Explain that if, during the interview, a student can't answer one or more questions, the partners will work as a team to research the answers using the library or Internet. Set a date for the completed interview reports and designate class time for interviewing, research, and writing.

Diversity

To facilitate the reporting procedure, create the following chart:

Student Name	Country of Origin	Interesting Fact About Country/Culture

Have each student report information learned about his/her partner's country of origin or region. Assign a recorder to add information to the chart as each report is given.

Discussion Questions

1. How can we all benefit from the various cultures represented in our class?
2. What do we gain by learning about the ethnic backgrounds of others?

Assessment

- Did the students successfully answer the majority of questions?
- Did the students work together cooperatively to complete the assignment?
- Did the students provide accurate information about countries and cultures?

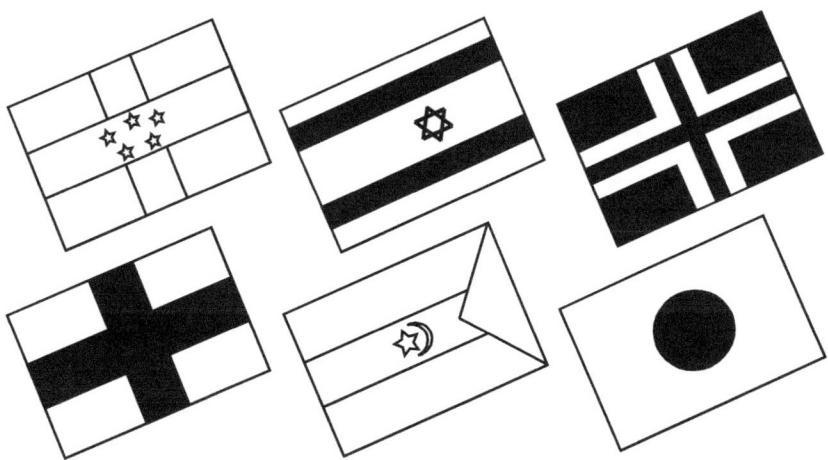

Cultural Background Interviews

Write down your partner's answers to the following questions. If your partner doesn't know the answer, research the question together using the library or Internet.

1. What is your family's country of origin?
   _____

2. What is the geographical location of the country?
   _____

3. Who are its neighbors on each side?
   _____

4. What is the name of the leader of the country at this time?
   _____

5. What form of government does the country have?
   _____

6. What foods are native to the country?
   _____

7. What types of music are common?
   _____

8. In what major industries do people work?
   _____

9. What arts and crafts is the country known for?
   _____

10. What customs are followed when someone is born, has a birthday, gets married, or dies?
    _____

11. What are some special holidays and how are they celebrated?
    _____

12. What is the name of one famous person (living or dead) who came from this country?
    _____

Diversity

Diversity

The Challenge of Disabilities

Objectives

The students will:
- Describe challenges and frustrations experienced by individuals with disabilities.
- Develop empathy for people with disabilities.
- Identify specific needs of people with disabilities.

ASCA Standards

PS:A2.3   Recognize, accept, respect, and appreciate individual differences.

Materials

Several each of blindfolds, cotton balls (or foam earplugs), shoelaces, and mirrors; index cards (one per student) labeled with the following disabilities:

- What is it like to be blind? Wear a blindfold.
- What is it like to be deaf or hard of hearing? Tightly insert cotton or earplugs in your ears.
- What is it like to have difficulty walking? Tie your legs together at the knees.
- What is it like to have difficulty talking? Keep your tongue on the roof of your mouth.
- What is it like to have difficulty getting your hands to do what you want? Use only your non-dominant hand.
- What is it like to have a learning disability? Do all of your reading by looking at the words in the mirror.

Procedure

Write the following list on the board. Ask the students to prioritize how important these things are to them:

1. the ability to hear
2. the ability to see
3. the ability to walk
4. the ability to talk
5. the ability to use your hands
6. the ability to read and understand the written word

Facilitate comments and discussion.

Next, explain that the students are going to experience what it is like to have some of these disabilities. Distribute the index cards, one per student. Explain that for the next couple of hours (or as long as you think is workable), the students are to do everything with the disability they have been assigned on the index card.

Diversity

Distribute blindfolds, cotton, shoelaces, and mirrors to the appropriate students and coach the students on how to proceed with their given disability. Be sure to provide assistance to the blindfolded students when they need to move around. Then proceed with your regular lesson. Allow enough time for the students to fully experience the difficulty of living with a disability. Going a full day, with the students exchanging disabilities halfway through, will provide the most powerful lesson on disability awareness.

When all the students have fully experienced one or more disabilities, conclude with a class discussion.

Discussion Questions

1. How did you feel living with a disability?
2. Would learning be more difficult if you had to live with a disability all the time?
3. What methods did you develop to cope with your disability?
4. How did other people help you?
5. What kinds of special considerations or treatment would help a person with your disability?
6. How did you feel about yourself?
7. Why do you think we did this activity?
8. What did you learn?

Assessment

- Did the majority of students play their disabled roles seriously and consistently?
- Were the coping methods employed by students realistic and thoughtful?
- Did the students express empathy for individuals with disabilities?

Diversity

Communicating with People with Disabilities

Objectives

The students will:
- Identify common mistakes communicating with people with disabilities.
- Practice effective methods of communication.

ASCA Standards

PS:A1.7   Recognize personal boundaries, rights, and privacy needs
PS:A2.3   Recognize, accept, respect, and appreciate individual differences
PS:A2.6   Use effective communication skills
PS: A2.7 Know that communication involves speaking, listening, and nonverbal behavior

Materials

One copy each of the five *Role Play Guidelines* on separate sheets of paper; props for the role plays (optional)

Procedure

Announce that the students are going to have an opportunity to contrast effective (and acceptable) and ineffective (and unacceptable) ways of communicating with people who have various disabilities.

On the board, write these general guidelines and discuss them with the students:
- See the person as an individual, not as a disability.
- Don't talk down to the person.
- Speak directly to the person, not to a companion or an interpreter.
- Treat adults as adults. Don't use first names unless you are invited to do so.
- Be considerate. Allow extra time for the person to say or do things.
- Relax. Don't worry about using common expressions like, "See you later," or "I've got to be running along," when talking to people with vision or physical limitations.

Diversity

Divide the class into five groups. Give each group a different sheet of "Role-Play Guidelines."

Explain that the groups are to read and discuss the communication guidelines for their category of disability and then develop a two-part role-play demonstrating:

1. Ineffective and/or unacceptable ways of communicating with a person who has that type of disability. These can be easily inferred from the guidelines and may be exaggerated for humor and effect.
2. Effective and acceptable ways of communicating with the same person.

Direct the groups to create whatever roles are necessary for the dramatizations they develop, including those of people with disabilities, friends, family, teachers, employers, health-care professionals, etc.

Allow the remainder of the class period for planning and rehearsing. At the next class meeting, have the groups take turns acting out their role plays, first demonstrating ineffective communication, then effective communication. Expect the ineffective methods to generate laugher among the audience.

After each role play, ask audience members to describe as many of the guidelines as they can identify from watching the dramatization. Then have one of the actors read the entire list of guidelines to the class.

At the conclusion of the role plays, post all of the guidelines on a bulletin board. Lead a follow-up discussion.

Discussion Questions

1. What did you learn as an actor in your role-play that you didn't realize before?
2. What was particularly striking to you as an audience member?
3. What are some of the most common mistakes we make when communicating with people who have disabilities?
4. How do you feel now about your ability to communicate with people who have disabilities?
5. If you aren't sure how to communicate with a person who has a disability, what can you do?

Assessment

- Did the students effectively demonstrate negative and positive communication skills?
- Did the students explain the reasoning behind specific guidelines for communicating with people who have various disabilities?

Role Play Guidelines

Communicating with Persons Who Have Hearing Loss

1. Get the person's attention. Wave your hand, tap the person's shoulder, or bang on the table, if necessary.
2. Speak clearly and slowly. Don't shout or exaggerate lip movements. Keep sentences short.
3. Be flexible in your language. If the person has difficulty understanding you, rephrase your statement using simpler words. Don't keep repeating. If difficulty persists, write it down.
4. Provide a clear view of your face and keep the light source on it. Keep hands, food, and other items away from your mouth when talking.
5. Be a lively speaker. Use facial expressions that match your tone of voice, and use gestures and body movements to aid communication.

Communicating with Persons Who Have Speech Difficulties

1. Give your complete attention to the person who has difficulty speaking.
2. Be patient. Don't correct and don't speak for the person. Allow extra time. Give help when needed.
3. Keep your manner encouraging.
4. Ask questions that require short answers, or a nod or shake of the head, when necessary.
5. If you have difficulty understanding, don't pretend. Repeat as much as you do understand. The person's reaction will clue you.

Communicating with Persons Who Have Vision Loss

1. Introduce yourself and others who are with you. Use a normal tone of voice.
2. Use the person's name when starting conversation, so the person knows you are speaking to him or her. Let the person know when you are ending a conversation or moving away.
3. Ask the person if he or she wants help. When giving assistance, allow the person to take your arm, which helps you to guide. Warn the person of any steps or changes in level. Use specifics such as *left* and *right*.
4. Offer seating by placing the person's hand on the back or arm of the seat.
5. Don't pet a guide dog. Remember to walk on the side of the person away from the dog.

Role Play Guidelines

Communicating with Persons Who Use Wheelchairs or Crutches

1. Don't lean or hang on a person's wheelchair. It is part of that person's body space.
2. Sit, squat, or kneel if conversation continues for more than a few minutes. Don't be a "pain in the neck."
3. Ask a wheelchair occupant if he or she wants to be pushed *before* you do so.
4. Allow a person who uses a wheelchair or crutches to keep them within reach. Many wheelchair users can transfer to chairs, car seats, etc. Some wheelchair users can walk with crutches part of the time.
5. Consider distance, weather conditions, and surfaces such as stairs, curbs, or inclines when giving directions.

Communicating with Persons Who Have An Intellectual Disability

1. Speak slowly and distinctly. *Show* might be more effective than *tell*.
2. Tell the person what to do, not what *not* to do.
3. Help the person feel comfortable. Maintain nonthreatening voice and facial expressions.
4. Treat the adult person who has an intellectual disability as an adult.
5. Base exceptions to rules on reason, not pity.

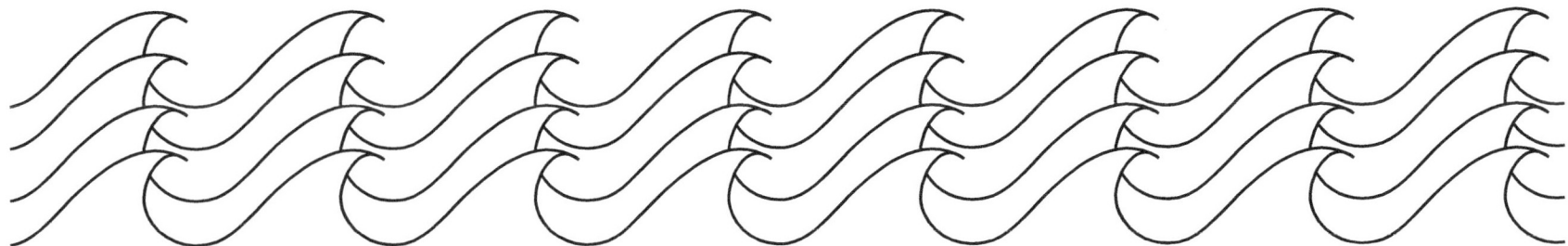

Diversity

Examining Discrimination

Objectives

The students will:
- Examine racial, cultural issues.
- Discuss causes and possible cures for discrimination.

ASCA Standards

PS:A1.2 Identify values, attitudes, and beliefs
PS:A2.3 Recognize, accept, respect, and appreciate individual differences
PS:A2.7 Recognize, accept, and appreciate ethnic and cultural diversity

Materials

One copy of the experience sheet, *How Would You Feel?*, for each student

Procedure

Distribute the experience sheets. Give the students time to answer the questions. If you want to encourage longer, more thoughtful responses, make this a homework assignment.

Allow the students to approach the questions in any way they choose. Some of the questions are worded so that they may represent the view of either a minority or a majority person. This ambiguity could add interest to the discussion.

Ask the students which question they want to discuss first. Give students who are particularly troubled or confused by an item the opportunity to air their concerns. Encourage the sharing of personal experiences similar to those described.

If your group is large, have the students share in dyads before convening the total group. As each item is discussed, ask the questions listed below along with other relevant open-ended questions.

Diversity

Discussion Questions

1. What is really going on in this situation?
2. What would your very first feelings be in this situation? What about later?
3. What do you think you would say or do in this situation?
4. What, if anything, would you like to see done about this kind of situation? What are you willing to do?

Assessment

- Did the students express empathy for the victims of discrimination?
- Did the students describe realistic causes and possible cures for discrimination?

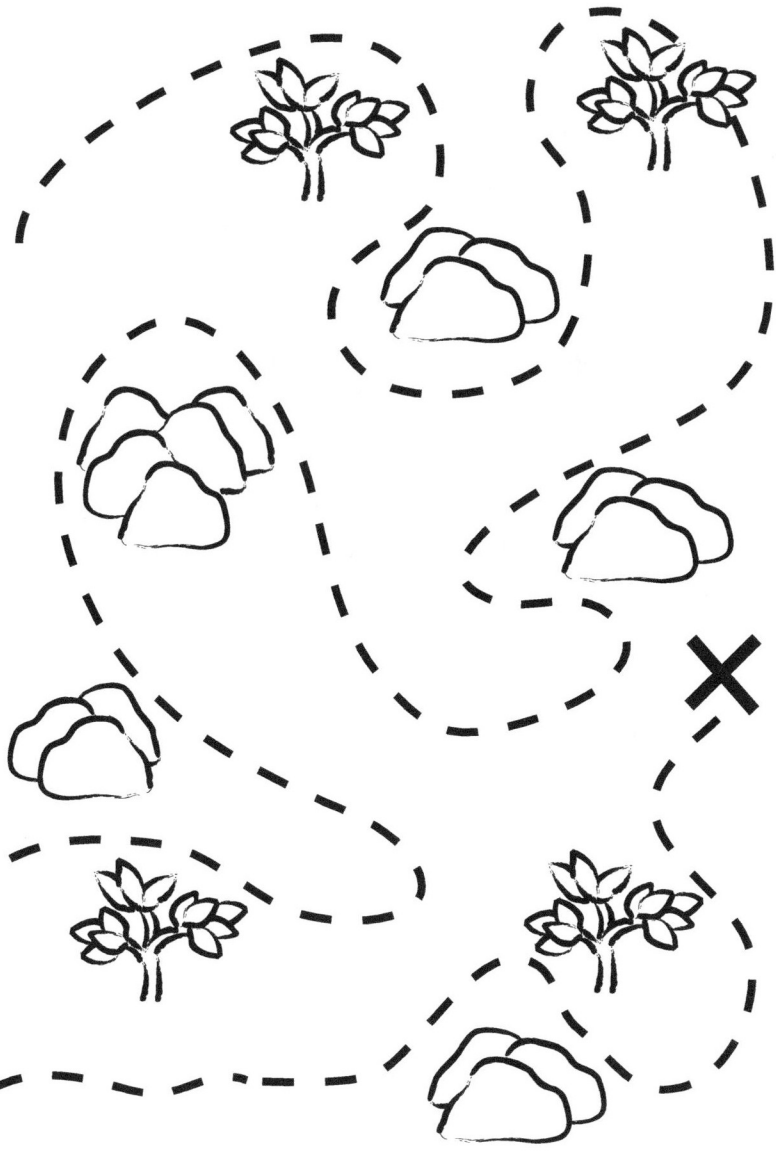

Diversity

How Would You Feel?

Read each situation and write down your feelings and thoughts. Use an extra sheet of paper if you run out of space.

1. You have to pay up front before being served at a restaurant.

   _____

   _____

   _____

2. The fences and walls in your once nice neighborhood are covered with graffiti.

   _____

   _____

   _____

3. You've been waiting in a long line and when it's your turn, the clerk ignores you and helps the next person.

   _____

   _____

   _____

4. Women visibly clutch their handbags tighter when you pass them on the street.

   _____

   _____

   _____

5. You can't get into your chosen college because the rest of the openings are reserved for minorities

   _____

   _____

   _____

6. You are stopped for no apparent reason other than your appearance and asked to prove your legal residency.

   _____

   _____

   _____

Diversity

7. Your little brother or sister doesn't understand the social slights and racial slurs of other kids and you have to explain them to him/her.

_____
_____
_____

8. Your parents won't let you date a person you really like because of his/her race.

_____
_____
_____

9. People are always getting impatient with you—even angry—because of your heavy accent in English.

_____
_____
_____

10. You keep getting passed over for promotions, which go to workers less qualified than you.

_____
_____
_____

11. You are never invited when your friends go swimming at a private club.

_____
_____
_____

12. Your parent gently suggests that you spend less time with your friend of a different race.

_____
_____
_____

Diversity

Recipes for Open-Mindedness

Objectives

The students will:
- Identify differences between open- and closed-mindedness.
- Describe advantages and disadvantages of each.
- Recognize areas where they may be closed-minded.
- Appreciate the value of different views.

ASCA Standards

PS:A2.2   Respect alternative points of view
PS:A2.3   Recognize, accept, respect, and appreciate individual differences
PS:A2.4   Recognize, accept, and appreciate ethnic and cultural diversity
PS:B1.7   Demonstrate respect and appreciation for individual and cultural differences

Materials

Writing materials for the students

Procedure

Introduce the topic by asking the students to define the term, *open-minded*. For example: *A person who is open-minded is receptive to new and different ideas and opinions of others.*

Contrast open-mindedness with *close-mindedness*, or lack of receptivity to new and different ideas and opinions of others. Suggest other synonyms: *broad minded vs. narrow minded, tolerant vs. intolerant hospitable vs. inhospitable, liberal vs. conservative.*

Explain that during the 1960s, a group of psychologists set out to study the similarities and differences between individuals with closed minds and those with open minds. They found that closed-minded thinkers strongly rejected beliefs different from their own and tended to build their own beliefs around the views of a trusted authority figure. The close-minded thinkers often saw the world as an unfriendly and dangerous place. Open-minded thinkers, on the other hand, were willing to consider viewpoints other than their own. They operated from a more nonrestrictive sense of time and space and saw the world as a friendlier place (M. Rokeach, *The Open and Closed Mind*, New York: Basic Books, 1960).

Facilitate a discussion using selected questions, below.

Have the students form small groups. Announce that each group is to create a recipe for open-mindedness. Explain that there are many recipes for open-mindedness, just as there are many recipes for chocolate cake. The recipes may share some of the same ingredients, but each is a unique blend producing a unique "flavor." Suggest that the students keep this analogy in mind as they develop what they consider to be the best possible recipe for open-mindedness.

Explain that every recipe must include three things. (Write them on the board):

1. Name of recipe
2. List of all ingredients (and amounts, if desired)
3. Clear directions

Have the groups share their completed recipes with the class. Encourage comments, questions, and further discussion after each presentation. Review the definition of open-mindedness and pose specific examples occasionally throughout the presentations.

Assign homework: Ask the students to watch TV news shows, read newspapers, news magazines, and reputable Internet news sources, and to write down 5 examples of open-mindedness and 5 examples of close-mindedness in the news. Tell them to record the date, news source, and enough details to accurately report the item to the class.

At a later class meeting, have the students take turns giving their reports. Facilitate further discussion.

Discussion Questions

1. Do you consider yourself open-minded?
2. Do your friends think of you as open-minded?
3. What kinds of behaviors and attitudes would an open-minded person display? How about a close-minded person?
4. How does open-mindedness apply to the way you think about people who are different from you?
5. Is open-mindedness always a good thing? Explain.
6. What did you learn about open-mindedness from your news items?
7. What subject, if any, could you never be open-minded about?
8. How difficult is it to be open-minded?
9. How can you judge the relative openness of your own mind in particular areas?

Assessment

- Did the students define and give examples of open- and close-mindedness?
- Did the students name a variety of key ingredients in open-mindedness?
- Did the majority of students successfully relate open- and close-mindedness to their own lives, and to events in the news?

Identifying Stereotypes

Objectives

The students will:
- Explain the nature of prejudice and stereotyping.
- Describe specific stereotypes and how they developed.
- Demonstrate ways in which stereotyping can be avoided.

ASCA Standards

PS:A1.2 Identify values, attitudes, and beliefs
PS:A2.3 Recognize, accept, respect, and appreciate individual differences
PS:A2.4 Recognize, accept, and appreciate ethnic and cultural diversity

Materials

One copy of the experience sheet, *Shattering Stereotypes*, for each student

Procedure

Ask the students to define the words *stereotype* and *prejudice*. Agree on definitions of both words, using a dictionary if necessary. Write the definitions on the board.

Point out that a prejudice often begins with a bad experience, which we then generalize into a stereotype. To illustrate this concept, ask the students to think of a person who is different from themselves with whom they have had a bad experience. The difference does not have to be racial or ethnic and the person could be anyone—dentist, doctor, police officer, teacher, etc.

Ask the students to describe some of their experiences (without using proper names). If they have difficulty grasping the idea, give some examples from your own experience. For example, tell about a doctor who was gruff and dismissive, or an auto mechanic who cheated you. If you became wary of all doctors, or suspicious of all auto mechanics, as a result of your experience, acknowledge that you developed a prejudice in that area.

DIVERSITY

Ask each volunteer who shares an experience to describe any generalizations or prejudices they developed as a result. For example, ask:
- *Do you feel differently about other (dentists) because of what happened?*
- *Are you prejudiced against all (motorcyclists) because of what that one did?*

Distribute the experience sheets and go over the directions. Stress the importance of writing down the *first* thing that comes to mind. Point out that stereotypes can be both negative and positive.

After the students have completed Part A of the experience sheet, ask volunteers to share some of their responses. Encourage discussion. Then give the students a few additional minutes to complete the experience sheet by listing exceptions (Part B).

Divide the class into small groups of 4 or 5. Assign each group one category from the experience sheet, with no duplications.

Have the groups brainstorm positive attributes for their particular category, writing down all their ideas. Circulate and offer assistance, as needed.

Note: Caution the students to avoid listing more stereotypes (e.g., "Blondes are fun," "Texans give great barbecues," "Blacks are athletic."). To avoid this trap, suggest that they think of specific people they know in each category and list qualities they've admired in those people.

When the lists have been completed, ask each group to demonstrate as many of the positive attributes as they can to the rest of the class. Tell them they can do this in any way the choose: with a skit, story, picture, etc. Whatever creative way they design will be fine. Announce a date time for the presentations.

Discussion Questions

1. Where did you learn the stereotyped ideas that you wrote down?
2. Which stereotypes bother you most?
3. How do stereotypes cause prejudice?
4. What can we do to eliminate stereotypes?
5. Which is easier to look at in a person, positive qualities or negative qualities? Why?
6. Why is it important to look at people as individuals rather than as members of a group?
7. Are you likely to become friends with someone if you only focus on what you see as that person's negative qualities? What do you need to focus on?
8. When were you completely wrong about a person because of a prejudice or stereotype?
9. How can we deal with people who tease others by using ethnic humor or slurs?

Assessment

- Did the students identify a variety of stereotypes?
- Did the students describe exceptions to common stereotypes?
- Were the students able to explain how stereotypes develop?

Shattering Stereotypes

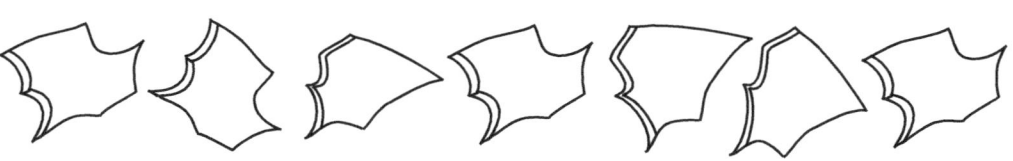

Part A: Write down your first reaction to each statement. Don't take time to think about it—just write.

_____ Indians all/always _____

_____ Mexicans all/always _____

_____ Blondes all/always _____

_____ Texans all/always _____

_____ Skinheads all/always _____

_____ Blacks all/always _____

_____ Italians all/always _____

_____ Arabs all/always _____

_____ Teens all/always _____

_____ Boys all/always _____

_____ Girls all/always _____

_____ Old people all/always _____

_____ Police all/always _____

_____ Asians all/always _____

_____ Whites all/always _____

_____ Americans all/always _____

_____ Hollywood stars all/always _____

_____ Millionaires all/always _____

_____ Politicians all/always _____

Part B: Identify at least one person for each category who doesn't fit the stereotype. It can be someone you know or a famous person. Write their name in the blank on the left.

Remember: Whenever you catch yourself thinking a prejudiced or stereotypical thought about a group or individual, stop and think of three exceptions to the prejudice or stereotype.

Diversity

Diversity

Fighting Prejudice

Objectives

The students will:
- Describe incidents of apparent racism, prejudice, and discrimination.
- Identify a variety of specific strategies that students can employ to curb racism and prejudice at school.

ASCA Standards

PS:A1.2 Identify values, attitudes, and beliefs
PS:A2.3 Recognize, accept, respect, and appreciate individual differences
PS:A2.4 Recognize, accept, and appreciate ethnic and cultural diversity

Materials

Writing materials, marking pens, several large pieces of poster paper or poster board

Procedure

In your own words say to the students:
Racism is a serious problem in many schools today. Our school is no exception. At times you may have witnessed name-calling, slurs, threats, and even fights. In some schools, racial hate groups like the skinheads spend their time harassing and terrorizing minority students.

Racism hurts everyone. It promotes stereotypes and prevents people from really getting to know each other. It can have a terrible effect on a person's self-worth and self-esteem.

What are some acts of racism, prejudice, or discrimination that you have witnessed here at school or elsewhere?

What could have prevented these incidents from occurring?

Facilitate discussion, cautioning students not to identify the people involved by name. As a total group, brainstorm some of the factors involved in overt and covert racism and intolerance. Write all ideas on the board. The students will need this list later while working in small groups. Try to elicit the ideas on the following page and other ideas:

Diversity

- Instead of objecting to racist remarks, people often ignore them. Some students snicker or laugh at racist jokes instead of saying, "That's not funny."
- Acts of discrimination and favoritism (for example, when most awards or elected offices go to students of one race) often go unnoticed and unchallenged. Vigilance and activism are needed to stem such practices.
- Kids tend to hang out with other kids who are like them, racially as well as in other ways. Reaching out to and befriending students from other groups promotes understanding and is personally rewarding.
- People are quick to label normal conflicts between individuals as "racially motivated" when in fact they are no different from conflicts between people of the same race. This retards communication and makes it difficult to resolve differences productively.
- People are afraid to talk about their racist feelings. We all have prejudices. Instead of pretending we don't, or ignoring them, we need to get them out in the open and discuss them.

Have the students form small groups of six to eight. Tell them that you want each group to brainstorm strategies that the entire student body can use to promote tolerance and diversity. Have each group appoint a recorder to write down all ideas. Suggest that each strategy begin with an "action word" that says what the individual student must do to carry out that strategy. Examples of action words are: *work, reach out, stand up, promote, accept, speak up, learn, talk to, join.*

Allow at least 15 minutes for brainstorming. Circulate and offer encouragement as needed. Then have each group read its ideas to the rest of the class. Using the questions below, facilitate discussion.

Have a team of two or three volunteers compile all of the strategies into a single list, combining similar items. Then at a later session, work with the class to reduce the list to no more than ten strategies. Be sure each of the final strategies is worded clearly and includes examples of specific behaviors. Have the same (or a different) team of volunteers make the final chart or poster. Display it in the classroom and elsewhere in the school.

Discussion Questions

1. Why is it important to fight racism actively and openly?
2. Why do so many people ignore racist remarks, jokes, and behaviors?
3. What impression does a racist person get when his or her remarks and actions are tolerated by others?
4. What can you do to help promote tolerance and diversity?

Assessment

- Did the students acknowledge and describe specific prejudiced and/or racist behaviors?
- Did the students verbalize the need to combat racism and prejudice?
- Did the majority of the group actively participate in developing strategies to curb discrimination and racism at school?

Conflict Management

Rules Help Prevent Conflict

Objectives

The students will:
- Observe rules in action and describe how they guide student behavior.
- Describe the importance of rules in preventing and resolving conflict.

ASCA Standards

PS:C1.2 Learn about the relationship between rules, laws, safety, and the protection of rights of the individual

Materials

Art paper and colored magic markers

Procedure

Begin with a general discussion of rules. Point out that everyone is expected to follow rules of one sort or another. For example, adults abide by workplace rules on the job and motor vehicle rules when they drive. Children have rules both at home and at school.

Ask the students to describe some of the rules they have in their families. Write the rules on the board and point out similarities and differences.

Assign the students the task of observing one another throughout the next recess or athletic break. Tell them to watch for situations in which behavior is guided by, and/or conflicts are settled by, specific rules. Give some examples, such as signing up for play equipment, waiting their turn, or tossing a coin to decide who is first.

After recess (or at the next session), generate a discussion concerning situations they observed in which the existence of rules prevented or resolved problems. Let the students tell about real or potential conflicts. If appropriate, use the opportunity to review existing school rules. List the rules on the board.

Conflict Management

Ask volunteers to act out situations that could occur if there were no rules and then reenact them, applying the rules. Discuss how rules are made to prevent problems and conflicts.

Distribute the art materials. Ask the students to illustrate one of the rules that helps prevent conflict at school and write a short story or anecdote to accompany it. Have the students share their stories and illustrations in small groups. Display them around the room.

Discussion Questions

1. Who develops the rules at school? …at home?
2. How do rules help prevent conflict?
3. What can you do if a conflict arises on the playing field and there is no rule to follow?
4. What can you do if you think a rule is unfair or impractical?
5. How does cooperation help people avoid conflict?

Assessment

- Did the students identify a majority of existing school or classroom rules?
- Were the students able to associate behaviors they observed on the playing field with the rules that govern those behaviors?

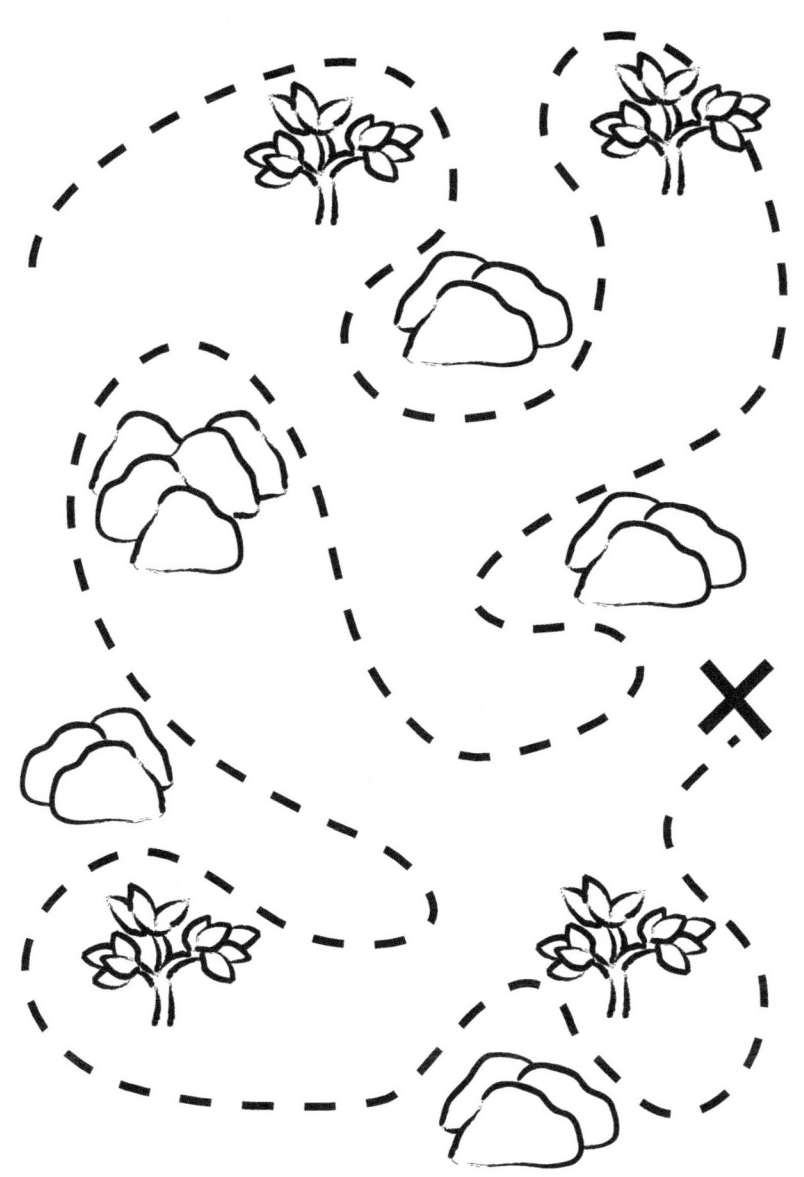

What Makes You Angry?

Objectives

The students will:
- Explore various causes of anger.
- Identify strategies to control anger.

ASCA Standards

PS:A1.5   Identify and express feelings
PS:A1.8   Understand the need for self-control and how to practice it
PS:B1.3   Identify alternative solutions to a problem

Materials

Whiteboard and markers

Procedure

Gather the students together and generate a discussion about why people get angry. Ask questions like these to help them explore the topic:
- What causes people to get angry?
- Why do *you* get angry?
- Do you tend to get annoyed with certain types of people?
- Do you get angry at yourself sometimes?
- Do you get angry when you don't get your way, or when you can't have something you want?
- Do you get angry when someone disagrees with you, criticizes you, or treats you unfairly?

Point out that not everyone gets mad at the same kinds of situations or people.

On the board, write these headings:

People   **Situations**   **Actions**   **Self**

Explain that for purposes of discussion, you are dividing the things that make people angry into these four categories. Give several examples of each. "People" might include loudmouths, whiners, or stuck ups. "Situations" might include missing a favorite TV show because of homework, being stuck in the house for five days due to rain, or getting a flat tire on your bike. "Actions" are specific annoying things that people have done, like cutting in line ahead of you, not returning borrowed items, or not doing their part of a team assignment. "Self" refers to things about yourself that often make you mad, like being clumsy or having thin hair.

Invite the students to notice what most often makes them angry: certain types of people, certain types of situations, specific actions, or disappointment in themselves. Explain that by knowing what most often angers them, the students will develop greater self-awareness. And understanding causes is a good starting point for managing anger.

In your own words, state: *Remember, you have control over your behavior. It's always hard to stay in control once you are very angry, but by knowing the kinds of things that tend to make you angry, you are less likely to blow up and lose control in the first place.*

Divide the students into four groups. Direct each group to choose a recorder. Assign each group one of the four categories (people, situations, etc.). Tell them to brainstorm ways to positively manage their anger in situations like those listed on the board.

Have each group share their top five anger-management strategies with the total group. Facilitate discussion.

Discussion Questions

1. How did the strategies differ from one group to another? How were they the same?
2. Why is it helpful to categorize the causes of anger?
3. We all get angry, but for different reasons. Why do you think that is?

Assessment

- Were the students able to identify personal sources of anger?
- Did categorizing sources of anger help the students to better understand how anger is generated?
- Did the students identify appropriate anger-management strategies?

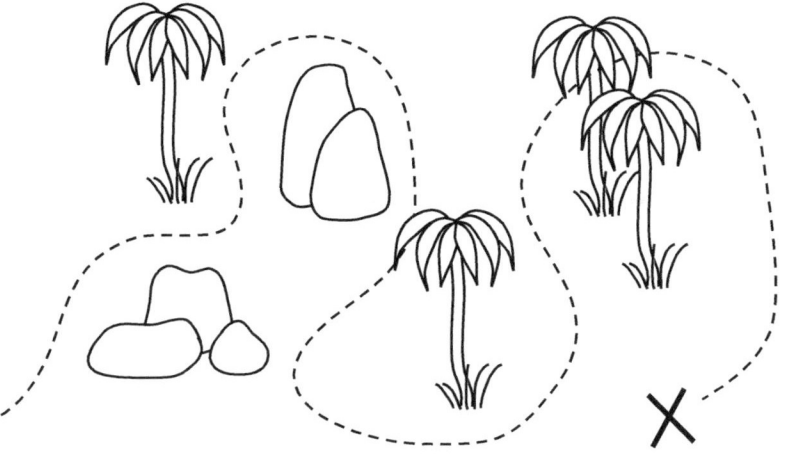

Conflict Management

A Ritual for Releasing Anger

Objectives

The students will:
- Understand that holding in anger can lead to emotional outbursts and illness.
- Practice releasing anger through writing.
- Learn to let go of daily gripes and grudges.

ASCA Standards

PS:A3.1   Take responsibility for their actions
PS:B1.4   Develop effective coping skills for dealing with problems
PS:C1.10   Learn techniques for managing stress and conflict
PS:C1.11   Learn coping skills for managing life events

Materials

An empty coffee can or large jar with lid; a paper label glued or taped to the can/jar printed with the words, "Gripes and Grudges"; note paper and pencils

Procedure

Talk with the students about the physical sensations that often accompany feelings of anger. Ask these questions to generate discussion:
- How does your body feel when you are angry?
- What happens to your energy level when you are angry?
- How does your body feel when you stay angry for several hours? …days?
- Have you ever held a grudge for several days or weeks? How did your stomach feel? How did being angry affect your schoolwork?
- How well do you play and sleep when you are angry?

Explain that holding on to gripes and grudges makes people lose energy and can lead to illness. In addition, when a student's attention is focused on being angry, the student doesn't learn as well in school.

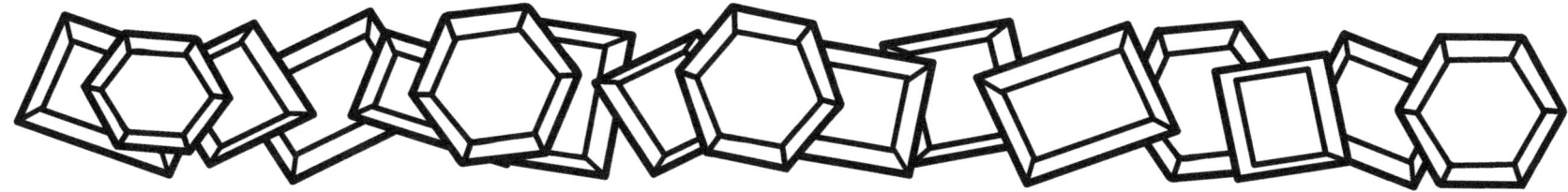

Show the students the can or jar and read aloud the label, "Gripes and Grudges." Ask if anyone can explain what a gripe is. (A gripe is a complaint, grievance, or criticism.) Ask a volunteer to explain what a grudge is. (A grudge is a deep-seated or enduring sense of bitterness or anger.) Clarify the explanations of the students and use them to develop simple definitions.

Announce that you are going to show the students a ritual for releasing, or getting rid of, gripes and grudges. (Explain that a ritual is a procedure that is repeated regularly or faithfully.)

Explain that throughout the day the students will write down on paper everything that irritates or annoys them. Instruct them to use a separate piece of paper for each gripe or grudge.

Periodically throughout the day, have the students deposit their papers in the can or jar, replacing the lid each time a new gripe or grudge is added.

At the end of the day, ask the students if they would like to get rid of their gripes and grudges or hold on to them. Give any student who wishes to keep a gripe or grudge the opportunity to remove the corresponding sheet of paper from the can. Treat this part of the exercise matter-of-factly and urge the students to be honest about their feelings. Pretending to let go of anger is not the objective.

Ceremoniously dispose of the remaining gripes and drudges. For example, use a paper shredder, throw the papers into an outside dumpster, or burn the papers in a hibachi or fireproof container. Invite the students to say goodbye to their gripes and grudges and be ready to start tomorrow fresh and clean.

Discussion Questions

1. How does it feel to let go of what is making you angry?
2. How do you feel when you hold on to anger versus when you release it?
3. How does writing down what makes you angry help to release the anger from your mind?

Assessment

- Were the students able to identify anger-producing incidents to write about?
- Did the students understand the concept of releasing anger?

Conflict Management

Tantrums and Tirades

Objectives

The students will:
- Describe what a tantrum looks like.
- Recognize that a tantrum is something that can be controlled.
- Discover methods for calming themselves and others.

ASCA Standards

PS:A1.6   Distinguish between appropriate and inappropriate behavior
PS:A1.8   Understand the need for self-control and how to practice it
PS:C1.11 Learn coping skills for managing life events

Materials

Whiteboard and markers

Procedure

Begin by asking the students if they have ever had a tantrum or seen someone else have a tantrum. When hands go up, ask, "How did you know it was a tantrum?" Encourage volunteers to describe what a tantrum looks and sounds like. List descriptors like the following on the board.
- Red face
- Loud crying or yelling
- Unreasonable demands
- Unable to stop
- Disruptive

Read the following scenario to the students:

Monica and her older brother, Sal, are standing at the bedroom window watching their father build a deck in the backyard. He is using power tools and lumber is piled everywhere. Sal asks their mother if he can go outside and help his father. Mother thinks about it for a few seconds and finally says, "Yes, if you promise to do only what he tells you to do and not touch anything without his permission." Sal agrees.

Conflict Management

Monica asks eagerly, "Can I help, too?"
Mother says, "No, Monica, you are too little. You stay inside with me."

As Monica watches her brother head for the door, she jumps up and down and cries, "I can help. I can help. I am not too little!" Again, Mother says, "No, Monica."

Monica looks out the window at her brother and father. Her face turns bright red and she starts to wail loudly. Then she begins beating her fists against the window and screaming, "I'm not too little to help. It's not fair, it's not fair!"

Ask the students to imagine that they are the "Super Tantrum-Breaker" and have the ability to say and do just the right thing to make a tantrum go away. Ask them what they would say or do to stop Monica's tantrum. Jot their ideas on the board. You will probably hear positive as well as punitive ideas. Write down all of them. For example:

- Distract her with a game or toy.
- Move her away from the window so she can't watch.
- Tell her to stop or you'll spank her.
- Slowly count with her to 20.
- Make her lie down in bed until she calms down.
- Make a loud noise to startle her.

Discuss the various ideas. Ask the students how they would feel if each method were used on them. Finally have volunteers act out several of the ideas to see how they work. Conclude the activity with a summary discussion.

Discussion Questions

1. How do you feel when you see a young child have a tantrum?
2. How do you feel when an older child, teenager, or adult has a tantrum?
3. What have you seen adults do to calm down a child during a tantrum?
4. What can you do to calm yourself down when you are about to lose control?

Assessment

- Did the students accurately describe tantrum behaviors?
- Did the students think of realistic ways to control tantrums in themselves and others?

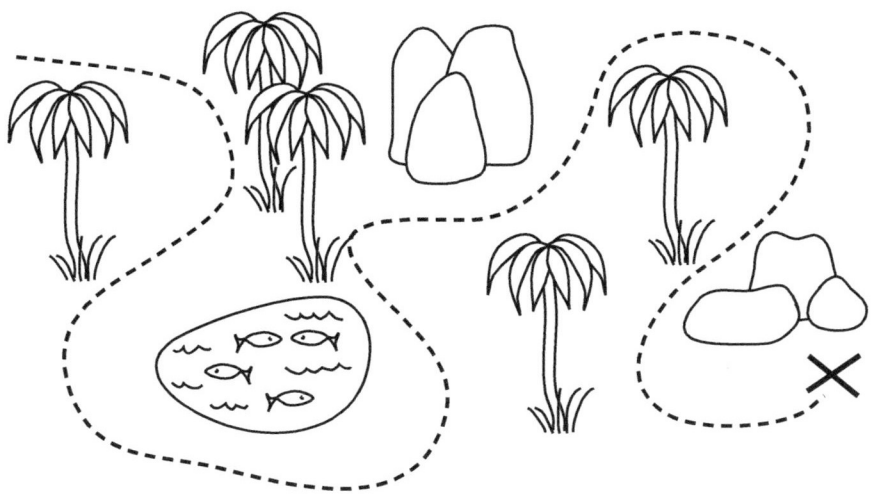

Conflict Management

Anger and Self-Control

Objectives

The students will:
- Understand that anger is normal and that they can learn to control their reactions to anger.
- Become familiar with a range of typical responses to anger.
- Observe and evaluate their own behaviors in anger-provoking situations.

ASCA Standards

PS:A1.6 Distinguish between appropriate and inappropriate behavior

PS:A1.8 Understand the need for self-control and how to practice it

PS:B1.4 Develop effective coping skills for dealing with problems

PS:B1.6 Know how to apply conflict resolution skills

Materials

One copy of the experience sheet, *Chart Your Anger,* for each student

Procedure

Begin by telling the students a real story about a recent time when you got angry. For example, you might say:

This morning I was waiting in a line of cars to get on the freeway and this person zoomed by me on the shoulder of the onramp. He was going so fast it looked like he was going to lose control of his car. He passed up all of us who were waiting patiently for our turns. I was furious. In fact, I still feel mad when I talk about it.

Ask the students if they ever get angry. Talk a little about the kinds of things that provoke anger in them.

Ask the students to take out a sheet of paper (or distribute paper) and write a list of events or situations that make them angry. Give the students 5 to 10 minutes to do this. When they have finished, tell them to go back through their list and number the items from Most Angry (#1) to Least Angry (highest number).

Conflict Management

Next, return to your earlier story and talk about your behaviors when you were angry. Continuing with the previous example, you might say:

When I was angry with that driver this morning, I started yelling. No one could hear me inside my car, but I was yelling anyway. The woman in front of me laid on her horn and I heard a couple of other horns blaring too.

Explain that you and the other people were expressing your anger or "blowing off steam." Point out that some ways of expressing anger are more effective than others. Also, some exhibit more self-control than others. Give the students an opportunity to talk about ways in which they express anger.

Then, have the students turn their sheet of paper over and, on the back, list things they do when they are angry. Give them another 5 to 10 minutes to complete this second list. When they have finished, tell them to go back through the list and number the items from Most Effective (#1) to Least Effective (highest number).

Ask volunteers to share their lists with the class. Discuss the effects of various expressions of anger and the relative amounts of self-control they require.

Distribute the experience sheets. Go over the directions and answer any questions about the use of the chart. Explain that the students are to chart their reactions to anger for 1 week. Name a specific due date.

On the scheduled due date, have the students discuss their charts in small groups. Suggest that they take turns sharing one or two events from their chart. Talk about which behaviors worked for them and which did not. Conclude the activity with a class discussion.

Discussion Questions

1. What similarities did you notice in the things that made us angry?
2. What were the most common reactions?
3. What are the benefits of being in control?
4. What are the dangers of reacting with low-self-control?
5. What high self-control behavior would you like to learn? How can you go about learning it?

Assessment

- Did the students recognize and record episodes of anger?
- Did the students distinguish between high self-control and low self-control reactions to anger?
- Did the students demonstrate willingness to learn greater control?

Chart Your Anger

Getting angry is a natural reaction. You hardly ever have to think about it — it just happens. Two things you *do* have to think about are:

1. How to control yourself when you are angry.
2. How to express your anger in constructive ways. That's much harder.

Event	Reaction

Use the chart provided for one week. Every time you get angry, write it down. In the EVENT column, describe what happened to make you angry. In the REACTION column, put the number of the reaction that comes closest to what you did. Choose from the list below. If you did two or more things, put two or more numbers. At the end of the week, answer the summary questions. Then, bring this experience sheet back to class.

1. Physically hurt someone.
2. Damage or destroy property.
3. Yell accusations or threats.
4. Call a person lots of bad names.
5. Use alcohol or drugs to forget about it.
6. Try to get someone in trouble by telling.
7. Ignore it and pretend nothing happened.
8. Take several deep breaths.
9. Count to ten.
10. Punch a pillow or a punching bag.
11. Go for a bike ride or play a sport or game.
12. Listen to music.
13. Take a walk, run, or swim.
14. Do a relaxation exercise or meditation.
15. Write about it in your diary or journal.
16. Share your feelings with someone you trust.
17. Calmly and assertively say what you think.

LOW SELF CONTROL HIGH

Summary Questions

1. Were any of the things that made you angry preventable? How?
2. Which high self-control actions work best for you?
3. Which high self-control actions would you like to learn?

Conflict Management

Rethinking the Situation

Objectives

The students will:
- Recognize how anger develops.
- Practice substituting moderate thoughts for angry thoughts as a way of reducing anger.

ASCA Standards

PS:B1.6   Know how to apply conflict-resolution skills
PS:C1.10   Learn techniques for managing stress and conflict
PS:C1.11   Learn coping skills for managing life events

Materials

One copy of the two-page experience sheet, *Change Your Thoughts!*, for each student

Procedure

Tell the students that in this activity they will have an opportunity to discover a new way of handling anger. Ask them to consider that angry feelings are not actually caused by situations and events, but rather by the *thoughts we have* about those situations and events. Once the thoughts about an event are identified, those thoughts can be replaced with different (more moderate) thoughts as one way of controlling anger. Demonstrate this concept using a chart on the board.

Write four headings across the top of the board:

Event   Thoughts   Feelings   Substitute Thoughts

Under the <u>Event</u> heading, write "Mom won't let me go to the party at my friend's house." Skip the second column and ask the students what their feelings might be in this situation. The students will probably suggest words such as *mad, furious, and sad*. Write several of these words in the <u>Feelings</u> column. Then go back to the <u>Thoughts</u> column and ask the students what their thoughts might be concerning this situation. Elicit answers such as, "She's being mean," "She doesn't understand how important it is to me," "She never wants me to have fun," and "She treats me like a baby."

Conflict Management

Explain to the students that it is not the event, but the *thoughts about the event*, that cause the feelings. Refer to the sentences in the second column and point out that any of these thoughts could create angry feelings. Explain that no situation, event, or person can force us to have a particular feeling. We *choose* our feelings by the thoughts we have, even if we are not aware of it.

Next, suggest that if the thoughts recorded in the second column are moderated, the feelings too will change. Help the students create new thought statements, such as, "Mom thinks she is looking out for my safety," "Mom has family plans the night of the party and wants me to be with the family," and "There will be more parties this year." Record them in the last column, <u>Substitute Thoughts</u>. Point out that these moderated thoughts will reduce the anger.

Distribute the experience sheet and go over the directions. Give the students a few minutes to complete the sheet, or have them complete it as homework.

Invite individuals to share one or more examples from their completed experience sheets. After each example, ask the group how their feelings might change as a result of the substitute thoughts. If the student had trouble thinking of substitute thoughts, ask the group to come up with some.

In a culminating discussion, emphasize that when the students find themselves reacting to a situation too strongly, they can improve their feelings by rethinking the situation. This ability takes practice and perseverance, but it works.

Discussion Questions

1. Why do we choose to feel angry in certain situations?
2. When you are angry, how does it help to rethink the situation?
3. What is easy about substituting new thoughts? What is difficult about it?

Assessment

- Were the students able to associate their angry feelings to the thoughts that precede them?
- Did the students successfully substitute moderate for extreme thoughts?

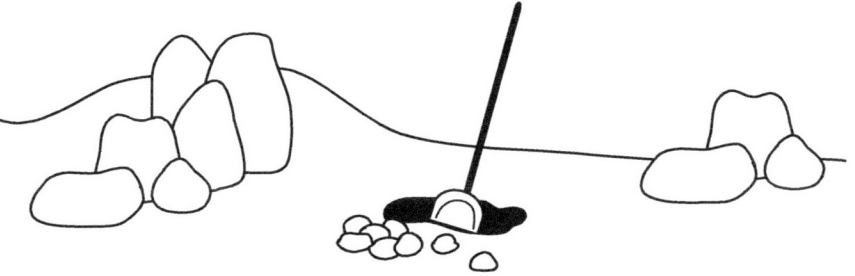

Change Your Thoughts

Directions

In the first column, list at least three real or made-up situations/events that are certain to make you angry. In the second column, write the thoughts that you have in each situation. In the third column, write the feelings that these thoughts create. In the fourth column, write new thoughts to help change your feelings.

Event	Thoughts
1.	
2.	
3.	
4.	
5.	
6.	

Conflict Management

Feelings	Substitute Thoughts
1.	
2.	
3.	
4.	
5.	
6.	

Here are some tips for changing your thoughts:
- Picture the situation from the other person's point of view.
- Don't take what happened personally. It just happened.
- Ask yourself what you can learn from the situation.
- Think about how you can handle it differently next time.

Bag Your Anger

Objectives

The students will:
- Brainstorm strategies for controlling anger.
- Practice selected anger-control strategies for an extended time period.
- Assess the effectiveness of selected strategies.

ASCA Standards

PS:B1.6   Know how to apply conflict-resolution skills
PS:C1.10 Learn techniques for managing stress and conflict
PS:C1.11 Learn coping skills for managing life events

Materials

One copy of the experience sheet, *My Bag of Tricks*, for each student

Procedure

Lead a group discussion on what happens when people lose their tempers. Talk about the destructiveness of volatile behaviors and how lack of self-control can increase stress and make a conflict or problem worse. Allow the students to share examples of what happens when someone loses self-control.

Explain to the students that effective solutions to conflicts and problems often require communication, negotiations with others, and long-term effort. However, it is sometimes necessary to gain control of ourselves before attempting such strategies. Instead of throwing tantrums and venting anger in other destructive ways, we can use anger-control strategies to put a band-aid on a bad situation until we have calmed down enough to work on positive solutions to the problem.

On the board, write the heading, "Anger Control Strategies." Ask the students to brainstorm positive ways in which they can regain self-control when they feel themselves getting angry. Write ideas on the board as they are suggested. The following items may be included as anger-control strategies:

- Run laps around the house (block, school, track).
- Leave the situation and take ten slow, deep breaths.
- Jump on a trampoline or tumbling mat, or with a jump rope.
- Punch a pillow, mattress, or punching bag.
- Look away and/or walk away from the cause of stress.
- Go get a drink of water, milk, or juice.
- Listen to soft music.

Conflict Management

- Talk to a trusted adult.
- Throw balls at a wall or rocks at a tin can (away from people).
- Count to 100 (or backwards from 100).
- Take a walk outside and observe nature.
- Take a nap.

After the students have brainstormed ideas and you have added items from the above list, review all of the items and ask the students to think of the pros and cons of using each strategy. Next, invite the students to choose three to five anger-control strategies to try out for themselves. Suggest that they include strategies that they have already found successful and new ones that they believe might be beneficial.

Give each student an experience sheet. Ask the students to write down their chosen strategies. Announce that the list is their "Bag of Tricks."

Explain to the students that their task is to field test their Bag of Tricks over the next few weeks, trying each strategy in several situations. Suggest that the students carry the sheet with them to serve as a reminder and that they mark the strategies that worked best and jot notes on the back of the sheet. Alert the students that some strategies may work in one situation and not in others, and strategies that work for one person may not work for others. Each Bag of Tricks will become individualized with time and practice.

Each week ask volunteers to report the results of their field testing. Frequently remind the students that anger-control strategies are just short-term controls, not permanent solutions to problems.

As field-test data are brought in and shared, summarize the information on a big chart. Eventually the students will be able to see graphically which strategies work best.

Discussion Questions

1. Why is it helpful to know ways of controlling anger?
2. What sorts of situations require strategies like these?
3. How do you know when you are losing control of your emotions?
4. What did you learn about your own emotions from testing these strategies?
5. How would you go about teaching these strategies to someone else?

Assessment

- Did the students articulate the need to control anger in conflict situations?
- Did the students describe useable strategies for controlling anger?
- Did the students report consistent use of the strategies during the testing period?

My Bag of Tricks

Directions

Write down three (3) to five (5) ways of controlling anger. Choose strategies that will help you calm down and maintain control when you have a conflict with someone.

Try one or more of the strategies every time you feel yourself getting angry. Notice how you feel and how well the strategy works. Write down the results on the back of the sheet. Keep the sheet in your notebook and refer to it often.

Conflict Management

Two Sides of Conflict

Objectives

The students will:
- Empathize with the point of view of the other person in a conflict.
- Appreciate alternative perspectives and behaviors.

ASCA Standards

PS:A1.5   Identify and express feelings
PS:A2.2   Respect alternative points of view
PS:A2.3   Recognize, accept, respect, and appreciate individual differences
PS:B1.6   Know how to apply conflict-resolution skills

Materials

Two chairs for each student

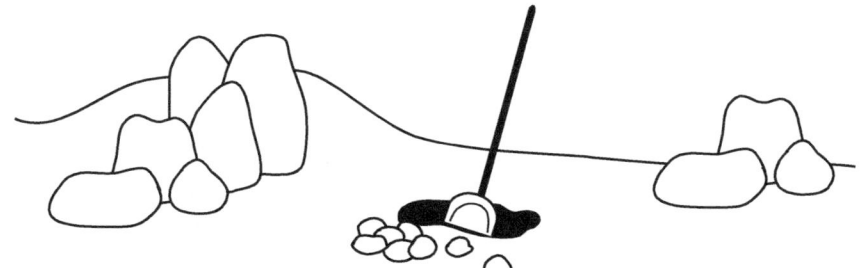

Procedure

Introduce the activity by pointing out that there are always at least two sides to a conflict, and that trying to understand the other person's perspective is one of the best strategies for resolving conflict. In your own words, explain:

When we are angry with another person, we often see only our own point of view. However, by putting ourselves in the other person's place and looking at the situation from his or her perspective, we can begin to appreciate and understand that person's motivations, feelings, and behaviors. This broadened point of view helps to reduce anger.

A good way to accomplish this change in perspectives is to act it out. Sit in one chair facing a second, empty, chair. Imagine that the other chair is occupied by the person with whom you are in conflict. Talk to the person from your point of view. Don't make accusations but calmly present your position. (If your students have an understanding of I-Statements, ask them to use I-Statements.) When you have said all that you need to say, change chairs and pretend you are the other person, talking from what you imagine to be her or his point of view.

Conflict Management

Have each student take two chairs and place them facing each other. Invite the students to sit in one of the chairs. Ask them to think of a time when they were angry at someone and imagine that person sitting in the opposite chair.

Tell the students to talk to the person in the empty chair, describing what the person did to upset them or make them angry. Suggest that they use I-statements or any other productive form of communication that expresses their feelings. Give the students two to five minutes to do this part of the activity.

Next, ask the students to switch chairs and pretend to be the other person. Tell them to explain that person's side of the conflict as though speaking in their voice. Again, give the students two to five minutes to finish.

Finally, ask the students to return to their original chairs, becoming themselves again. Tell them to respond to what the "other person" said.

Encourage the students to continue switching back and forth until they think they understand the other person's point of view. Some students may actually resolve their conflicts in the course of the exercise.

Circulate and coach the students to really confront their invisible partner, playing both roles with as much sincerity and honesty as they can.

Debrief the students and facilitate a summary discussion.

Discussion Questions

1. How did it feel to take both sides in a confrontation?
2. How did pretending that you were the other person help you to understand that person's point of view?
3. How did switching roles help you to clarify your own position?
4. When and how can you use this process away from school?

Assessment

- Did the students effectively articulate their own point of view?
- Did the students demonstrate empathy for the other person's point of view?

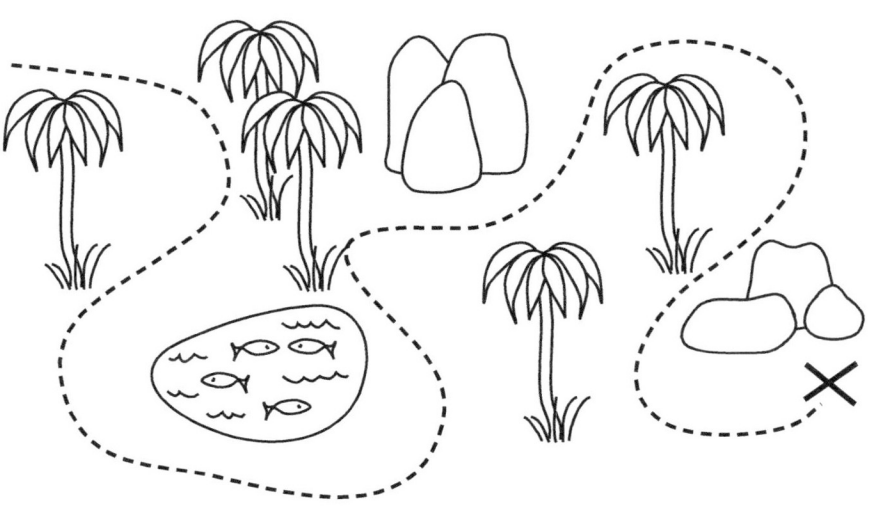

Misperceptions Lead to Conflict

Objectives

The students will:
- Demonstrate how faulty perceptions can lead to conflict.
- Explore ways of resolving conflict caused by differing views.

ASCA Standards

PS:A2.2   Respect alternative points off view
PS:A2.3   Recognize, accept, respect, and appreciate individual differences
PS:C1.11   Learn coping skills for managing life events

Materials

One copy of the experience sheet, *Misperceptions*, for each student

Procedure

Write the word "perception" on the board and ask the students to explain its meaning. Definitions might include:

- A mental image or picture
- A unique way of seeing and interpreting something based on past experiences

Then write the word "misperception" on the board. Ask the students to explain its meaning. (A misperception is a perception, or interpretation, that is untrue or wrong.

Point out that we often misinterpret what we see or hear, or read meaning into situations that isn't actually there. Our perceptions are colored by many things — past experience, fears, hopes, personal values, insecurity, even jealousy. Jumping to the wrong conclusion based on our perception can lead to disagreements, intolerance, and conflict.

Distribute the experience sheets and go over the directions. Give the students a few minutes to complete the cartoons. Have them share their completed cartoons in groups of four or five. Conclude the activity with a total group discussion.

Conflict Management

Discussion Questions

1. What are people likely to do when their perceptions clash?
2. Is there always one right way of seeing something and does that way make all other perceptions wrong? Explain.
3. How can you find out if you are perceiving a situation correctly?
4. What kinds of things might cause several of us to see the same incident differently?
5. What can you do to help two people resolve conflicting perceptions?

Assessment

- Did the students correctly define perception and misperception?
- Did the students demonstrate in their cartoons how conflicts arise from misperceptions?
- Did the students explain how to avoid and resolve conflicts caused by misperceptions?

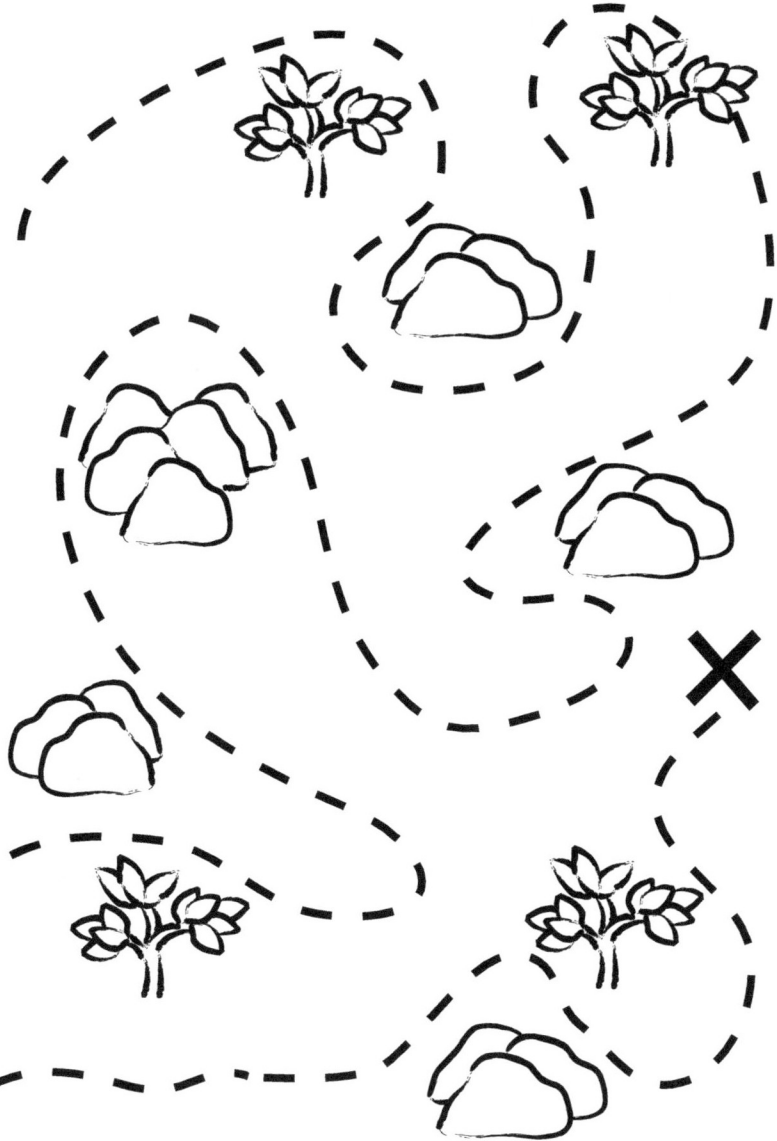

Conflict Management

Misperceptions

Perceiving things wrongly can lead to conflict. Examine the following cartoons. Draw in the next frame for each cartoon, showing how misperceptions can lead to conflict.

Conflict Management

Conflict Management

Describing Two Perceptions

Objectives

The students will:

- Describe two different perceptions of a conflict.
- Understand that every conflict has more than one point of view.
- Describe how understanding all points of view can help resolve conflicts.

ASCA Standards

PS:A2.2 Respect alternative points of view
PS:A2.3 Recognize, accept, respect, and appreciate individual differences
PS:C1.11 Learn coping skills for managing life events

Materials

One copy of the experience sheet, *My Moccasins*, for each student; colored markers, pencils, or crayons; scissors (optional)

Procedure

Begin the activity by stating in your own words:
When you are in a conflict, the other person's point of view, or perception, is often overshadowed by your own.

Making an effort to understand the other point of view may help to resolve the conflict. An old Indian saying states that you can't judge another person until you have walked two moons (months) in his moccasins. In this activity, you will put yourself in the moccasins of another person and try to imagine his or her side of a conflict.

Distribute the experience sheets and give the students a few minutes to decorate their moccasins with illustrations of beads in various designs. Urge them to personalize their designs with symbols that are meaningful to them. For example, a soccer player might include the image of a beaded soccer ball.

Decide in advance whether to have the students cut out their moccasins or leave them as a single sheet. Experiment on your own with this to determine which way is best for your students.

When the moccasins are finished, ask the students to think of a conflict that they have had with another person—one in which they had a very clear point of view. Caution the students to choose a conflict that they are willing to share with a partner. Give the students time to think carefully about the conflict, writing it down on paper if necessary.

Conflict Management

Explain that the students are going to look at their conflict from the other person's viewpoint, like "walking in his or her moccasins."

Have the students form dyads. Give these instructions:

Place your paper moccasins on the floor toe-to-toe with your partner's moccasins. Stand on your moccasins, facing your partner. Decide who is A and who is B. A's you will tell your conflict story to your partner. Express your point of view very clearly to your partner, including any feelings you have about the conflict. B's, your job is to suggest ways in which the story can be told from the other person's viewpoint. What would the other person in this conflict want? How would he or she feel?

Give the students time to carry out your directions. Then continue:

Now I want you to switch places with your partner. Stand on your partner's moccasins. A's retell your conflict, this time from the perspective of the other person. Recall the ideas your partner gave you and try to express the other person's thoughts, opinions, and feelings. B's listen carefully. When your partner is finished telling the story from the other persons' perspective, tell your partner how you think he or she did. Was your partner convincing? Did your partner really seem to be walking in the other person's moccasins?

Have the partners return to their own moccasins and repeat the activity with the B's acting as storytellers. When both partners have had a turn as conflict storyteller, ask several volunteers to share their stories with the whole group. Coach each volunteer to tell his/her story from both perspectives. Debrief the activity with a discussion concerning the importance of seeing the other person's point of view—particularly in a conflict.

Note: To ensure the success of this activity, you may need to demonstrate the dyad procedure with a volunteer.

Discussion Questions

1. Was it easy or hard to "walk in the other person's moccasins" and tell the story from his or her point of view? Why?
2. Why is it important to think about a conflict from different perspectives?
3. How can thinking about the other person's point of view help you avoid or resolve a conflict?
4. If you can't imagine the other person's point of view in a conflict, how can you learn what it is?

Assessment

- Did the students articulate both sides to their conflict story?
- Would you conclude from their statements that the students appreciate the importance of understanding the other person's perspective in a conflict?

My Moccasins

Decorate your moccasins with colored dots to symbolize beaded designs and symbols.

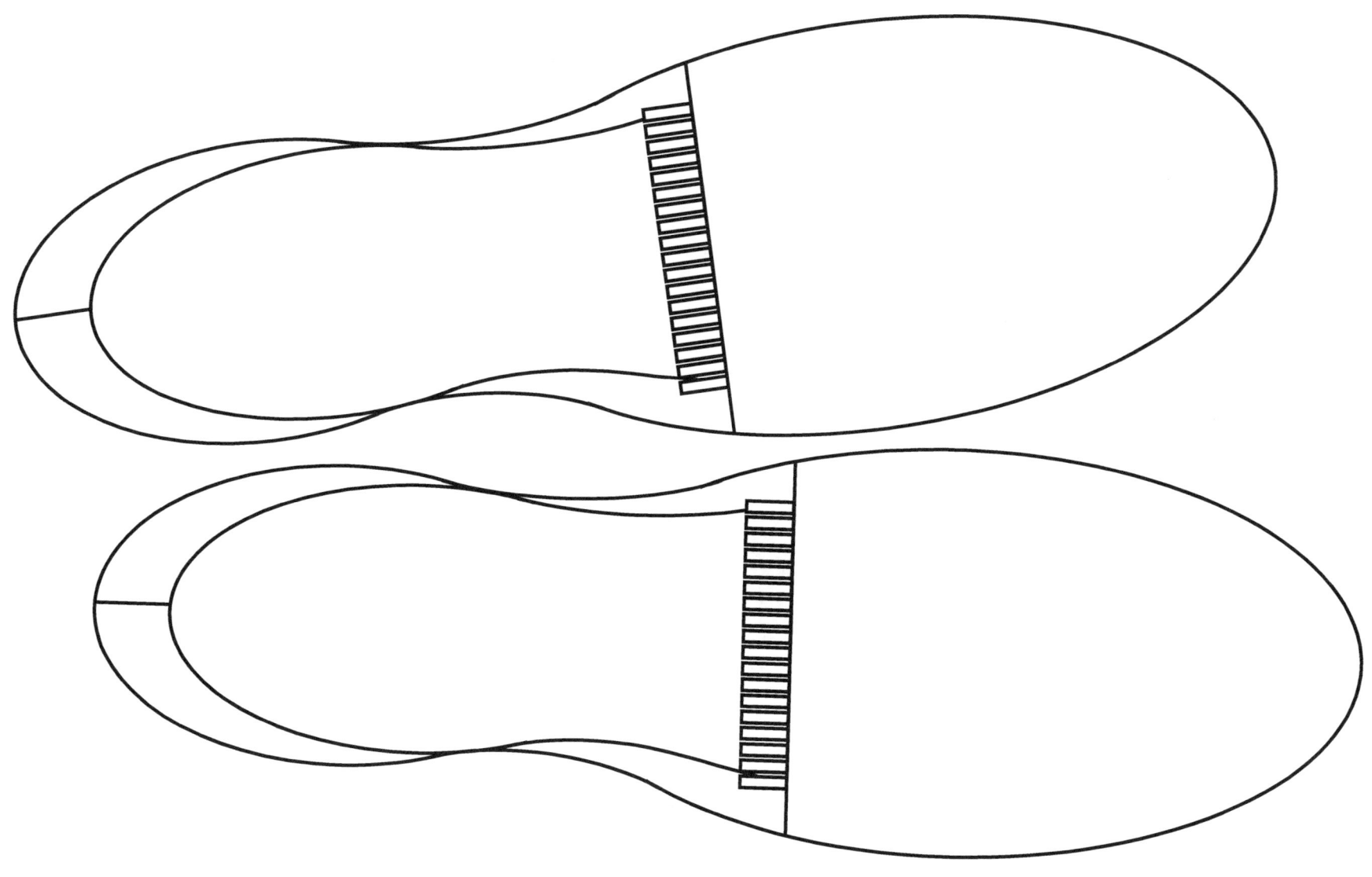

Conflict Management

The Rise and Fall of Conflict

Objectives

The students will:
- Identify behaviors that escalate and de-escalate conflict.
- Practice using communication skills to control the escalation of conflicts.

ASCA Standards

PS:A2.6 Use effective communication skills
PS:B1.2 Understand consequences of decisions and choices
PS:B1.6 Know how to apply conflict-resolution skills

Materials

Paper and black marking pens

Procedure

In your own words, introduce the concept of conflict escalation and de-escalation. For example, say:

Imagine an escalator, such as the kind you use in department stores. An escalator moves people up and down from one level to another. The same is true with behaviors that escalate and de-escalate conflict. Some words and actions raise, or escalate, the conflict to higher levels; other behaviors lower, or de-escalate the conflict, to lower levels. In judging the effects of certain behaviors on conflict, try to picture whether the behavior is making the conflict go up or down.

Distribute paper and marking pens. Ask the students to draw a large, bold arrow on the paper. When they have finished, tell them that you are going to read them two scenarios. As you read, they are to listen closely to the statements and actions of each character in the scenario. When they hear a statement or action that is likely to escalate the conflict, they should hold their arrow high, pointing up. When they hear a statement or action that is likely to de-escalate the conflict, they should hold their arrow pointing down.

Conflict Management

Read each scenario slowly, allowing time for the students to respond. Notice if any of the behaviors draw mixed reactions from the students. After you have read each scenario, go back and role-play the parts that caused disagreement, with volunteers taking the two roles. Demonstrate and discuss how voice tone, facial expression and body posture contribute greatly to determining whether a specific behavior is escalating or de-escalating.

Conclude the activity with a general discussion.

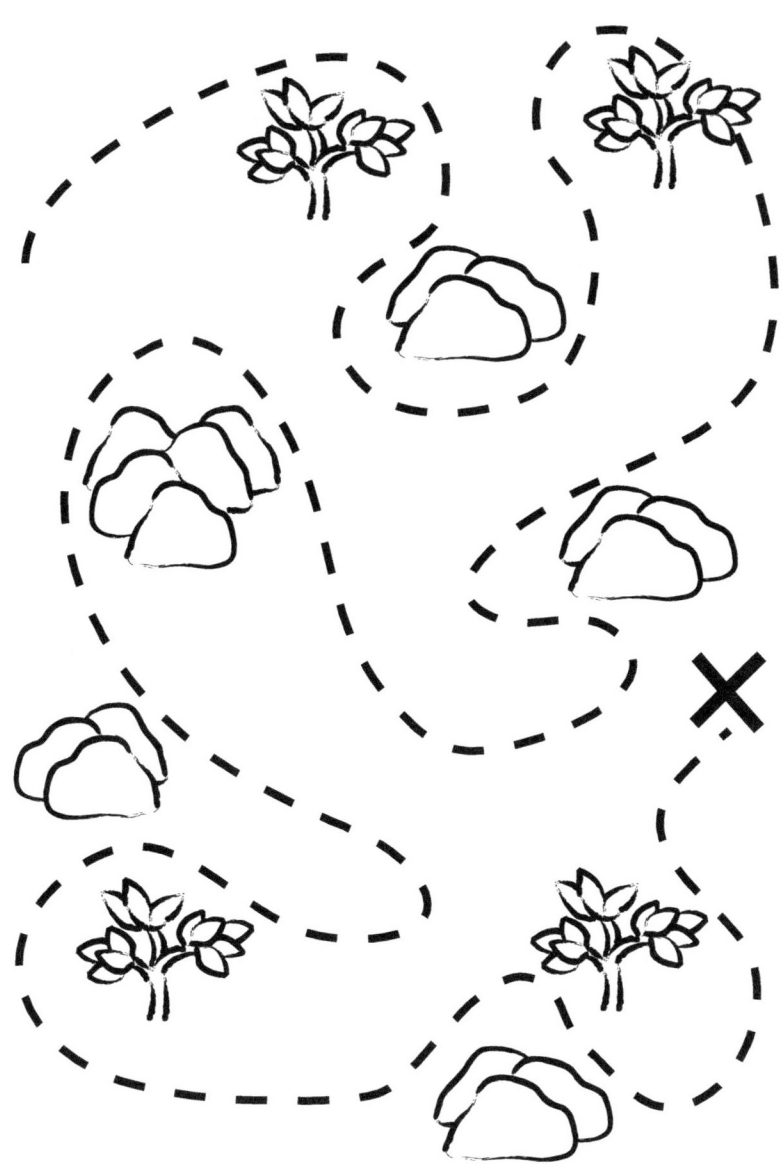

Discussion Questions

1. What types of behaviors almost always escalate a conflict?
2. What types of behaviors have a good chance of de-escalating a conflict?
3. How can being aware of whether a conflict is escalating or de-escalating help you manage the conflict?
4. What have you learned from this activity that will make a difference in the way you handle conflict?

Assessment

- Did the students accurately identify behaviors that raise and lower conflict?
- Did the students demonstrate how nonverbal behavior effects the way behaviors are perceived?

Conflict Management

Scenario 1

Ken and Sue are supposed to be working together to solve a math problem. Ken takes the problem sheet and starts to write his solution on it.

Sue: "Here, let me have that. I think I know how to do this." (Slides the paper away from Ken and starts to write on it.)

Ken: "Hey, I was right in the middle of something. Give that back to me." (Reaches over, pulls the paper back and continues writing.)

Sue: "You're not doing it right, dummy. You're going to have to erase the whole thing."

Ken: "I'll erase your face in a minute if you don't stop bugging me."

Sue: "We're supposed to be doing this together, and you're not listening to me!"

Ken: "Maybe I'd listen if you weren't so pushy. Anyway, I've finished it. There!"

Sue: "It's wrong. You can't prove your answer."

Ken: "Sure I can."

Sue: "Show me, Mr. Smarty. You couldn't prove it if you worked all day. (Loudly) Ha, ha, ha."

Ken: "Shut up, Sue. You always think you know everything, but you don't" (Pushes Sue away.)

Scenario 2

Sergio and Livier are brother and sister. Sergio is watching TV. Livier walks in, picks up the remote and changes the channel.

Sergio: "Why did you change the channel? I was watching that show!"

Livier: "I don't have time to argue with you. I have to watch this show for my science homework."

Sergio: "I don't care what it's for. That was my favorite show. Change it back right now!"

Livier: "You can't make me. I have just as much right to this TV as you do."

Sergio: "Not if I'm here first. I'm telling Mom!"

Livier: "Go ahead and tell Mom, crybaby. She'll just make you go do your homework."

Sergio: "I finished mine. What's the science program about?"

Livier: "Insects. (Grinning) Like you, creepy brother."

CONFLICT MANAGEMENT

A Process for Resolving Conflict

Objectives

The students will:
- Learn and practice a conflict-resolution process.
- Verbalize the benefits of resolving conflicts collaboratively.

ASCA Standards

PS:B1.1 Use a decision-making and problem-solving model
PS:B1.3 Identify alternative solutions to a problem
PS:B1.5 Demonstrate when, where, and how to seek help for solving problems and making decisions

Materials

One copy of the experience sheet, *Steps for Resolving a Conflict*, for each student

Procedure

Distribute the experience sheets. Read and discuss each step of the conflict-resolution process with the group.

Steps for Resolving a Conflict

1. **Stop all blaming.** Blaming each other will not solve the problem. It's a waste of time. Put your energy into working out a solution.

2. **Define the conflict.** Ask each other this question: "How do you see the conflict?" Then listen to each other's answer.

3. **Consider asking for help.** Sometimes a third person needs to work with you to resolve a conflict. Choose someone who will listen to both of you and not take sides.

4. **Think of alternative solutions.** Write down as many ideas for resolving the conflict as you can think of.

5. **Evaluate the alternatives.** Ask yourselves, "What will happen if we try this one?" Be very honest with yourselves and each other.

6. **Make a decision.** Choose the alternative that looks like it has the best chance of working. Don't hesitate to combine parts of two or more alternatives.

Conflict Management

7. **Follow through.** Stick with your decision for a reasonable length of time. If it doesn't work, get together and choose a different solution. If the decision causes more problems, resolve those, too.

Ask the students to form groups of four. Instruct them to think of a conflict situation between two people that might be resolved using the conflict-resolution steps. (Conflicts from their own experience are okay, as long as the other parties involved remain anonymous.) Tell the students that two members of the group are to go through the conflict resolution steps while the other two coach them. If time permits, have the students switch roles and practice the steps again using a different conflict. Conclude the activity with a class discussion.

Discussion Questions

1. What happens when you get bogged down in the blaming game?
2. Why is it so important to know exactly what the conflict is about?
3. When should you ask a third person to help you?
4. What is the advantage of thinking of alternative solutions?
5. Why not just do the first thing that comes to mind?
6. Why is it important to imagine what will happen as a result of trying each alternative?
7. If you can't make a decision, which steps should you repeat? (2, 4, 5, and 3, in that order. The conflict may be incorrectly defined; you may need to think of more alternatives; the consequences may need more thought; or help may be called for.)

Assessment

- When coaching, did the students demonstrate understanding of the conflict-resolution steps?
- Did the groups resolve their mock conflicts using the steps?

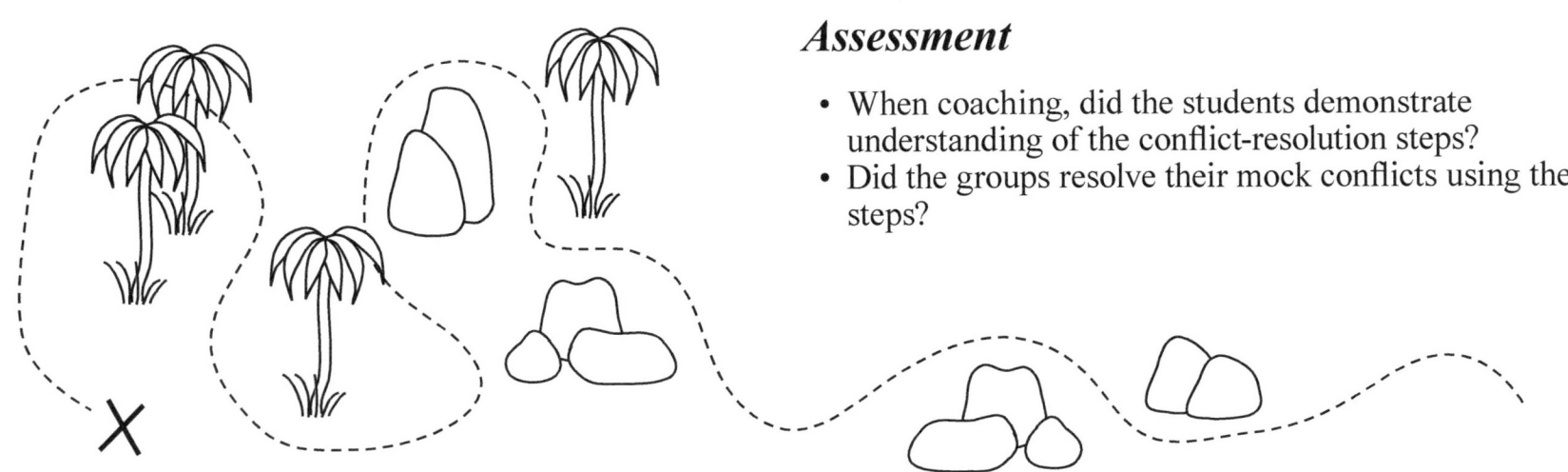

Conflict Management

Steps for Resolving a Conflict

7. Follow through. Stick with your decision for a reasonable length of time. If it doesn't work, get together and choose a different solution. If the decision causes more problems, resolve those, too.

6. Make a decision. Choose the alternative that looks like it has the best chance of working. Don't hesitate to combine parts of two or more alternatives.

5. Evaluate the alternatives. Ask yourselves, "What will happen if we try this one?" Be very honest with yourselves and each other.

4. Think of alternative solutions. Write down as many ideas for resolving the conflict as you can think of.

3. Consider asking for help. Sometimes a third person needs to work with you to resolve a conflict. Choose someone who will listen to both of you and not take sides.

2. Define the conflict. Ask each other this question: "How do you see the conflict?" Then listen to each other's answer.

1. Stop all blaming. Blaming each other will not solve the problem. It's a waste of time. Put your energy into working out a solution.

Conflict Management

What to Do?

Objectives

The students will:
- Describe in writing a personal conflict.
- Identify and evaluate strategies for resolving conflicts.

ASCA Standards

PS:B1.3   Identify alternative solutions to a problem
PS:B1.5   Demonstrate when, where, and how to seek help for solving problems and making decisions
PS:B1.6   Know how to apply conflict-resolution skills
PS:C1.10   Learn techniques for managing stress and conflict

Materials

Writing materials

Procedure

Ask the students to think of conflict situations they have experienced in which it was hard to decide what to do. Discuss a few examples, including one from your own experience.

Explain the writing assignment: ask the students to write about one personal conflict experience without putting their names on the stories. Announce that the students will have 30 minutes to complete the writing. Students who finish writing their stories before time is up may write about a second conflict.

Collect the stories. Prepare for the second part of this activity by reading all of the stories to yourself and selecting four or five to review aloud. Try to select stories that:
1. Describe typical conflicts that the students can relate to.
2. Provide enough detailed information to give the reader/listener most or all pertinent facts.

Begin the second session by reading one of the stories aloud. Emphasize that the identity of the student who wrote the story is not important.

Have the class brainstorm possible ways to resolve or manage the conflict described in the story. Write at least 10 suggestions on the board. On a second board, list ideas that come up about conflict and conflict resolution in general.

Conflict Management

Circle the suggestions that the students generally agree are best. If time allows, repeat the procedure with other stories you have selected. Conclude with a class discussion.

Discussion Questions

1. What methods of responding to conflict are most effective? What methods are least effective? Why?
2. What kinds of things determine which conflict resolution strategy works best?
3. How can you control your feelings in a conflict situation?
4. What have you learned about conflict and conflict resolution from this activity?

Extension

Have volunteers role play the best solutions for each conflict.

Assessment

- Did the students describe five or more conflict resolution strategies covered in previous activities?
- Did the students apply conflict management strategies effectively?

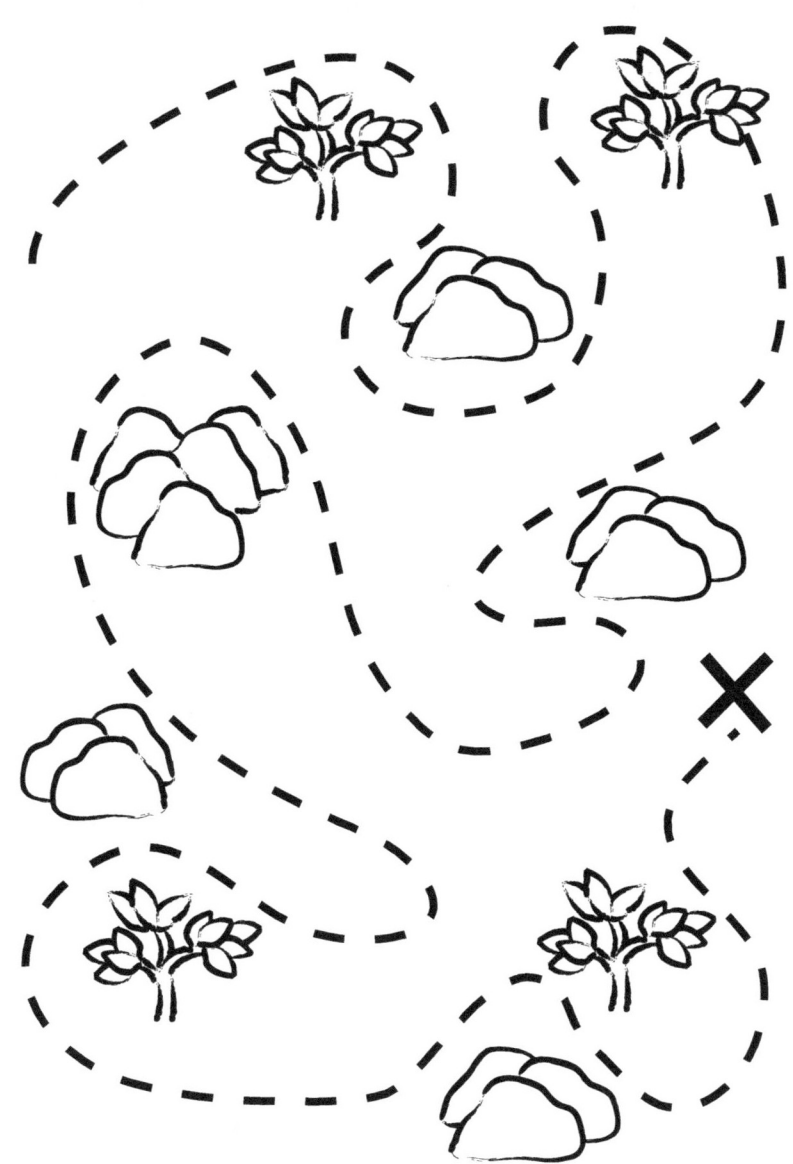

Conflict Management

Eight Conflict Management Strategies

Objectives

The students will:
- Learn and practice strategies for resolving conflict.
- Explain why some strategies are better than others in specific situations.

ASCA Standards

PS:B1.3   Identify alternative solutions to a problem
PS:B1.5   Demonstrate when, where, and how to seek help for solving problems and making decisions
PS:B1.6   Know how to apply conflict-resolution skills
PS:C1.10 Learn techniques for managing stress and conflict

Materials

Five conflict sheets, each printed with a different scenario from the list below; one copy of the experience sheet, *Conflict Resolution Strategies*, for each student

Procedure

Introduce the activity by inviting the students to think about a time when they were involved in a conflict, or observed a conflict. Suggest that they think about the events leading up to the conflict and the feelings of the people involved.

Have the students choose partners and tell each other their conflict stories. After the pairs have shared, invite a few volunteers to retell their experiences to the entire group.

Explain that certain behaviors can help people to handle disagreements more positively and to resolve their conflicts. These behaviors are called *strategies*.

Distribute the experience sheets. On the board, write the heading "Strategies for Resolving Conflict." List the strategies shown below, while the students follow along on their experience sheets. Give examples and ask the students to describe problems that might be resolved using each alternative.

Conflict Management

1. **Sharing:** Using/doing something with another person.
2. **Taking turns:** Alternatively using/doing something with another person.
3. **Active listening:** Hearing the other person's feelings and opinions.
4. **Postponing:** Deciding to put off dealing with the conflict until another time (for example when you have calmed down).
5. **Using humor:** Looking at the situation in a comical way; making light of the situation.
6. **Compromising:** Giving up part of what you want in order to get the remainder of what you want.
7. **Expressing regret:** Saying that you are sorry about the situation without taking the blame.
8. **Problem solving:** Discussing the problem; trying to find a mutually acceptable solution.

Discussion Questions

1. Why is it better to practice positive alternatives, rather than wait for a conflict to occur and then try them?
2. Which strategies are hardest to use and why? Which are easiest? Which work best and why?
3. When do you think you should get help to resolve a conflict?

Assessment

- Did the students effectively demonstrate the five conflict resolution strategies?
- Were the students able to assess the effectiveness of various strategies in specific situations?

Divide the class into small groups and give each group a printed conflict scenario. Instruct the groups to discuss the scenario and pick a conflict management strategy from the list of alternatives on the board. Have the members of each group act out the conflict and its resolution while the rest of the class tries to guess which alternative they are using. At the conclusion of the role plays, lead a class discussion.

Scenarios

- Cherie and Jonelle agree to meet on the playground after school and walk home together. Just before the bell rings, Jonelle remembers that her mother is picking her up out front to take her to a dental appointment. There is no time to stop by the playground. Cherie waits 30 minutes and then goes to Jonelle's classroom to ask the teacher if Jonelle has left yet. The teacher says that Jonelle ran out of the room as soon as class was dismissed. When the two girls see each other the next day, Cherie is so angry and hurt that she ignores Jonelle. Jonelle runs after her, saying, "Let me explain, please!"

- Arturo thinks that his classmate Kenny is to blame for the class losing 20 minutes of free time. Kenny was talking to someone in his group about the homework after the teacher told the class to be quiet. Others were talking and giggling, too, but Arturo only saw Kenny talking. After school, Arturo tries to pick a fight with Kenny by calling him names.

- Mr. Cruz is returning homework and test papers. Mindy glances at the paper that is passed back to her. Thinking that it is her homework, she begins to tear it up. When Ahmad looks over her shoulder and sees that it is his math test, he shouts, "Hey, what are you doing with my test? My dad wants to see all of my test grades." Surprised and embarrassed, Mindy becomes defensive and tries to blame Mr. Cruz.

- When Jessica strikes out at bat in the bottom of the ninth inning, she feels terrible. Her friend and classmate, Tina, makes it worse by blaming her for the team's loss. "We could have won, Jess," yells Tina. "Why didn't you try a little harder to hit that ball? Geez, now we're out of the playoffs!" Jessica wants to cry, but she knows that the team's loss isn't her fault alone.

- When Kyle accidentally trips over Andy's foot walking into the assembly, he doesn't have a chance to apologize because the teacher is hurrying the class to their seats. He feels nervous because he knows that Andy has a bad temper. On the way back to class, Andy goes up to Kyle, pushes him and accuses Kyle of kicking him deliberately. When Kyle tries to explain, Andy pushes him again.

Conflict Management

Conflict Resolution Strategies

Have you ever been in a conflict? Of course! No matter how much you try to avoid them, conflicts happen. They are part of life. What makes conflicts upsetting is not knowing how to handle them. If you don't know something helpful to do, you may end up making things worse. Study these strategies and the next time you see a conflict coming, try one!

1. **Share**
   Whatever the conflict is over, keep (or use) some of it yourself and let the other person keep (or use) some.

2. **Take Turns**
   Use or do something for a little while. Then let the other person take a turn.

3. **Active Listen**
   Let the other person talk while you listen carefully. Really try to understand the persons' feelings and ideas.

4. **Postpone**
   Decide to put off dealing with the conflict until another time. For example wait until you have calmed down.

5. **Use Humor**
   Look at the situation, but not the person, in a comical way. Don't take it too seriously.

6. **Compromise**
   Offer to give up part of what you want and ask the other person to do the same.

7. **Express Regret**
   Say that you are sorry about the situation, without taking the blame.

8. **Problem Solve**
   Discuss the problem. Try to find a solution that works for both of you.

Conflict Management

Bullying Hurts

Objectives

The students will:
- Define, describe, and understand bully behavior.
- Share experiences they have had with bully behavior.

ASCA Standards

PS:A1.2   Identify values, attitudes, and beliefs
PS:A1.5   Identify and express feelings
PS:A1.7   Recognize personal boundaries, rights, and privacy needs
PS:C1.4   Demonstrate the ability to set boundaries, rights, and personal privacy

Materials

One copy each of the experience sheets, *Bullying Hurts* and *Let Off Some Steam*, for each student

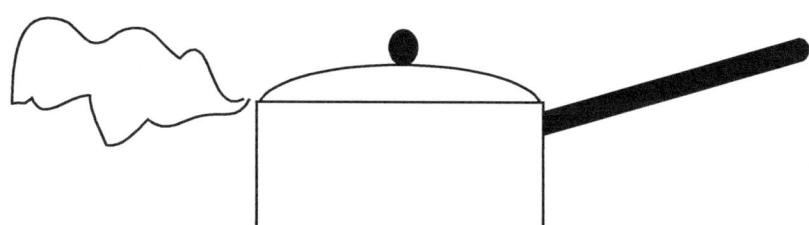

Procedure

Ask the students to help you brainstorm a list of typical bully behaviors. Write them on the board. Add the following if they are not suggested by the group:

- demanding money or other objects
- hitting
- ridiculing or humiliating
- name-calling
- damaging personal belongings
- stealing
- repeatedly excluding from activities
- forcing to do something
- threatening to harm
- gossiping and telling lies about

Go back over the list and ask for a show of hands from students who have been hit, threatened, ridiculed, etc. Point out that all of these hurtful experiences can be considered bullying.

Distribute the experience sheet, *Bullying Hurts*, and go over the directions. Allow time for the students to complete the sheet.

Conflict Management

When the students have finished writing their stories, ask volunteers to tell (or read) their stories to the group. Remind them to talk about what happened and how they felt, but not to use names. Break the ice by sharing a personal story of your own related to bullying.

Facilitate discussion following each story. Stress that it is important for students to come forward if they are bullied, or witness someone else being bullied. Let the students know that bullying will not be tolerated; however, before bullying can be stopped, incidents of bullying must be reported. Assure them that you will respect their need to remain anonymous.

Give a copy of the experience sheet, *Let Off Some Steam*, to any student who has actually experienced bullying. Go over the directions. Suggest that these students wait until a time when they can be alone and undisturbed to write their letter. Tell them to be as open as possible about their anger, hurt, humiliation, or frustration, telling the bully exactly what they think of him or her. Stress, however, that the letter must not be delivered.

Discussion Questions

1. How do you feel when you see someone acting like a bully? What do you usually do?
2. What have you done to stop bullying behavior?
3. If you haven't done anything, what is stopping you?
4. Why is it important to let bullies know that their behavior is unacceptable?

Assessment

- Were the students able to describe bullying behavior?
- Did the students explain why bullying behavior is wrong?
- Were the students willing to take responsibility for helping to reduce or eliminate bullying in their classroom/school?

Note: What you can do for victims:
Connect with victims, allowing them to share their experiences and vent their feelings. More than anything else, victims need to feel safe and secure, so address the fear first. Let victims know that you are there to help put an end to the bullying. They don't have to face it alone. Being bullied is not their fault.

Bullying Hurts

In the space to the right, write about one of the following:

- A time you were bullied.
- A time you saw someone else being bullied.
- A time you bullied someone.

Please don't use any names. Just tell what happened and how you felt.

Let Off Some Steam

Dear Bully,

_____

Is there a bully in your life? Write a letter to the bully and let him (or her) know exactly how you feel about what is happening.

By putting your feelings down on paper, you can "let off some steam." Write anything you want to say. You are not going to deliver this letter.

When you are finished, keep the letter or throw it away. It's up to you.

Now write about some positive and peaceful ways that you might get the bully to leave you alone.

Conflict Management

The Bully Mask

Objectives

The students will:
- Recognize that bullies are often insecure, with low self-esteem.
- Identify some of the things that motivate bullies.

ASCA Standards

PS:C1.7 Apply effective problem-solving and decision-making skills to make safe and healthy choices

PS:C1.11 Learn coping skills for managing life events

Materials

One copy of the experience sheet, *Behind the Bully Mask*, for each student

Procedure

Ask the students to help you brainstorm a list of reasons why bullies do what they do. Accept all contributions and jot them on the board. You will probably hear things like, "They think they're tough," "They like to boss people around," and "They think they're better than everybody else." All of these contributions are valid and describe how bullies are often perceived by their peers.

Help the students to recognize underlying causes of bullying that might not be apparent to them. Add these causes to the list, making the following points in the process:

- Bullies usually lack friends and other healthy support.
- Bullies are often fearful and angry.
- Some bullies are being bullied themselves (perhaps by an older child or adult).
- Bullies may not have love and support at home.
- Bullies usually have learned poor ways of relating to others and don't know how to change their behavior.
- Bullies lack empathy for their victims and other people.

Provide examples wherever possible. To prompt thinking on the part of the students, you may want to refer back to the stories written about bullies in the previous activity. Ask the students to try to understand what motivated the bully in their story.

Distribute the experience sheet and allow time for the students to complete it. Then facilitate additional discussion.

Conflict Management

Discussion Questions

1. What are bullies usually trying to do to their victim?
2. How do bullies usually feel deep inside?
3. Are most bullies well liked and popular? Why or why not?
4. Are bullies brave? Why or why not?
5. Do bullies have high self-esteem? Why or why not?
6. Do bullies pick on strong, self-confident kids? Why or why not?

Assessment

- Did the students identify factors that motivate bullies?
- Did the students recognize that the outward demeanor of bullies is often a mask for insecurities of various kinds?

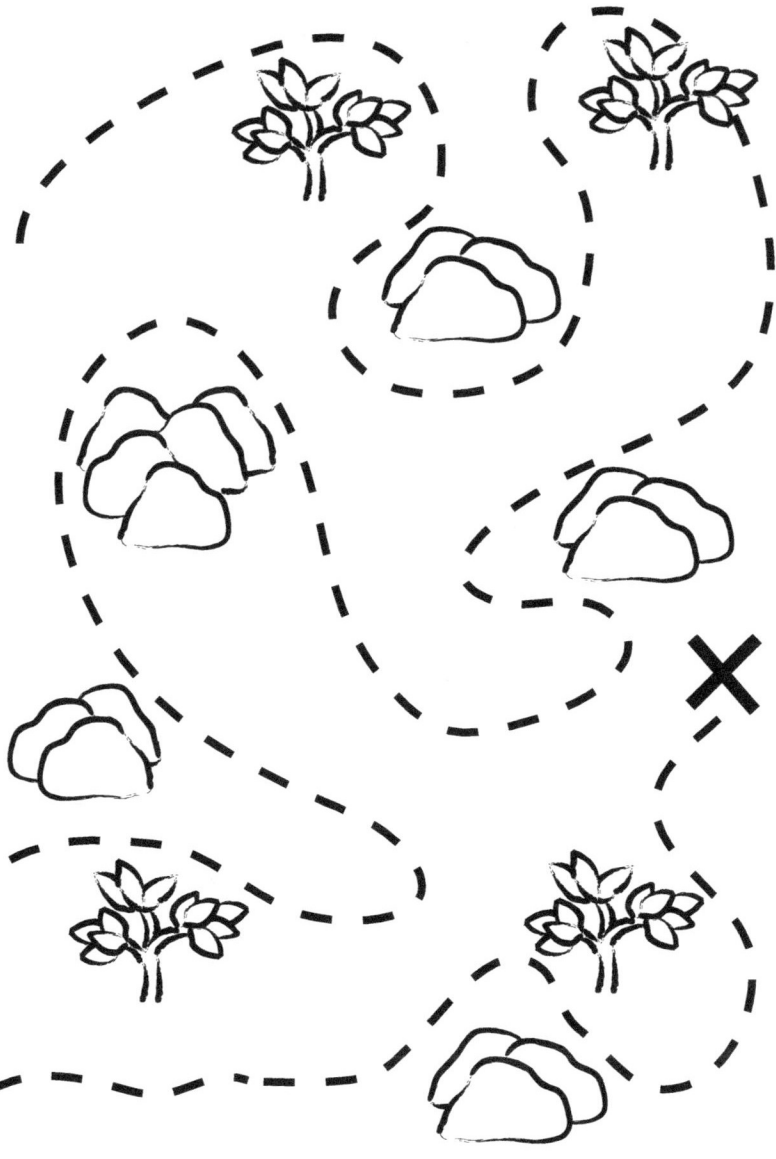

Conflict Management

Behind the Bully Mask

Who is the real person behind the bully mask?

Bullies try to appear big, tough, and mean. They push kids around as a way of dealing with their own feelings of fear, hurt, or anger. They think that by intimidating others, they will feel better about themselves.

Think of a bully you know. If you could rip away the bully's mask, what do you think you would find underneath? Inside the body, write words that describe what is going on deep down inside the bully you know. Write as many words as you can.

Conflict Management

Down With Bullies

Objectives

The students will:

- Recognize that stopping bully behavior is everyone's responsibility.
- Learn ways to safely intervene when someone is being bullied.
- Agree to help the victim by reporting bullying behavior.

ASCA Standards

PS:B1.5   Demonstrate when, where, and how to seek help for solving problems and making decisions

PS:C1.5   Differentiate between situations requiring peer support and situations requiring adult professional help

Materials

One copy of the experience sheet, *Stopping Bullies Is Everyone's Responsibility*, for each student

Procedure

Point out that bullying incidents that happen at school often occur in busy places, like hallways, lunch areas, in front of the school, and on playgrounds. Although adults don't usually see these incidents, very often other kids are nearby and do witness them, but don't know what to do.

Ask the students to help you brainstorm things that witnesses can do to stop bullies. Add the following four ideas if they are not mentioned by the group.

1. Refuse to watch a bullying incident. Bullies want an audience.
2. If appropriate and safe, distract the bully and/or victim.
3. Create safety in numbers. If you know that someone is being bullied, make sure that the victim is not alone in places where he or she may be vulnerable.
4. Report bullying incidents.

Stress that reporting the incident is very important. Even if the students try other strategies to stop the bully, they should always tell a responsible adult what happened.

Conflict Management

Write the following headings on the board:

Who   How

Stress that students should talk to an adult about every bullying incident that occurs. Under "Who," list appropriate adults.

Discuss ways of reporting that guard the safety of students, such as writing an anonymous note, going to the office after school when the rest of the kids have gone home, or calling a teacher/counselor from home. List these ideas under "How." Make a distinction between tattling or snitching and reporting an incident. Tattling is about wanting to get someone in trouble. Informing an adult is about wanting to help the victim.

Distribute the experience sheets and go over the directions. After allowing the students time to complete the sheet, ask volunteers to read their top five ideas. Facilitate discussion. Try to honor and implement ideas that seem workable, developing action plans as needed.

If you want to ensure that students report the next bullying incident that occurs, you must show them that you (and other adults) will take action. The students must see that telling is relevant and rewarding and ideas that they put forth are honored and implemented.

Discussion Questions

1. What have you done in the past when you saw someone being bullied?
2. Why is it everyone's responsibility to report bullying behavior?
3. What do bullies think when no one is willing to stand up to them or report them?
4. What are some safe ways to stop a bully from harassing someone?

Assessment

- Did the students demonstrate empathy for the victims of bullying?
- Did the students describe effective ways to reduce or stop bullying behavior at school?

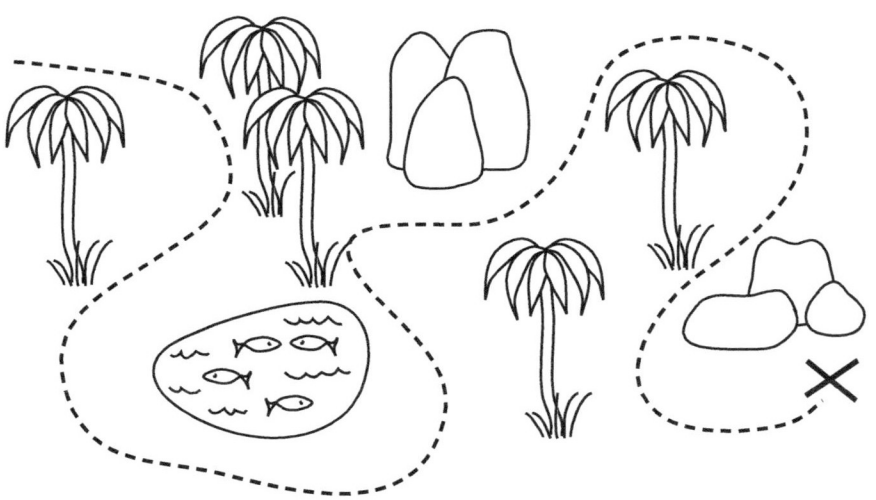

Stopping Bullies Is Everyone's Responsibilty

It is up to everyone in the school to stop bullies. When you and other kids decide that it is time to stand up to a bully, you can really make a difference. You can help put an end to bully behavior. Wouldn't you like to have a school with no bullies?

What can be done to stop bullies from harassing others? List your ideas here:

_____

_____

_____

_____

_____

_____

_____

What can *you* do to stop bullies, all by yourself?

_____

_____

_____

_____

_____

_____

Cross out any ideas that involve violence or retaliation. When you use violence against a bully, you are doing the same thing you want him (or her) to stop doing. Besides, violence usually makes things worse.

Go back and look at each of your ideas. Ask yourself, "Will this idea really work to stop a bully?" Put parentheses ( ) around any ideas that probably will not work.

Now pick your five best ideas and number them #1 to #5. Make your very best idea #1. That's the idea you should try first!

Conflict Management

Character Education

Learning to Care

Objectives

The students will:
- Identify and discuss a variety of caring behaviors.
- Explore the concept of caring.

ASCA Standards

PS:A1.2　Identify values, attitudes, and beliefs
PS:B1.7　Demonstrate respect and appreciation for individual and cultural differences

Materials

Copies of fairy tales and fables

Procedure

Read or tell a fairy tale to the students. A tale such as *Cinderella* has many cultural versions and lends itself well to this activity. Other good ones include *The Ugly Duckling, Snow White,* and *The Wild Swans*. You might also select one of the many Aesop's fables, such as *The Lion and the Mouse*.

After telling the story, identify and discuss the caring behaviors of various characters. Talk about those who risked their lives to help others, like the sister in Andersen's *The Wild Swans*. Expand the discussion to include all of the characters, both good and bad, and the motives for their actions.

After the discussion, ask volunteers to dramatize the key events in the story. Review the story sequence and allow the students to improvise the dialogue. After the first dramatization, ask a new group of volunteers to dramatize the same story.

In the upper grades, divide the class into cooperative groups and give each group a fairy tale or fable to read, discuss, sequence, and dramatize. After a rehearsal, have the groups take turns performing in front of the class. Then lead the class in a discussion of the events and character motivations.

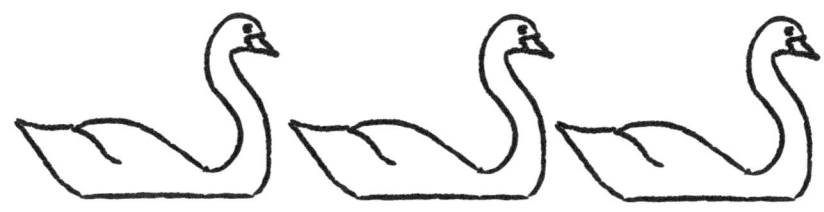

Character Education

After the dramatizations, extend the discussion to actual historical figures and events. Talk about real people who performed caring and courageous deeds. Examples are:

- Harriet Tubman, who risked her life many times to help her people escape slavery.
- Sequoya, the Cherokee Indian who worked for 12 years to create an alphabet of 86 signs to put the Cherokee language into writing.
- Florence Nightingale, who nursed many people back to health.
- John Muir, who helped to preserve the natural beauty of the land by collaborating in the creation of the national parks.
- Dr. Martin Luther King, Jr., who lost his life working for the equal rights of all people.
- Peter Zenger, a colonial newspaperman who dared to print the truth about the wrongdoings of a public figure.

Ask the students to share about people they know who have performed caring deeds. Summarize the activity by asking some thought-provoking questions and facilitating discussion.

Discussion Questions

1. Why do people dedicate or risk their lives for the sake of others?

2. How can you be a more caring person at home? ...at school? ...in the neighborhood?

3. When we care about someone or something, what feelings do we typically experience?

4. How do we learn to be caring?

5. What are some good ways to spread caring and kindness?

Assessment

- Did the students accurately identify the caring behaviors of story characters?
- Was the concept of caring clearly demonstrated in the majority of dramatizations?

Character Education

Good Character in Action

Objectives

The students will:
- Identify specific ways of demonstrating good character.
- Successfully work together in small groups.

ASCA Standards

PS:A1.2 Identify values, attitudes, and beliefs
PS:A1.9 Demonstrate cooperative behavior in groups
PS:A2.1 Recognize that everyone has rights and responsibilities

Materials

Index cards, chart paper, and marking pens

Procedure

Choose several character traits from the following list (adding or substituting others, if you wish). You will be asking the students to work in groups of three and will need a separate trait for each group, so divide your total number of students by three. Choose that number of distinct traits.

- Honesty
- Kindness
- Responsibility
- Respect
- Fairness
- Citizenship
- Charity
- Forgiveness
- Excellence
- Integrity

Label three index cards with each of the selected traits. Each selected trait should have three index cards labeled with that trait. You will end up with one card for each student and each trait will be lifted three times on three separate cards. Put the cards in a box or basket and have each student draw one card.

Tell the students to get together with the two classmates who drew the same trait as they did, forming groups of three. (If necessary, you may have one group of either two or four.) Distribute chart paper and marking pens.

Have the groups work together to list at least three specific ways that their character trait can be demonstrated:

- In the classroom (three ways)
- On the playground (three ways)
- At home (three ways)
- With friends (three ways)

All together, each group should have a list of 12 specific ways of demonstrating their chosen character trait.

Offer some examples to get the groups going, e.g., responsibility is demonstrated at school by completing assignments, on the playground by returning play equipment after recess, at home by making one's bed, and with friends by returning borrowed items.

Allow at least 15 minutes for group work. Circulate and assist the groups as necessary.

Finally, bring the class back together and ask each group to present its list. After the group has shared, ask the class to suggest additional ideas for the group to add to their list.

Post all of the completed lists around the room. Lead a follow-up discussion.

Discussion Questions

1. Why is it important to develop the character trait you chose?

2. What does it mean to have good character?

3. What might happen if you had an irresponsible mail carrier? …an unfair teammate? …a dishonest doctor? …an unkind principal? …an unforgiving neighbor?

4. What character traits did you demonstrate while working in your small groups?

Assessment

- Did the students name specific behaviors for each character trait?
- Did the students satisfactorily explain why good character is important?

The Importance of Rules

Objectives

The students will:
- Develop classroom rules.
- Explain why having rules is important.
- Practice a democratic group process.

ASCA Standards

PS:A1.8   Understand the need for self-control and how to practice it

PS:A2.1   Recognize that everyone has rights and responsibilities

Materials

Large sheets of art paper, colored markers, and a prepared bulletin board on which to display the finished classroom rules

Procedure

Decide in advance the kinds of rules needed for the classroom so that you can guide the students in appropriate directions during the activity.

Begin the activity by discussing with the students the need for rules in games and in group situations where people work together on a regular basis. Ask them, *"What is the purpose of having rules in a game?"*

Write suggestions on the board. For example, game rules:

- Keep players safe.
- Ensure that play is fair.
- Give everyone an equal chance to participate.
- Promote the purpose of the game.
- Ensure that the game is always played the same way.

Ask, *"Why do we have rules in the classroom?"*

Again record responses. For example, classroom rules:

- Keep students safe and secure.
- Promote learning.
- Give everyone an equal chance to participate.
- Ensure the best use of time.
- Encourage everyone to cooperate.
- Promote order and predictability.

When the students appear to have a good understanding of the need and purpose for rules, divide the students into small groups of four or five. Tell the groups that they have 10 minutes to brainstorm a list of rules that they think will help the classroom run smoothly and achieve the purposes listed on the board.

Ask each group to read its list of rules to the class. Write the suggested rules on the board. After all of the groups have reported, go back over the list to eliminate duplications. Then discuss and vote on each rule. Suggestions that receive a majority of votes become classroom rules.

Go back over the final list of rules and ask the students to help you identify rules that are worded negatively and rewrite them so that they are positive. For example, if a rule says, "No cutting in lines," it could be rewritten to say, "Always take your proper turn in line."

Have the students return to their small groups. Distribute the art paper and marking pens. Divide the rules evenly among the small groups (indicating assignments on the board adjacent to the rules). In your own words, explain the next step:

Print one rule on each sheet of paper. Make the letters large enough to be seen from a distance. Then, draw a picture to illustrate the rule. Decide as a group how you want to divide up these responsibilities. You'll have 15 minutes to complete your rule sheets.

Ask each group to show its rules to the class before posting them on the bulletin board. Complete the activity with a brief discussion.

Discussion Questions

1. How do you think this list of rules will help you personally?

2. What do you think the consequences should be for breaking a rule?

3. How does it feel to have a part in making the rules you live by?

4. If you act against a rule, whose rule are you actually breaking?

5. How is this process the same as or different from what happens when elected representatives make the rules that govern our city, state and nation?

Variation

Take this activity a step further by allowing a group of students to bind the rules into book form. The rule book could then be available throughout the year for review by students who break rules and for revisions if rules need to be changed, added or deleted.

Assessment

- Did the students state several valid reasons why rules are needed?
- Did the majority of students participate in developing appropriate rules for the classroom?

Solving Current Events Problems

Objectives

The students will:
- Summarize a current-events issue.
- Work in groups to identify alternative solutions to a problem.

ASCA Standards

PS:B1.2   Learn and apply critical-thinking skills
PS:A2.2   Respect alternative points of view
PS:B1.3   Identify alternative solutions to a problem

Materials

A news article about an issue or problem that clearly relates to the moral value of citizenship

Procedure

At the session before you lead this activity, ask the students to cut a current-events article from a newspaper or news magazine and bring it to school, or to print an article from a respected online news source. Require that the articles deal with issues or events of civic importance. Bring an article of your own dealing with a problem for which creative solutions are obviously needed.

Talk to the students about the importance of being well informed. Explain that the community, nation, and world are made up of individuals just like them. Communities are shaped by the interest and participation of individual people working together. People build, produce, feed, govern, and educate. In the process, they create conflicts and problems that they also must solve. Ask the students what kinds of issues, events, and problems they discovered while reading the news. Ask two or three volunteers to briefly tell the class about their articles.

Have the students share their article with a partner. Allow about 5 minutes for this.

Read your article aloud to the class. Define terms used in the article and discuss the problem. Ask these questions:

- What is the problem?
- Whose problem is it?
- What moral values are involved in this problem?

Character Education

Announce that the students are going to work in small groups to find solutions to the problem featured in your article. Have the students form groups of three to five. Give the groups 1 minute to choose a leader and a recorder. Then announce that the groups will have 10 minutes to brainstorm solutions to the problem.

Call time after 10 minutes and have the groups discuss and evaluate their suggestions, one at a time. Their task is to choose one solution to present to the class. Suggest that they answer these questions:

- Will this solution solve the problem?
- Can this solution actually be done?
- Will combining any suggestions make a better solution?

Allow a few minutes for discussion. Urge the groups to find a solution that everyone in the group can agree to. Have the group leaders report to the class. Then lead a culminating discussion.

Discussion Questions

1. What was the hardest part about finding a solution to this problem? What was the easiest part?

2. If your group was not able to come to a decision, why not?

3. How were disagreements or conflicts handled in your group?

4. Is there any way for individuals or nations to avoid having problems? Explain.

5. How will learning to solve problems here in the classroom help prepare us to solve them in the outside world?

Assessment

- Did the majority of students select appropriate news articles?
- Were the students able to summarize the main issues of the articles?
- Did the groups identify appropriate solutions to the problem?

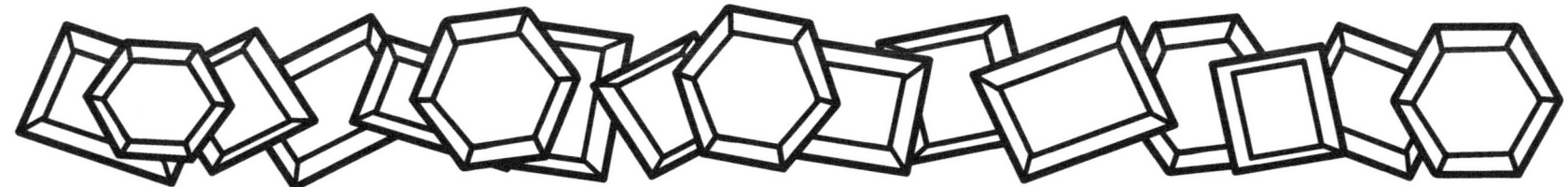

An Exercise in Empathy

Objectives

The students will:
- Put themselves in the place of someone who has been rejected or excluded.
- Understand the feelings of others.

ASCA Standards

PS:A1.2   Identify values, attitudes, and beliefs
PS:A1.5   Identify and express feelings
PS:A2.3   Recognize, accept, respect, and appreciate individual differences

Materials

Writing materials

Procedure

Explain to the students that you would like them to write about the topic, "How It Feels to Be Left Out." Emphasize that they will need to use their imaginations, because they are going to write from the viewpoint of a person of a different race or culture, or a person with a disability.

In your own words, explain to the students:

Imagine a situation in which a person might be excluded. Think about how you feel when you are left out of a group or activity in which you really want to participate.

Now ask yourself: How might the situation or your feelings be different if you were a different race or culture, or had a disability? Would you have the same feelings, or would you feel other feelings?

Begin your story when the person is just starting to think about joining the group or activity. Describe what happens and leads to the rejection, and concentrate on expressing your feelings throughout.

Ask the students to indicate at the end of their papers whether or not they would be willing to read their story to the class. Collect the papers and evaluate them in your usual manner. Then return them to the students. Ask volunteers to read their stories to the class. Facilitate a discussion after each reading. Base your questions on issues presented in the story. Conclude the activity with a general discussion.

Discussion Questions

1. What are the feelings of most people in response to rejection? How are they different for people who belong to a minority race or culture? ...for people who have a disability?

2. What did you discover about your own attitudes towards people who belong to minorities or have disabilities?

3. What good does it do to try to understand each other's feelings?

4. What new ideas did you get about rejecting others? ...about handling rejection? ...about including others?

Assessment

- Did the students describe how it feels to be rejected or left out?
- Did the majority of students express empathy for individuals who are rejected because of race, culture, or disability?

Character Education

Knowing Right From Wrong

Objectives

The students will:

- Distinguish between right and wrong behaviors.
- Discuss different perceptions of the same behavior.
- Distinguish between thinking about doing something and actually doing it.
- Consider how values and ethics are formed.

ASCA Standards

PS:A1.2 Identify values, attitudes, and beliefs
PS:A1.8 Understand the need for self-control and how to practice it
PS:A2.1 Recognize that everyone has rights and responsibilities

Materials

Chart paper, marking pens, masking tape, and three signs prepared prior to the session (see procedure)

Procedure

Ask the students if they know what the term *ethics* means. Write the word on the board, listen to any ideas that the students voice and clarify that ethics are principles or values having to do with right and wrong.

Ask the students: *Who can tell us about a good thing they have done in the last few days?*

Call on volunteers. After each person shares, ask him or her: *How did you know that what you did was a good thing?*

Discuss various ways of knowing: because it feels good, because parents say it is good, because anything else would feel bad, etc.

Next, ask the students: *Who would like to tell us about a bad thing they have done recently?*

Again, ask each volunteer: *How do you know that what you did was bad?*

Character Education

Be sure to take a turn yourself and share something that you are not proud of having done. Emphasize that all people do bad things at times. That doesn't mean that they are bad people, only that they are human and made a mistake or a bad decision. The most important thing is to recognize and admit that you've done something wrong and learn from the experience.

Place these three signs (prepared ahead of time) on the wall:

- I think that was a <u>very good</u> thing to do.
- I'm <u>not sure</u> whether that was good or bad.
- I think that was a <u>very bad</u> thing to do.

Tell the students that you are going to read them some situations, and you want them to go and stand in front of the sign that matches what they think or feel about the behavior of the people in the situation. One at a time, read selected items from the list below. (Choose situations that are appropriate for your students.) Give the students time to decide and position themselves. Then walk up to each group and ask individual students, *"Why did you decide to stand here?"*

Interview the students about their reasons for deciding the way they did. Underscore examples that demonstrate different perceptions of what happened in the situation. When values have played a clear role in someone's decision, discuss with the class how values are developed.

Have the students return to their seats. Conclude the activity with a general discussion.

Discussion Questions

1. What's the difference between having a bad thought or feeling and actually doing a bad thing?

2. Have you ever wished someone were dead? Suppose the person died soon after you had that thought. Would it be your fault? How do you know?

3. Have you ever felt like running away? Was it bad to feel that way? Would it be wrong to do it?

4. When you find yourself thinking about doing something bad, how do you stop yourself from doing it?

5. How do we learn the difference between good and bad, right and wrong?

6. If you know a friend is about to do something bad, should you try to stop him or her? Why or why not?

7. To what lengths should you go to stop someone from doing something wrong?

8. How about just saying, "It's not my problem" and looking the other way?

Situations

- Sarah, whose parents have threatened to ground her for six months if she doesn't get an A, cheats on the final exam.

- Kevin beats up a smaller kid because the kid was bothering Kevin's sister.

- A woman whose elderly husband has been suffering for months from an incurable disease helps him to commit suicide.

- Jennifer does her very best work on a school project, but is so tired the next day that she messes up badly during a soccer playoff and her team is eliminated.

- Juan spends all evening helping his mom clean the kitchen and teaching his younger brother to play the guitar, so he doesn't get his homework done.

- A teacher makes the class stay after school and causes Lucy to miss her music lesson. On the way out the door, Lucy yells, "Thanks a lot, witch!"

- The next day, the teacher refuses to accept Lucy's homework and gives her an F for the day.

- Lucy's parents (hearing only what the teacher did) write letters to the principal and the school board and threaten to sue the district.

- Several children taunt a man and play tricks on him because he has a disability that makes him look and talk "funny."

- The parents of one of the children find out about it, but don't do anything. They think it's just "innocent fun."

- The man gets fed up, traps one of the children during a prank and holds him captive for several hours before finally letting him go.

Assessment

- Were the majority of students able to distinguish between good and bad behavior?
- Did the students distinguish between thoughts about bad actions and the actions themselves?

Character Education

Cheaters Are Big Losers!

Objectives

The students will:
- Examine the concept of cheating.
- Explain why cheaters are the ultimate losers.

ASCA Standards

PS:A1.2   Identify values, attitudes, and beliefs
PS:A1.5   Identify and express feelings
PS:A1.6   Distinguish between appropriate and inappropriate behavior

Materials

Large pieces of butcher paper; drawing paper, art supplies, and writing implements

Procedure

Begin by asking the students: *Do you know what cheating is?*

Discuss the meaning of cheating, inviting the students to share their perceptions. Add to their ideas by explaining that cheating is getting something in a dishonest way. Ask the students to think of some examples of cheating in school.

List their suggestions on the board, adding ideas of your own. The list should include:

- Copying answers from someone else's paper instead of doing your own work.
- Erasing someone's name from a paper and putting your name on it.
- Taking the teacher's answer book and getting answers to an assignment.
- Getting someone else to do your work for you.
- Downloading something from the Internet and saying you wrote it.

Have the students form groups of three or four. Explain that their task is to brainstorm as many reasons as they can think of why cheaters always lose in the long run. Have them focus on the possible effects, or consequences, of cheating in school.

Give each group a sheet of butcher paper and a colored marker. Ask them to select a scribe to record their ideas in large lettering on the butcher paper. Allow 5 to 10 minutes to complete the task. When time is up, ask one member from each group to report to the whole class. Post the lists around the room.

Character Education

If the following reasons are not included on the student lists, discuss them with the students while recording them on a separate list of your own. Post this list also.

- You lose the teacher's trust that you will do your own work.
- If you cheat in school, you may find it easier to cheat outside of school.
- You lose your self-respect and pride.
- Cheating is a lie because it causes people to think you know more than you do.
- Cheating may lead to other forms of lying.
- Cheating is not fair to students who are honest.
- If you get into the habit of cheating when you are young, you will find it easier to cheat when you are older.
- Cheating is taking something that you haven't earned and may lead to other forms of stealing.

Announce that the students are going to have an opportunity to express one of their ideas about cheating in poster form. Distribute the art materials. Suggest that the students choose one reason why cheaters lose from a posted list and try to express that idea in as few words as possible, combining the words with a picture or symbol to complete the poster. For example, the words might read:

- Choose to Cheat? Lose Self-respect!
- Cheating Is Lying
- Cheating: Unfair to Others!
- Cheat in School? Cheat Out of School.
- Young Cheaters Become Old Cheaters

When the posters are finished, invite the students to share them with the class. Then display the posters on a bulletin board in the school auditorium or library under the heading, "Cheaters Lose Because..."

Conclude the activity with discussion.

Discussion Questions

1. How would you feel if someone cheated on a test and got a better score than you?

2. How would you feel if someone took your work and put his or her name on it?

3. How does cheating hurt the community? ...the country? ...the world?

4. How does cheating hurt the cheater?

Variation

In primary classrooms, allow the children to brainstorm their ideas while you record them on the board. Write a list of five or six short phrases for the children to choose from when making their posters.

Assessment

- Did the students identify several negative effects of cheating?
- Did the students explain how cheaters lose, even if they don't get caught?

The Lying Trap

Objectives

The students will:
- Examine motivations and consequences of lying.
- Describe how lying hurts the liar and others.

ASCA Standards

PS:A1.2   Identify values, attitudes, and beliefs
PS:A1.5   Identify and express feelings
PS:A1.6   Distinguish between appropriate and inappropriate behavior

Materials

One copy of the experience sheet, *The Big Lie*, for each student

Procedure

Distribute the experience sheets and give the students a few minutes to read the story.

Ask the students to help you sequence the events in the story. Write the sequence on the board and discuss how events and Suzie's reaction to those events led to her decision to lie.

Create dialogue for each event by talking about what Suzie and the other characters might have said in each scene and why. Write the dialogue on the board adjacent to the events.

Next, ask for volunteers to act out the story.

After the first group of students has dramatized the story, ask a second group to role-play the same story. Explain to the actors:

We're going to do this role play a little differently. Sometime during each scene, I will say, "Freeze." When you hear that word, hold your positions and stop talking. I will walk among you and tap different actors on the shoulder. When you feel a tap, tell us what your character is thinking and feeling at that moment. I may tap just one person or I may tap several during each of these "freeze" periods. Continue with the role play when you hear me say, "Continue."

Have several groups of volunteers act out *The Big Lie*. Conclude the activity with a discussion.

Character Education

Discussion Questions

1. How do you feel when you know that someone has lied to you?

2. If you frequently lied about yourself and your accomplishments, how do you think other people would react if they found out?

3. Do you think that lying can become a habit—something a person does without thinking? If so, how can that habit be changed?

4. Why should we make truthfulness a habit?

Assessment

- Did the students demonstrate negative consequences of lying?
- Did the students express appropriate feelings during the role plays?

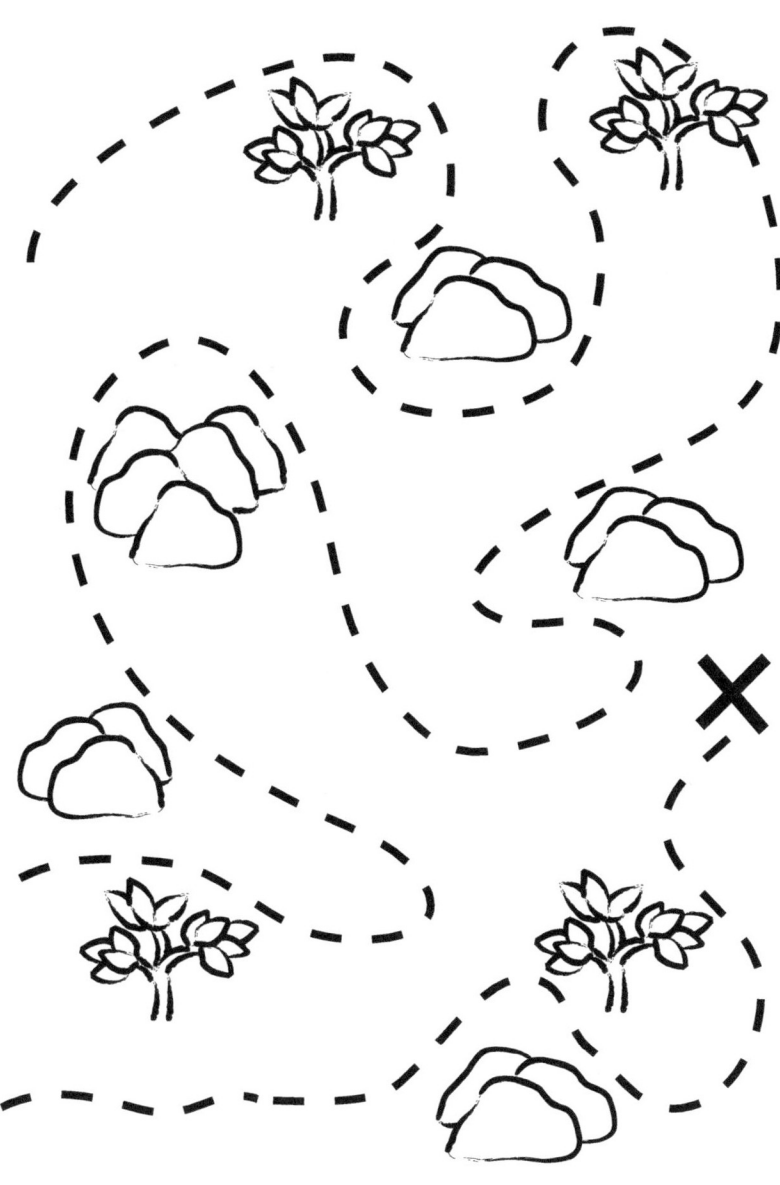

Character Education

The Big Lie

Suzie wiggled excitedly during breakfast. She couldn't eat fast enough. Neither could her mom and the aunts and uncles she was visiting for the summer. There was a big fair in town and today they were all going to it. In her mind, Suzie could already see the clowns, feel the thrill of the rides, smell the cotton candy and popcorn and hear the barkers crying, "Knock over just three ducks and win a fabulous toy," or "Step right up and let me guess your weight."

When the family was finally ready, Suzie's mom said to her, "You may choose one present for yourself at the fair and I will buy it for you." Suzie couldn't wait to see all of the displays and toys so she could make her choice.

At the fair, Suzie was dazzled by the many beautiful things. As she strolled in front of the booths, she narrowed her choices to a heart-shaped ring and a soft, cuddly teddy bear. Oh, what a difficult choice. Suzie really wanted them both. At last Suzie told her mom that she wanted the ring, so her mom bought it for her.

As they walked around other parts of the fair, Suzie admired the ring on her finger, but she kept thinking of the teddy bear. Then she had an idea. Without anyone noticing, Suzie slipped the ring in her pocket.

Just before stopping for lunch, Suzie cried, "I've lost my ring!" Everyone searched on the ground, but the ring was gone.

Suzie's mother felt so sorry for her that she offered to buy her another ring. Suzie sniffled, "No, I want the teddy bear." So her mom took her to the booth with the teddy bear and bought it for her. Suzie was delighted that she had fooled her mom and family and now had both presents.

When Suzie sat down to lunch with her family, she reached in her pocket to check if the ring was still there. Satisfied that the ring was safe, she pulled out her hand. However, the ring accidentally came out with her hand and fell on the ground. When the family saw the ring drop to the ground, they knew what Suzie had been up to. They knew that she lied about the lost ring. "You lied to us," her aunt said severely. "How could you have done such a thing?" her mom asked as she stared at Suzie in disbelief. "What a bad girl you are," an uncle scolded.

For the rest of the day, the family acted very cool toward Suzie. She felt awful. She wished she hadn't lied. Her behavior ruined the day for her family. Suzie vowed to herself that she would never lie again, no matter how tempting it might be.

Character Education

Character Education

Animal Chit Chat

Objectives

The students will:
- Empathize with the feelings of pets.
- Recognize that pets need care and attention.

ASCA Standards

PS:A1.2 Identify values, attitudes, and beliefs
PS:A1.5 Identify and express feelings
PS:A2.3 Recognize, accept, respect, and appreciate individual differences

Materials

Drawing materials

Procedure

In this activity, the students will assume the role of their pet in order to understand the animal's perspective on the kind of care it receives.

Begin by discussing the various pets that the students have or would like to have. List them on the board. Then discuss the care that each animal requires in order to stay healthy and happy.

Be sure to include exercise, shelter, food and water, companionship, affection, pest control, cleanliness, and medical care. This will help the students identify the needs of each type of pet, so that the students can more easily role play their chosen animal.

Ask the students to think about their own pet, or the pet they would like to have. Say to them:

Now that we have listed various kinds of pets and the care each needs to receive, put yourself in the place of your pet and think about what it would say if it could talk. What would your pet turtle say? Would your dog say that you take her for a run every morning and evening? Do you think your guinea pig would brag about how clean you keep his cage? Pretend that you are your pet and talk with a partner who is taking the role of his or her pet.

Ask volunteers to come before the group, two or three at a time, to role play their pets in an animal "chit chat." Encourage them to say what their animals would really say if they could talk. Suggest that they assume the mannerisms of the animals, and focus on how well they are cared for. Allow two to three minutes for each conversation.

Character Education

Distribute the art materials and give the students a few minutes to draw a picture of their pet. Suggest that they use cartoon bubbles to show what their pet is thinking or saying about its care. Post the drawings around the room.

Discussion Questions

1. What did you learn about your pet by pretending to be its voice?

2. What would happen to your pet if you didn't properly care for it?

3. How is having a pet a big responsibility?

4. What does it take to understand what another is feeling?

Assessment

- Did the students empathize with the feelings of their pets?
- Did the students seem to judge honestly the level of care they provide?

Character Education

Identifying Moral Values

Objectives

The students will:
- Identify moral values to which they adhere.
- Recognize that they have choices.
- Understand the consequences of not being true to moral values.

ASCA Standards

PS:A1.2 Identify values, attitudes, and beliefs
PS:B1.2 Understand consequences of decisions and choices

Materials

One copy of the experience sheet, *Choosing Moral Values*, for each student

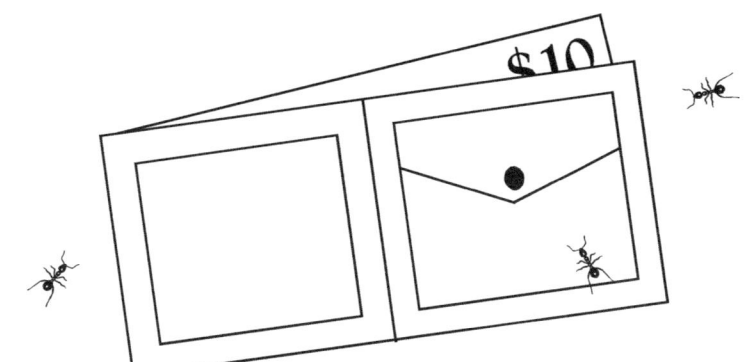

Procedure

Introduce the topic by asking the students these questions:

- As you are walking home from school you find a wallet on the sidewalk with $100 and credit cards inside. What would you do?
- You are invited to a party on Friday night and say yes. Then you are invited to another function that sounds like more fun. What do you do?

As the students answer these questions, help them identify the moral values upon which their opinions are based. For example, returning the wallet and all its contents would be an act of *honesty*. Keeping any of the items would be *dishonest*. Keeping your commitment and going to the party would show *respect* for the other person, *integrity* and *honesty* (keeping a promise). Lying to get out of the party would be *dishonest, disrespectful,* and *unkind*. Another option would be to say that you have changed your mind and plan to do something more fun. While this would be *honest*, it might also be *unkind* and *disrespectful*.

Character Education

Tell the students that honesty, respect, integrity, and kindness are moral values. Write these words on the board. Explain that a moral value is a principle or standard of good character.

Ask the students to think of other moral values. Write their suggestions on the board. For example, other moral values might include:
- Fairness
- Friendship
- Responsibility
- Truthfulness
- Promise-keeping
- Charity
- Humility
- Service
- Courage
- Duty
- Environmentalism
- Good citizenship

Explain that moral values often guide our decisions, choices and interactions and help us determine what is important in our lives. For example, people who value friendship will usually try to be a good friend to others.

When we ignore the moral values that we have been taught and say we believe in, we experience inner conflict, stress, guilt, and emotional confusion. Those feelings come from what we call our *conscience*.

Distribute the experience sheets. Give the students a few minutes to complete them.

Conclude the activity with additional discussion.

Discussion Questions

1. Why is it important to be clear about our moral values?

2. What happens when people don't live up to their moral values?

3. How do we learn moral values?

4. What would our class be like if we had no moral values?

5. What are some ways that moral values are expressed in our community? …in our country?

6. What are some examples of dishonesty? …irresponsibility? …poor citizenship? …unkindness?

7. What is the difference between a moral value and a "lifestyle" value? (A lifestyle value is not a standard of good character, it is simply a personal preference. For example, to greater or lesser degrees people value sports, music, socializing, privacy, gardening, hiking, fishing, painting, cooking, eating out, and so on.)

Assessment

- Did the students name a variety of moral values?
- Did the students distinguish between moral values and lifestyle values?
- Did the majority of students describe at least one specific behavior for each of their top five moral values?

Character Education

Choosing Moral Values

From the list of moral values created by the class, choose the five that are most important to you. Write them below. (You may list values that are not on the board.)

Now, describe one thing that you have done this week that expresses each moral value. For example, feeding your pet is an act of responsibility. Helping a classmate could be an act of kindness, responsibility, service, friendship, or all four. Telling your parent that you didn't do well on a test is an act of honesty and truthfulness.

Moral Value

1. _____

2. _____

3. _____

4. _____

5. _____

Moral Action

1. _____
   _____

2. _____
   _____

3. _____
   _____

4. _____
   _____

5. _____
   _____

Character Education

Careers

Careers

Careers

Family Tree of Occupations

Objectives

The students will:
- Identify and discuss a variety of occupations.
- Describe changes in occupations over time.
- Trace the occupational histories of their families.

ASCA Standards

C:A1.2   Learn about the variety of traditional and nontraditional occupations

C:A2.3   Demonstrate knowledge about the changing workplace

Materials

One copy of the experience sheet, *My Family Occupation Tree*, for each student; a long sheet of butcher paper; magic markers in various colors

Procedure

Ask the students if they know what a family tree is. Listen to their answers and expand upon their ideas. Explain that a family tree is a way of showing a person's "roots." It lists parents, grandparents, great-grandparents, and so on, as far back as you can go. It can also list sisters, brothers, aunts, uncles, and cousins.

Tell the students that they are going to make a family tree. However, theirs will be different from most family trees in that it will show the name and occupation of each person.

Distribute the experience sheets and go over the directions. Ask the students to take the sheet home and ask their parents to help them complete it. Tell them to list both paid and unpaid occupations. For example, a grandmother who worked at home taking care of family should be listed as a homemaker or housewife. However, if the same grandmother worked as a secretary for most of her adult life and is now retired, she should be listed as a secretary.

When all of the students have returned their completed occupation trees, have each student take a few minutes to show their tree to the class and talk about the occupations of listed family members and ancestors. Facilitate discussion.

Careers

Discussion Questions

1. Which occupations are you interested in learning more about?
2. What did you learn about your family's occupations that you didn't know before?
3. What are you learning now that your father had to learn in order to do his job?
4. What did your mother have to study in order to do her job?
5. How many of you have parents who use computers in their jobs?
6. Which occupations we've talked about didn't exist when our grandparents' were working?
7. Which occupations we've talked about no longer exist today?
8. What things cause occupations to change over time?

Extension

Have the students (or a small team of students) transfer the information from the completed experience sheets to a large mural. With colored magic markers, have them draw a large tree for each student and write the various occupations on the branches of the tree. Put the name and a photo of each student on the trunk of his or her tree. Entitle the mural, "The Occupation Forest."

Assessment

- Did the majority of students identify three or more generations of family occupations?
- Were the students able to describe features of the occupations they listed?

My Family Occupation Tree

Directions

Write your name at the base of the tree.

Write the occupation of your mother, your father, your aunts, your uncles, your grandmothers, and your grandfathers in the spaces.

Take the tree home with you and have your parents help you. Bring the completed tree back to class with you.

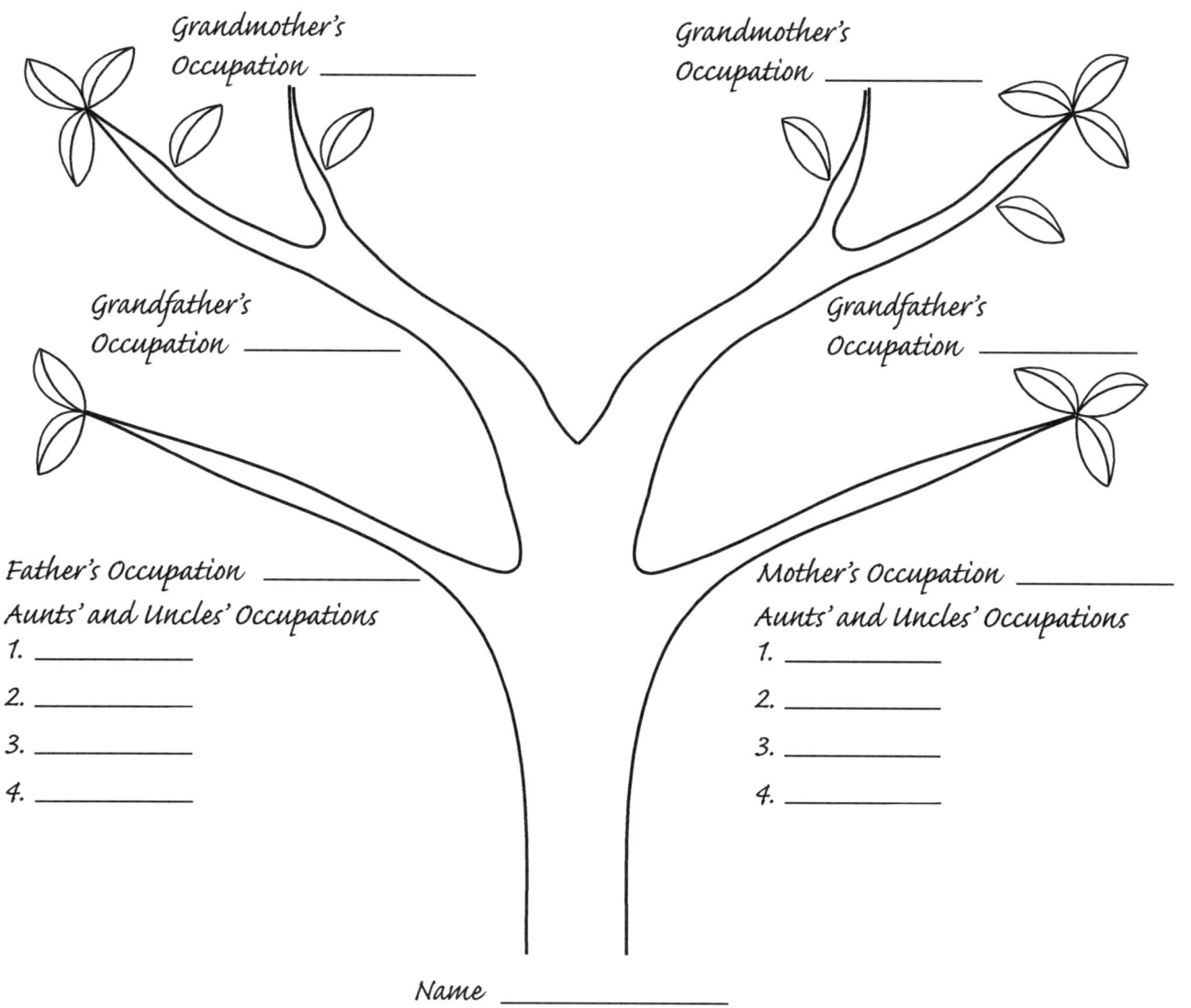

Grandmother's Occupation _____

Grandmother's Occupation _____

Grandfather's Occupation _____

Grandfather's Occupation _____

Father's Occupation _____
Aunts' and Uncles' Occupations
1. _____
2. _____
3. _____
4. _____

Mother's Occupation _____
Aunts' and Uncles' Occupations
1. _____
2. _____
3. _____
4. _____

Name _____

Careers

Careers

School Is My First Job

Objectives

The students will:
- Describe how the role of student is like that of adult worker.
- Describe how current learning relates to future careers.
- Identify skills essential for both school and career success.

ASCA Standards

C:A2.8   Understand the importance of responsibility, dependability, punctuality, integrity, and effort in the workplace
C:C1.1   Understand the relationship between educational achievements and career success
A:C1.3   Understand the relationship between learning and work
A:C1.5   Understand that school success is the preparation to make the transition from student to community member

Materials

One copy of the experience sheet, *Job-Responsibility Puzzle*, for each student

Procedure

Explain to the students that just about everyone has jobs to do. Even very small children are given things to do that can be called jobs. Announce that the class is going to talk about responsibilities that are essential both to learning and job success. Ask them to think about learning as though it were their job.

On the board, write the heading, "Job Responsibilities." Ask the students to think of some responsibilities they have in their job of learning that adults also have in their jobs. Demonstrate by contributing several items to the list yourself. As the list develops be sure to include these seven items from the experience sheet:

1. Be positive.
2. Complete all work assigned.
3. Be honest.
4. Be on time.
5. Help others.
6. Do the best job I can.
7. Cooperate with others.

When the list includes at least 10 items, underline the seven listed above. Tell the students that they will have an opportunity to use these items to solve a puzzle.

Careers

Distribute the experience sheets and go over the directions. Explain that to solve the puzzle, the students must figure out where each of the seven responsibilities fits. Assure them that every item fits perfectly into one of the rows or columns. Remind them to use as clues the letters that have already been filled in.

Circulate and offer assistance.

After all of the students have completed the puzzle, facilitate a discussion.

Discussion Questions

1. How does being positive help you learn?
2. What are ways in which you cooperate with others?
3. What happens when a company employee doesn't complete assigned work?
4. Why is it important to help others here at school?
5. What does it mean to do the best job you can?
6. Why is honesty important at school? ...at work?
7. What problems are caused by being late to school? ...to work?
8. What other responsibilities are important in most jobs?

Assessment

- Did the students identify a variety of responsibilities essential to both school and job success?
- Did the students describe how things they are learning in school can relate to future jobs?

Careers

Job-Responsibility Puzzle

Directions

Read the list of seven sentences below. Each sentence describes a very important responsibility. People who make a habit of doing these things are almost always successful in their jobs. If you make a habit of doing these things at school, there's no puzzle about it—you will be successful.

Fill in the blank spaces with the sentences. Some letters are already there. Use them as clues to help you complete the puzzle.

Be positive.
Complete all work assigned.
Be honest.
Be on time.
Help others.
Do the best job I can.
Cooperate with others.

Careers

301

Careers

A Block of Businesses

Objectives

The students will:
- Identify and discuss different types of businesses and jobs.
- Learn the purpose of various businesses.

ASCA Standards

C:A1.2   Learn about a variety of traditional and nontraditional occupations

Materials

Two 8.5-inch by 11-inch maps for each team of students (see below), plus numerous extra copies; chart paper and markers

Procedure

Choose a block of businesses and stores near your school that most of the students have seen many times. Try to select an area that includes at least one store (like a convenience-food store) where the students have shopped. Make a very simple map of the block, showing the street and the stores or businesses on it. Depending on the configuration of businesses you choose, show either one or both sides of the street. Label the street, but do not label the businesses. Using simple floor plans, approximate the relative size and shape of the buildings, so that the students will be able to identify them . If you are artistic or ambitious, draw elevations (fronts) of the stores instead of floor plans.

Part 1

Tell the students that they are going to have an opportunity to become more familiar with some of the stores and businesses in the neighborhood around the school.

Form teams of two or three and distribute at least two maps to each team—one working copy and one for the finished map.

Orient the students to the map. Point out the name of the street and make certain that the students know which block they are looking at. Then explain:
Your job is to write in the names of the businesses and stores on the block. Start by filling in those that you can remember. Then find out the names of the rest.

Decide how to handle the research involved. One way is to encourage the teams to collaborate—to get information from one another. A second way is to have the teams send at least one member to the block to copy down the names of the businesses. A third

Careers

method is to designate one investigative team to make the visitations and share findings with the rest of the class.

Have the teams share their completed maps with the class. If the teams come up with different results (for example, different names for the same business), resolve those differences before launching the second part of the activity.

Part 2
In a follow-up session, announce that the teams are now going to take a closer look at the stores and businesses on the their completed maps. Assign a different business to each team and have the teams research the purpose of the business and the types of work people do there. Offer several research alternatives: Students may phone the business, visit the business, or get the information from the company's web-site. Tell them to obtain job titles along with brief descriptions of what people do in those jobs.

When the research has been completed, have the teams take turns reporting on their businesses (you might want to do this over a period of several days). Make a chart listing the name of the business, purpose of the business, and the types of work that people do there. For example, if the block contains a bank the chart might show:

People's Union Bank
Purpose:
A bank is a safe place for people to keep their money.

Types of Bank Employees:
Teller
Branch Manager
Loan Officer
Clerk or Data Processor
Supervisor
Marketing Director
Personnel Director
Security Guard

Throughout the sharing process, use the information gained to facilitate discussion.

Discussion Questions

1. Have you or a family member gone to this store or business?
2. What kind of work is done there?
3. What products or services are sold there?
4. Why do you think the owner chose this location?
5. Which, if any, stores on this block sell the same products or services?
6. What kinds of skills are needed in this job?
7. Why are there so many different kinds of work?
8. What would you have to learn in school in order to do that job?

Assessment

- Did the majority of students correctly identify the designated businesses?
- Did the students provide adequate explanations of the kinds of work done at each business?
- Did the students identify skills needed to perform a variety of jobs?

Work I Can Imagine Doing

Objectives

The students will:
- Describe school tasks that are similar to skills essential for success in a career.
- Identify and discuss different types of work.
- Describe the importance of preparing for an occupation.

ASCA Standards

C:A1.2	Learn about the variety of traditional and nontraditional occupations
C:B1.4	Know the various ways in which occupations can be classified
C:B2.1	Demonstrate awareness of the education and training needed to achieve career goals
C:C1.1	Understand the relationship between educational achievement and career success
C:C1.3	Identify personal preferences and interests influencing career choice and success.

Materials

Writing or drawing materials

Procedure

Remind the students of the different types of work they learned about in previous activities. If the students completed the map-making activity, suggest that if one city block contains so many different kinds of work, there must be thousands of different kinds of jobs in the whole country.

Tell the students that you want them to select one type of work that they learned about and write a one-page story describing themselves doing that job. (Have younger students draw pictures of themselves doing the job.) In your own words explain:

Imagine that you have learned all the things you need to know in order to do the job. Mentally place yourself in the office or store, see yourself using the tools, working with the other employees, serving customers or clients, and completing the tasks and projects assigned to you in the job. Then write (or draw) about the experience in general, or about one particular event in the course of your imaginary workday.

While the students are working, circulate and talk to them individually. Ask them questions such as:
- What are you doing in your imagined job?
- Why did you choose this job?
- What would you have to learn in school in order to do this job?

When the students have finished their stories (or drawings) have them write identifying titles on the sheets (e.g., Josh: Insurance Agent). Display the stories (or drawings) around the room along with the maps and charts from previous activities.

Assessment

1. Were the majority of students able to imagine themselves doing a specific job?
2. Did the students describe specific job experiences in writing (or art)?
3. Did the students identify school learning tasks necessary for various jobs?

Discussion Questions

1. What other blocks or centers of business would you like to investigate?
2. Did you learn about jobs that you might like to do someday? Which ones?
3. Why is it important to start learning about different occupations while you are still in school?
4. What kinds of skills must the manager of a business have?

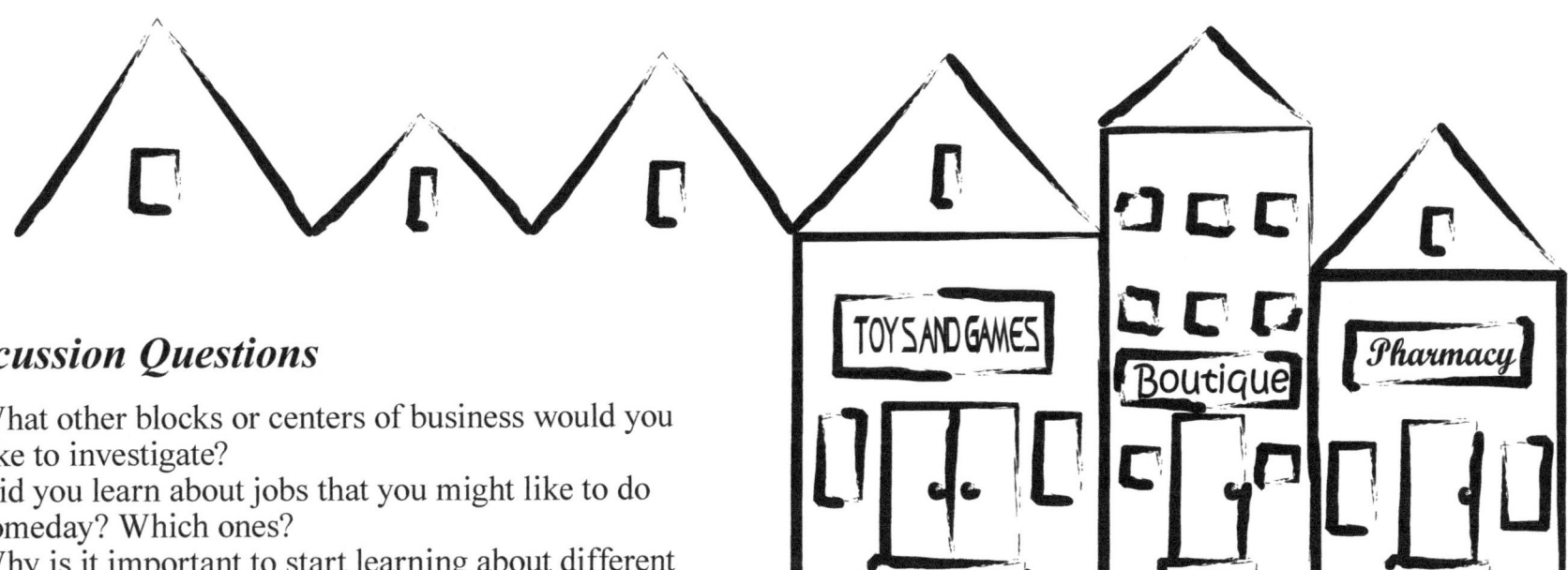

Want-Ad Research

Objectives

The students will:
- Identify different classifications of jobs.
- Describe jobs in their own community.
- Use a variety of resources to learn about careers.

ASCA Standards

C:A1.2	Learn about the variety of traditional and nontraditional occupations
C:B1.4	Know the various ways in which occupations can be classified
C:B2.1	Demonstrate awareness of the educational and training needed to achieve career goals
C:C1.1	Understand the relationship between educational achievement and career success
C:C2.1	Demonstrate how interests, abilities and achievement relate to achieving personal, social, educational, and career goals

Materials

Several copies of the help-wanted section of the Sunday newspaper; highlighting pens, paper and pencils; computers with web access, if available.

Procedure

Ask the students to tell you what they know about want-ads. Discuss the purpose of want-ads, where they can be found, who uses them, and how employers list jobs. Ask if anyone knows a person who has obtained a job through a newspaper or online want-ad.

Tell the students that they are going to use the want-ads to learn more about the jobs that are available in their own community. Have the students form groups of three. Give a newspaper help-wanted section to each group, or have them access a specific job-search site on the Internet (for example, *Craig's List*).

Assign each group a unique task. For example:
- Identify jobs that involve working mostly with people.
- Identify jobs that involve working mostly with things (tools, equipment, etc.).
- Identify jobs that involve working mostly with ideas.
- Identify jobs that don't require experience and include on-the-job training.
- Identify jobs that require a college degree.

While researching the jobs that fit their category, have the students compile a list of unfamiliar terms. In addition, give them some calculations to perform. For example, have them compute the percentage of jobs in their category that require:

- more than three years experience
- specific computer skills
- advanced degrees
- travel
- working at night
- a second language

Compare the findings of the different groups. Talk about the distinction between careers that involve working primarily with people, things, and ideas. Ask the students which category they prefer and why. Discuss the importance of technology in jobs. Focus on the education, training, and experience required for different jobs and the implications of those requirements to schooling.

Discussion Questions

1. What did you learn about jobs from this activity?
2. Why are different jobs appealing to different people?
3. What relationship is there between the amount of education required for the job and the job pay?
4. What, if any, jobs are more appropriate for men than for women, or vise-versa?
5. What is a resumé and how important were resumés in the ads you studied?

Assessment

- Did the students thoroughly research their assigned category?
- Did the students learn about a variety of jobs?
- Did the students identify skills required in a variety of jobs?

The Card Factory

Objectives

The students will:
- Simulate assembly line participation and production.
- Work as a team to make a product.

ASCA Standards

C:A1.4   Learn how to interact and work cooperatively in teams

C:A2.1   Acquire employability skills such as working on a team, problem-solving and organizational skills

C:C2.3   Learn to work cooperatively with others as a team member

Materials

Numerous construction paper cut-outs depicting various holiday symbols (hearts, Christmas trees, turkeys, birthday cakes, shamrocks); half-sheets of construction paper; pre-printed verses; glitter, glue, stars, stickers, and other decorative items; one or more long tables; job titles printed on slips of paper and stored in a bag or box (see procedure)

Procedure

In order to allow for mistakes and waste, prepare enough supplies to enable the assembly of several more greeting cards than there are students in your class. In addition to the decorative items, construction paper and glue, identify and duplicate several appropriate verses. Trim the verses to fit the inside of the construction paper when folded. Arrange the tables end-to-end, designate workstations (see below), and stock them with appropriate supplies. If you are assembling more than one type of greeting card, consider having a separate assembly line for each type.

Talk to the students about assembly-line jobs and production. Explain that an assembly line consists of a group of workers (or robots in automated factories) who have among them the necessary tools and parts to manufacture a particular product. Often, a moving belt called a conveyor belt moves the product from worker to worker. Each worker performs a job or adds a part. For example, if the factory manufactures bicycles, one worker might add the pedals, another worker the handle bars, another the front wheel, and another the back wheel. Other workers fit each part tightly in place.

When a product reaches the end of the line, it is finished. Workers on an assembly line must know how to do *their* job, but they don't have to know *everything* about making the product.

Tell the students that they are going to work on an assembly line. However, on this assembly line there is no conveyor belt, so each worker must pass the product to the next worker. Say to the students:

Imagine that you are applying for a job at a greeting card factory. We need the following workers on each assembly line: a <u>folder</u> to fold the colored paper; a <u>pattern selector</u> to choose the size and color of a cut-out; a <u>gluer</u> to squeeze glue on the outside of the card; <u>designers</u> to paste on cut-outs, glitter, lace, and other decorations; a <u>gluer</u> to squeeze glue on the inside; a <u>message selector</u> to add a verse to the inside; an inspector to check the cards; and a <u>supervisor</u> to see that everyone has enough supplies and that things are running smoothly on the assembly line.

Have the students draw job titles from a bag. If you have ample time, select the supervisors first and let them interview and assign applicants to the other jobs.

Begin the work day. As the students are assembling the cards, encourage the supervisors to look for problems on the line. Stop occasionally and let the supervisor make adjustments, switch workers, etc. Coach the supervisor and encourage all the workers. Allow the assembly line to continue until more finished cards have passed inspection than there are students on the line. Blow a whistle to end the factory day.

Gather the students together and look at the cards. Have the students display the cards on a bulletin board and around the room. Conclude the activity with a discussion.

Discussion Questions

1. What did you like about working together to make the cards?
2. Did anyone want to work alone to make an entire card?
3. What problems did you experience on your assembly line? How were they handled?
4. What do you think would happen if an assembly-line worker didn't come to work one day?
5. What happens when an assembly-line worker works much faster than everyone else? …much slower than everyone else?
6. Do you think you would enjoy working on an assembly line in a factory? Why or why not?
7. What are some products that are made or prepared on assembly lines?
8. What advantages are there in having seven people work together to produce seven products rather than have each person make one product from beginning to end?

Assessment

- Did the students demonstrate effective team attitudes and skills?
- Did the students resolve team problems when they arose?
- Did the students satisfactorily explain the advantages of teamwork over individual work when producing a product?

Cover-Art Competition

Objectives

The students will:

- Describe the importance of cooperation among workers.
- Demonstrate the ability to work in teams.

ASCA Standards

C:A1.4   Learn how to interact and work cooperatively in teams

C:A2.1   Acquire employability skills such as working on a team, problem-solving, and organizational skills

C:C2.3   Learn to work cooperatively with others as a team member

Materials

Drawing paper, marking pens or crayons, one sheet of tracing paper, and at least 100 sheets of copy paper

Procedure

In the first part of this activity, students work in teams to design a magazine cover to submit to a contest.

In the second part (on a subsequent day) the teams compete to see who can mass produce the most copies of the winning cover in a given period of time.

Decide the type of magazine in advance, based on the interests of your students. Possibilities include zoo animals, surfing, computers, fashion, and music.

<u>Part 1</u>
Have the students form teams of five to seven. Ask each team to choose a manager. Give each team several sheets of paper and marking pens or crayons. Explain the assignment:

You will have 40 minutes to finish and submit a design for the cover of _____ magazine (add name). It should be simple and easy to mass produce, with large blocks of color and not too much detail. Use lines to show where the magazine title (masthead) and other words will go, but don't add the words. The magazine publisher will do that. Plan to submit three copies of your final design. How you accomplish all of this is up to you.

At the end of 40 minutes, have the teams submit their final designs. Facilitate discussion regarding the experience.

Careers

Part 2
Select one design to be mass produced in the second part of the activity. Using tracing paper, draw a black-line master of the winning design and reproduce at least 100 copies of it. Post the three original designs around the room where the teams can see and refer to them easily.

Divide the copies equally among the teams, along with plenty of drawing materials. Explain the assignment:

You will have 20 minutes to produce as many exact copies of the model design as you can. The winning team is the team that produces the most. Since I have provided line copies, your main task is to add the color, texture, and zones for letters and other elements. Copies of poor quality will be eliminated prior to the final count. Once again, you must decide how to proceed.

Give the groups 10 minutes to get organized. Announce the start of production and call time after 20 minutes. Tally the results and announce the winning team.

Lead a follow-up discussion.

Discussion Questions

1. How did you organize for the first job? …the second?
2. How did you get ideas for designs?
3. Did all members of your team do the same thing, or did you specialize? How did you specialize?
4. How did you select your final design?
5. How well did the members of your team cooperate?
6. What problems did you encounter and how were they handled?
7. What did you learn about working with others from this activity?
8. If you could do the production phase again, what would you change about your process and why?

Assessment

- Did the students demonstrate effective problem-solving skills in deciding how to work together?
- Did the teams work well together?
- Did the students sacrifice quality to win, or sacrifice winning to produce quality, or achieve a balance between the two?

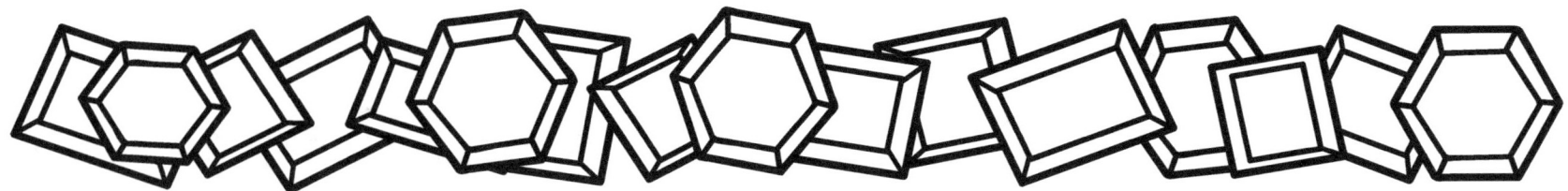

A School Newsletter

Objectives

The students will:
- Learn about the variety of jobs that create a functioning school.
- Practice effective teamwork skills.
- Obtain "real world" knowledge about careers

ASCA Standards

C:A1.1 Develop skills to locate, evaluate, and interpret career information

C:A1.2 Learn about the variety of traditional and nontraditional occupations

C:A2.4 Learn about the rights and responsibilities of employers and employees

C:A2.5 Learn to respect individual uniqueness in the workplace

C:A2.8 Understand the importance of responsibility, dependability, punctuality, integrity, and effort in the workplace

C:A2.9 Utilize time- and task-management skills

Materials

Writing materials, computer(s), appropriate software (word processing, drawing, page layout, etc.), digital camera.

Procedure

Time Note: After making the initial assignments, allow time each day to work on assignments over a minimum two-week period.

Tell the students that the class is going to publish a newsletter about the careers that are represented at the school. In addition to providing career information, the newsletter will have the added benefit of giving recognition to people who work at the school.

Brainstorm a list of articles/features. Here are some possibilities: An interview with the principal; articles about teachers who are involved in special projects, are team-teaching, work with handicapped students, or have received special recognition; people "behind-the-counter" in the cafeteria or office; an article about how people get hired, with quotes from the district personnel manager; articles about custodians, bus drivers, nurse, playground, and instructional aides.

Make assignments. Have reporters work in teams of two. Appoint at least two editors, a photographer, a computer-production team to do keyboarding, layouts, illustrations, etc. Tell the reporters to plan their articles carefully. Brainstorm a list of interview questions and post it for reference.

Keep the writing/production process going. Have the reporters submit their completed articles to an editor for corrections. After rewriting and approval by the editor-in-chief (you), have the articles sent to the production team for keyboarding and layout. Upload, select, edit, and caption the photographs.

When the newsletter is complete, either send it out for printing, or print a high-quality master and reproduce additional copies on a school copier. Distribute copies throughout the school.

Lead a follow-up discussion.

Discussion Questions

1. Why do employees specialize at school?
2. What would happen if the principal were also a teacher and drove the school bus besides?
3. Could we have produced a newsletter without specializing?
4. What did you learn about the working conditions at our school?
5. Describe one way in which the workers at our school cooperate to get something done? Be specific.
6. How well did we cooperate to write and produce the newsletter?
7. What could we have done better?

Variation

For a greater challenge, move the subject of the newsletter off campus and feature a business or community agency. Feature the careers within the particular organization you choose.

Assessment

- Did the students complete their assigned roles in a timely manner?
- Did the students describe a variety of jobs and career information?
- Did the students demonstrate effective teamwork skills?

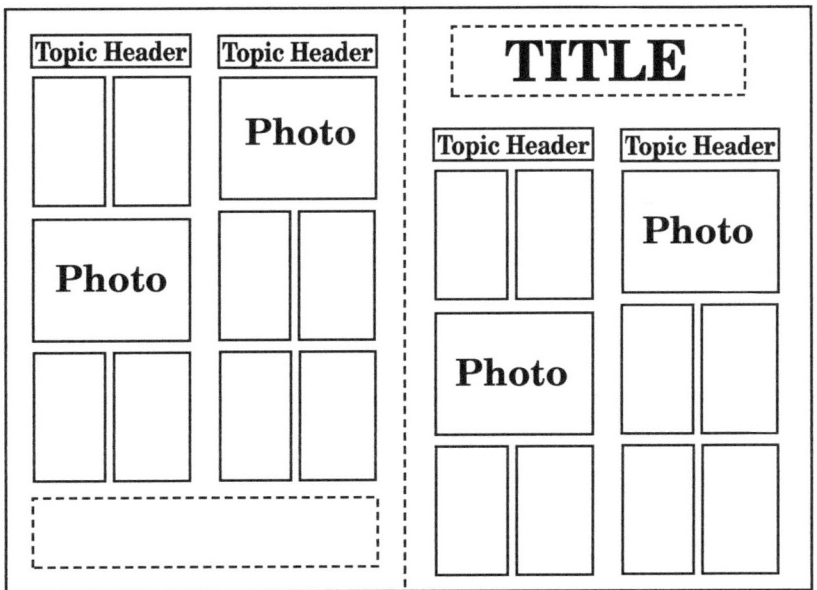

Careers

Career Path Interviews

Objectives

The students will:
- Describe work of family members, school personnel, and community workers.
- Describe the relationship of beliefs, attitudes, interests, and abilities to careers.

ASCA Standards

C:A1.3	Develop an awareness of personal abilities, skills, interests, and motivations
C:B1.3	Demonstrate knowledge of the career-planning process
C:B2.1	Demonstrate awareness of the education and training needed to achieve career goals
C:C1.4	Understand that the changing workplace requires lifelong learning and acquiring new skills
C:C1.7	Understand that work is an important and satisfying means of personal expression

Materials

Copies of the *Career Path Worksheet*, drawing paper, marking pens in assorted colors, and rulers

Procedure

Tell the students that you want each of them to interview a person who has a job or career that interests them. However, instead of writing a paper about the career, they will construct a career path showing how the person got to where he or she is. Explain:

You may interview one of your parents, an aunt or uncle, a neighbor, or a friend. You might also consider interviewing your doctor, the coach of your team, or someone in a business that interests you. Try to find out what led the person to choose his or her career. You will probably discover that the person was already doing related things at your age. Write down important dates and learn as much as you can about the person's career path.

Distribute the worksheets and go over the directions. As necessary, help individual students decide whom to interview.

Have the students draw career paths. When the students have completed their interviews, have one or two volunteers share their findings with the class. Use these examples to draw sample career paths for the students to use as models. Here are two different approaches..

1. Quite literally, draw a path (yellow-brick road style). At the end of the path, create a symbol or cartoon to represent the individual's present job and label it. At different points along the path, place flags or other symbols to indicate important milestones on the way to the career, such as a childhood hobby, college degree, preparatory job, etc. Label these, too.

2. Develop a linear timeline. Working backward from the present, mark off the years in five-year increments to the person's childhood. Using a contrasting color, write in important milestones. Use very simple symbols, if any.

While the students work, circulate and offer assistance. Display the completed career paths around the room. Over the next several days, give each student an opportunity to share his or her career path with the class, elaborating about the information it contains.

Facilitate discussion before and after sharing periods.

Discussion Questions

1. How did such things as special interests and likes/dislikes affect the career choices of the person you interviewed?
2. When do you think a person's career interests begin to show?
3. Looking at your own likes/dislikes, what career areas do you think you might choose?
4. How, besides through interviewing, can you find out about careers?
5. Where would you find career information in the library? …on the Internet?

Assessment

- Did the students demonstrate understanding of the career path concept?
- Did the students gather sufficient information to construct informative career paths?
- Did the students learn about a variety of jobs and careers?

Career Path Worksheet

Directions

Interview someone who works in a job that interests you. Ask the questions on this sheet. It's okay to ask other questions, too. Write down what the person says.

Name of the person interviewed: _____

Job title: _____

Company/Organization: _____

1. How long have you held this job? _____

2. How many other jobs did you have along the path to this job? _____

3. What were the most important ones? _____

4. What interests led you to choose this career? _____

5. What did you study in school that helps you in this career? _____

6. How much schooling did you have?
   High school _____
   College _____
   Graduate school _____

7. What special training did you have? _____

8. What ongoing training do you receive in your job? _____

Careers

Careers

If your heart is in
Social-Emotional Learning,
visit us online.

Come see us at
www.InnerchoicePublishing.com

Our web site gives you a look at all our other Social-Emotional Learning-based books, free activities, articles, research, and learning and teaching strategies.

Siubscribe to our weekly blog and every week you'll get a new activity or Sharing Circle topic and lesson.

 **INNERCHOICE Publishing**
15079 Oak Chase Court
Wellington, FL 33414

www.InnerchoicePublishing